RABBIS, LAWYERS,
IMMIGRANTS,
THIEVES

RABBIS, LAWYERS, IMMIGRANTS, THIEVES

Exploring Women's Roles

RITA J. SIMON

 PRAEGER

Westport, Connecticut
London

Library of Congress Cataloging-in-Publication Data

Simon, Rita James.
    Rabbis, lawyers, immigrants, thieves : exploring women's roles /
Rita J. Simon.
        p.   cm.
    Includes bibliographical references and index.
    ISBN 0–275–94410–7 (alk. paper)
    1. Women—United States—Social conditions.   2. Women in the
professions—United States.   3. Women immigrants—United States.
4. Female offenders—United States.   I. Title.
HQ1421.S595   1993
305.42′0973—dc20   92–41618

British Library Cataloguing in Publication Data is available.

Library of Congress Catalog Card Number: 92–41618
ISBN: 0–275–94410–7

First published in 1993

Praeger Publishers, 88 Post Road West, Westport, CT 06881
An imprint of Greenwood Publishing Group, Inc.

Printed in the United States of America

♾️™

The paper used in this book complies with the
Permanent Paper Standard issued by the National
Information Standards Organization (Z39.48–1984).

10   9   8   7   6   5   4   3   2   1

COPYRIGHT ACKNOWLEDGMENTS

The author and publisher thank the following for permission to use their material:

"On Nepotism, Marriage, and the Pursuit of an Academic Career," with Shirley M. Clark, colleague, and Larry Tifft, graduate student at the University of Illinois, in *Sociology of Education*, Vol. 39, No. 4, Fall 1966, pp. 344–358.

"The Productivity of Female Scholars," unpublished manuscript, 1991.

"Career Patterns Among University of Illinois Women Law Graduates," with Kathryn Gardner, Registrar at the Law School, University of Illinois, *Women Lawyers' Journal*, 1981, pp. 19–27.

"A Survey of Gender Bias Among Corporate/Securities Lawyers: Does It Exist?" with Mona Danner, graduate student in Department of Justice, Law and Society, and Linda Matarese, law student in Washington College of Law, The American University, in *The Journal of the Legal Profession*, University of Alabama School of Law, Vol. 14, 1989, pp. 29–72.

"Female Corrections Officers in Men's Prisons," with Judith D. Simon, corrections officer and daughter, in *It's a Crime, A Critical Look at Women's Issues in Criminal Justice*, (eds.) Roslyn Muraskin and Ted Alleman, Prentice-Hall, forthcoming.

"Rabbis and Ministers: Women of the Book and Cloth," with Pamela Nadell, colleague, and Angela M. Scanlan, graduate student at The American University, in *Sociological Analysis*, forthcoming.

"Sociology and Immigrant Women," in *Seeking Common Ground*, (ed.) Donna Gabaccia, Greenwood Press, 1992.

"The Social and Economic Adjustment of Soviet Jewish Women in the United States," with Louise Shelley, colleague in the Department of Justice, Law and Society, and Paul Schneiderman, undergraduate student in School of Justice, The American University, in *International Migration: The Female Experience*, Rowman and Littlefield Publishers, Lanham, MD, 1986, pp. 76–94.

For Ida, Abe, and Bessie
and for
Julian, David, Judith, and Daniel

Contents

Introduction

Women rabbis, professors, criminal offenders, immigrants, and lawyers are some of the roles performed by women that are described in this book. Altogether the work represents more than twenty-five years worth of studies, ideas, and observations about women in American society. Part I focuses on women in academia and the professions. Chapter 1, published originally in 1966, examines the impact that nepotism rules had on the employment of women with Ph.D.'s at American universities. That piece represented one aspect of a larger inquiry into the work life and scholarly productivity of women in academia. Chapter 2, on the productivity of female scholars, originated with that study; but it has recently been revised and updated to compare the scholarly productivity of single and married women Ph.D.'s from 1957 to 1990 against the productivity of men who earned their doctorates in the same fields over the same time span.

Other chapters in this part focus on women attorneys, rabbis, ministers, and corrections officers. In contrast to women rabbis and ministers, the woman lawyer is a well-established role going back more than a century. The ordination of women as ministers and rabbis did not begin until the late 1960s and early 1970s. And employment of women corrections officers in men's prisons only began slightly more than a decade ago, in the early 1980s.

Even though women were admitted to law school and permitted to take the bar exam for more than a century, a big change occurred in the late 1960s, when the proportion of female law students increased from about 6 percent to over 40 percent. Chapter 3 traces a cohort of male and female graduates of a major law school from its founding in 1897 until 1978. The study surveyed all the women who received their law degrees up to 1978 and compared them to a sample of male graduates over the same time period. Respondents were asked to describe the professional positions they held and the types of law they prac-

ticed. The chapter compares the experience of male and female graduates and
shows rather dramatically the big changes in women's professional experiences
beginning in the 1960s. Chapter 4 is based on a survey that compared status,
responsibility, and rewards between men and women in large law firms in the
late 1980s.

Chapter 5 portrays women who work as guards in men's prisons. It describes
who these women are, why they chose their work, how their male colleagues
and the male inmates regard them, and the impact that women guards have had
on the inmates and the institutions.

Chapter 6 examines and compares women who function as professional religious leaders in the United States. These women hold pulpits, lead congregations, and provide counseling, guidance, and spiritual comfort to their flock
or members. They conduct religious rites of passage ceremonies at birth, marriage, and death. They are spiritual spokespersons for their religious community.
The study describes the motivations of women who seek roles as rabbis and the
similarities and differences among the Protestant and Jewish religious leaders.
It also allows the women to explain in their own voices how and why they
perform their roles differently than do male colleagues of the same faith. It
describes how the women's sermons, relationships with congregants, and teaching differ from those of men in style and content.

Chapters 1, 2, and 5 developed out of personal interests and experiences. As
a spouse of a faculty member at the same university in the early 1960s, I had
more than a professional interest in how a nepotism rule then on the books at
the university at which I worked might impact on my career. Having also recently
given birth to my first child, I wondered how I would combine my professional
and personal life. I did not intend to interrupt my professional life and become
a full-time mother when the first of our three children was born; but I knew that
some changes and adjustments would have to be made. The physical circumstances, I realize in retrospect, were very important. We lived in a university
community; our home was a fifteen-minute walk to the campus and a five-minute
drive by car. We were able to hire a babysitter/housekeeper who arrived from
the country at 7:30 A.M. and left at 4:30 P.M. Monday through Friday. She stayed
with us for ten years. With my car parked in front of the building in which I
worked, I could make the trip from home to the university and back in about
ten minutes. Thus in the first year after David was born, I could nurse him at
6 A.M., teach a 9 A.M. class, and return home for a 10 A.M. feeding. It worked
the same way when Judith came along twelve and a half months later. With
Daniel, it was a little more complicated. He was born in Jerusalem when Julian
and I were teaching at the Hebrew University.

When the babies started coming I wondered how much research I would get
done and how much time I would have to write. There was a lot I wanted to
do: time, organization, and energy would be key factors. I also made a rule that
I worked hard at keeping. When I left the university at 4:20 in the afternoon in
time to say good-bye to Vi, our housekeeper, and shift roles, I put university

affairs, my lectures, my research, and my relations with students and colleagues literally "out of my mind." I focused on the children and on getting dinner ready. It was not until they were in bed for the night, usually around 9 o'clock, that I shifted gears and became once again a professor and a researcher. The pattern worked pretty well. As I think back over those years, mostly from 1964 to 1975 (when we returned after a third year of teaching in Israel, by which time all the children were in school), and as I look over my vita, I see that there were no long periods in which a book or articles were not published. Somehow, it all got done.

Since they have become adults, my children tell me, usually humorously, but with a strong note of seriousness, "Thank goodness you had your work to think about and take care of, otherwise you would have driven us crazy with all your ideas about what we could and should do after school and on weekends. You had too much energy. If all of it was directed at us, we would have been worn out with music, art, Hebrew lessons, field trips, sporting events, and holiday celebrations." So yes, I was more than "professionally" interested in finding out how women with Ph.D.'s managed their personal and professional lives and how productive they were.

The piece on women corrections officers (one of three on the topic I wrote with Judith) was also rooted in biography—my daughter's. Before Judith started law school she worked as a corrections officer in a medium security men's prison. As a sociologist with a strong interest in the work that women do in law and crime-related issues, I was excited about the opportunities her job would provide for us to do some interesting research together. In my role as her mother, I was worried, nervous, and scared about having my twenty-year-old, 5'3", 110-pound daughter working inside a men's prison. Getting involved in a research project that examined the legitimacy of the role of women guards in men's prisons helped me control my nervousness and my fears.

WOMEN IMMIGRANTS TO THE UNITED STATES

The first chapter in Part II offers an overview of the numbers, countries of origin, and demographic characteristics of women who have migrated to the United States. It points out that since the end of World War II more women than men have come to this country. In the second half of the 1940s, shortly after the war, many of the women were brides of G.I.'s stationed in Europe and the Far East. But in the later decades, many women came on their own. They came for the same reasons that men came and for the same reasons that people have migrated from one country or part of the world to another since the beginning of time: they were seeking better lives, better jobs, and more opportunities for themselves and their children. The data show that many of the women came with education and technical skills, and that, once in this country, a higher proportion of all immigrant women enter the labor force and work full-time than do native women.

Three chapters focus on female migrants from different parts of the world: Mexico, the Soviet Union, and Vietnam. The latter two were admitted as "refugees"; most of the former entered illegally. The type, amount, and circumstances under which these women migrants worked, as well as the wages they received, are important themes in all these chapters. Their mobility, skills, and aspirations are explored, as are how satisfied they were with their new lives in this country, how their personal circumstances changed vis-à-vis spouses and children, and what their hopes and aspirations were for themselves and their children.

Biography had some input in the decision to study immigrants generally, and women immigrants especially. I grew up in the house of my maternal grandmother, who arrived in the United States in 1903, when she was seventeen, from a village in eastern Poland, close to Bialystok. She traveled steerage class with a younger brother who was fifteen. They had relatives in New York who met them at the boat. My grandmother worked as a maid in a cousin's house until she met my grandfather, a recent immigrant from Poland, and married him. Years later, she was still bitter about how her relatives treated her.

Some of my earliest memories are sitting with my father in my grandmother's kitchen when I was three years old and listening to his stories about his childhood in Kobrin (a small city now in the Ukraine), in a family in which he was the oldest of nine children. In addition to working a small plot of land, his parents ran a saloon. Before his operation (when I was nine years old) my father had a deep and dramatic-looking scar that took up most of his forehead from his right eyebrow to his hairline. It looked as if a foot had smashed into him, and in fact that is exactly what had happened. When he was fourteen, he was doing something his father had warned him over and over again not to do: teasing the horse that pulled the plow for the land that his parents and grandparents were allowed to work. The horse kicked him in the head. My father used to say it was a miracle he did not lose at least one eye and suffer brain damage.

Most of my father's stories were about the troubles between the Jews and the larger Polish community (Kobrin was part of Poland until World War II) that often resulted in pogroms; about a diet that consisted mostly of potatoes; about beatings from his father, because as the oldest he was supposed to be responsible and diligent; about the arrival of a new brother or sister every year of his life that he could remember; and about his classes in Hebrew and Yiddish with the local rabbi.

At sixteen, he and his fifteen-year-old sister, Mollie, were sent steamship tickets by their "rich uncle" to come to New York. They made the trip by land to the port city of Danzig, where they boarded a ship, arriving in New York in 1920. Over the years, and before Hitler invaded Poland, my father helped bring over his parents and his seven younger siblings. The stories my father told of his young adulthood in New York City described the pleasures and joys of youth. He told about Sunday afternoons rowing on the lake in Central Park, going to the Yiddish Theater on Second Avenue, picking up girls at cafés on the Lower

East Side where the customers drank mostly tea in tall glasses and sang and danced to Russian folk music, and going to Farband (a Zionist socialist fraternal order) meetings. To my father, America was the land of opportunity. After the state of Israel was established he visited often, but for him the United States was home. His favorite retort to custom officials when they would ask him what he had to declare after returning from a trip abroad (no matter where he had been: Argentina, Mexico, Italy, Poland) was always: "I have nothing to declare. Anything I want, I can buy in New York." For him, America was the greatest country in the world. He could and did live out his dreams here.

But it was from my grandmother that I experienced what I came to see in my study of immigrant mothers and daughters. It did not matter that some of the mothers in the study were illiterate and lacked technical skills; their aspirations and hopes for their daughters were as high as those of educated, skilled immigrant mothers, and even higher than those of native-born mothers. I still remember, when I was nine or ten years old, my grandmother telling me on long summer days, when all the kids on the block were away in the mountains or at the beach with their families, and I would complain about not having anything to do or anyone to play with: "Look, you have those encyclopedias [The Wonderland of Knowledge]. Sit down and read or go to the library and take out some books." Even though she spoke English poorly and could barely read or sign her name in English, she knew when I was six years old that I must finish college, and then study to become a doctor (not a nurse) or a judge. When I was twelve and decided I would be a foreign correspondent and travel all over the world, she approved.

WOMEN IN CRIME

There is no biographical component to my work on women offenders. Nor was I a self-starter for the work I subsequently did about women in crime. In 1973, after I served on the reviewing council for the National Institute of Mental Health (NIMH) Section on Crime and Delinquency, a staff member called and asked if I would consider preparing a monograph on female offenders. She said that the staff thought it was a much underresearched area, and that with the growing interest in women, it might turn out to be important. I thought about it for a few days, checked some bibliographies, and agreed with her. In 1975 *Women and Crime* appeared in print. In 1991 *The Crimes Women Commit, The Punishment They Receive*, a revised and updated version of the women and crime study, was published. In the intervening years, I have written more than twenty articles on various aspects of women's criminal behavior.

The theme that runs through the work is that women are likely to commit crime as a function of their status and roles in society and the opportunities those characteristics provide them. Thus, as more and more women In the United States entered the labor force from the 1960s on, and assumed mostly white-collar, clerical positions, women's arrest rates went up. But not for all crimes:

almost exclusively for property offenses involving larceny, fraud, and embezzlement. The female arrest rates for violent offenses, such as homicide and aggravated assault, declined slightly over the years. Robbery arrests showed a slight ascent, but among all of the arrests for robbery, the rate for women never reached more than 10 percent. Having established a pattern for the types of offenses women were likely to commit, the subsequent analysis included a comparison of male and female conviction rates, the punishments handed down, and women's experiences in prison. More than 70 percent of women inmates are mothers of young children. More work should be done about the relationships mothers maintain with their children during their incarceration and whether there are any opportunities in U.S. prisons for infants or very young children to remain with their mothers in the prison. The educational and work opportunities available to women in prison are additional areas for study.

During the late 1960s and early 1970s a few women figured prominently in acts of international terrorism and sensational crimes of violence. These events prompted the chapters on terrorism and on the media's treatment of the Angela Davis, Patty Hearst, and Jean Harris trials.

Methodologically, the work in Part III differs from most of the other studies reported in this volume. Secondary analysis of census and other archival data (e.g., the annual FBI reports as well as judicial statistics) is the basis of the work on female offenders and their subsequent treatment by the courts and prisons. The international data are derived from statistics collected by the International Police Organization. In contrast, the coauthors and I collected almost all of the empirical data in the sections about women in academia and the professions, and on women immigrants.

FRIENDSHIPS, IMAGES, AND PUBLIC OPINION ON GENDER ISSUES

Part IV is less focused than the preceding three in both content and method. It includes two chapters on women's friendships. Chapter 16 compares working- and middle-class women using a random sample survey design. Chapter 17 is based on a snowball sample that asked successful professional women about whether they have close and intimate friendships, with whom, and how important such relationships are in their lives. The latter has biographical roots. Friends of the same and opposite sex with whom I can talk about personal as well as professional matters, seek advice in both spheres, and share disappointments and successes have been an important part of my life. I like to think I always make time for my friends, be it late at night over the telephone, over lunch or a drink when they come to town, or on a walk on Saturdays. Some of them go back to graduate school days, to the years we lived in Jerusalem, and to my life in Champaign-Urbana. I have worked closely with a few on research projects over many years; with some I have shared experiences: their and my divorce, the birth of children, professional setbacks or successes. In the study of intimate friendships I wanted to find out whether other busy professional women, especially those with spouses and children, also thought one-on-one friends were important, and whether they managed to find time for them and to maintain friendships over long periods of time even when their own or their friends' personal or professional circumstances might have changed.

Chapter 18, which compares men's and women's attitudes on salient issues in the contemporary women's movement, is part of a larger work that Gloria Danziger and I have done on the history of women's movements from the 1830s to 1990. Our research focuses on two points: first, men and women in the United States mostly see eye to eye on women's issues, including the Equal Rights Amendment, abortion, family size, and affirmative action; but some of the leaders of women's groups do not reflect or share the same priorities and views that most women hold. Second, many of the positions taken by the post-1960s women's organizations have reflected the interests and beliefs of professional, upper-middle-class white women. The leaders of such groups speak and listen mostly to themselves. Rather than confronting each other with hostility and anger, the majority of men and women agree with each other; and both are annoyed and at times amused at the way "women" are portrayed by the leaders of women's movements. Using national poll data over a fifty-year time span, the opinions and attitudes of a national sample of men and women are compared. The data are then juxtaposed against the goals, objectives, and rhetoric of the spokesperson for NOW and other women's organizations.

A few closing comments about where, when, and with whom the work in this volume was done. Ten of the chapters were written in collaboration with sociology graduate students at the University of Illinois and with law students and graduate students in Justice, Law and Society at The American University. Two of the coauthors were undergraduates; my daughter is another coauthor. Six of the students and my daughter subsequently completed their Ph.D.'s or J.D.'s and are working in their respective fields.

Colleagues at the University of Illinois or the American University were coauthors of six of the pieces. One was a Georgetown student who served as copy editor of *Justice Quarterly* during my term as editor. Each part includes research that was carried out both at the University of Illinois and at the American University.

Finally I want to express my thanks and appreciation to Gloria Danziger for reading and editing much of the manuscript. Her comments were invaluable. Thanks also to Linda Ireland, an undergraduate in the Department of Justice, Law and Society at The American University, who scanned many of the original pieces onto disks and then helped prepare final copy. Tanya Golash and Frances Norwood also provided much-needed clerical skills. My colleague on the "Women of the Book and the Cloth" project, Pamela Nadell, also deserves special thanks. She thought up the title for this book as she has the titles of several of our joint efforts.

PART I

Women in Academia and the Professions

1

On Nepotism, Marriage, and the Pursuit of an Academic Career

This chapter was part of a 1966 study of the social and professional characteristics of women who had been awarded Ph.D.'s. We reported that about 15 percent of married women with Ph.D.'s believed that their careers had been hurt by antinepotism regulations. These regulations, as it turned out, were not barriers to entry into the academic market but did serve as barriers to advancement, to the gaining of tenure, and to salary increases. The data show that women who claimed that their careers were affected by antinepotism rules were as productive as male Ph.D.'s, holding year and field constant, and more productive than other women Ph.D.'s, married as well as unmarried.

Historically and literally, nepotism means the bestowal of patronage by reason of relationship regardless of merit. Antinepotism regulations were passed at academic institutions largely in response to the institutions' conflicts with state legislatures over which body should have final control over faculty appointments. From the viewpoint of the university, the purpose of an antinepotism rule was to protect itself from being used as a dumping ground for patronage appointees and to bar officials from firing professors for their views on controversial issues.[1]

The passage of antinepotism rules at colleges and universities paralleled the passage of civil service reforms and the introduction of the "merit system" in government agencies and other institutions. It represented one aspect of a more general reform movement whose primary objective was to endow government departments, agencies, and other public institutions with autonomy over personnel and with freedom to hire on the basis of merit.

In recent years, however, the antinepotism regulations passed by colleges and universities have had unanticipated and perhaps unintended consequences. They have been applied, primarily, to prevent the hiring of married women whose distinguishing characteristic is that they are the wives of men already on the faculty. In this context, the rules have little connection with their original purpose: preventing incompetent or unqualified persons from gaining positions as a result of political influence.

Three recent studies have investigated the frequency and extensiveness of antinepotism rules as barriers to college or university employment among married women whose husbands are employed at academic institutions. The latest and most comprehensive study was conducted by the American Association of University Women (AAUW) in 1959–1960.[2] The AAUW sampled 363 public and private institutions. Each of the institutions was asked to describe its personnel policies and specifically to tell whether it had antinepotism regulations and, if so, whether they were enforced, the extent of enforcement, and so on. Two hundred eighty-five, or 79 percent of the institutions contacted, responded. Among those that responded, 26.3 percent replied that they have antinepotism regulations, 18.2 percent said that they have no written restrictive regulations but do have restrictive practices relevant to some situations, and 55.4 percent indicated that they have no antinepotism regulations or practices.[3]

When schools were ordered by size, it was found that schools with smaller enrollments had more liberal hiring policies than those with larger enrollments, and that private universities were more likely than public ones to have no restrictions on hiring. The schools that admitted to restrictive practices without specific antinepotism regulations usually discriminated against the second family member in one or more of the following ways: (a) full faculty status or tenure was withheld, rendering employment (of wives) "temporary" in nature; (b) when married women were hired, they were considered as stop-gap faculty rather than career personnel; (c) on matters of policy decision, two-member family employees working in the same area could exercise only one vote; (d) fringe benefits, retirement and medical insurance plans, sabbatical leaves, and so on, were denied. The authors of the study concluded that the employment or status of potential women faculty is affected in nearly half of our institutions of higher learning.

As part of a larger study of the professional characteristics and productivity of the woman Ph.D., described in the next chapter, we asked our respondents whether they believed that their own careers had been affected by antinepotism regulations and, if so, to explain the circumstances.[4]

Of the 2,433 women who returned their questionnaires, half are unmarried, 28 percent are married but have husbands who are not employed at academic institutions, and the remaining 22 percent are married and have husbands who are employed at academic institutions. Among those in the latter category, slightly more than one in every three say that they are affected by antinepotism regulations. Thus, about 15 percent of the married women claim that antinepotism rules are interfering with their careers.

Among those women who maintain they are affected by antinepotism rules, 84 percent report they are presently employed; of those employed, 60 percent are employed full-time. This figure, as we shall see later, is not significantly lower than the figure reported by other married women. Thus, we note immediately that women who claim to be affected by antinepotism rules are just as likely to be employed as other married women. Antinepotism rules, then, are not an effective barrier to professional entry. Among the women who claim to be affected by nepotism and who are employed, about 40 percent are employed in the same department as their husbands. Eighty percent of the time, the husbands hold a higher rank and earn more money, and in 60 percent of the cases were hired first. These factors apply when husbands and wives received their degree in the same year.

The ways in which antinepotism regulations affect the respondents' careers have been summarized by the following situations, listed according to the frequency with which they were reported.

Situation 1

Women claim they can work at the same university, in some instances in the same department as their husbands, but only under "special" circumstances. These special circumstances involve such things as temporary employment with no possibility of being considered for tenure; part-time employment; semester by semester hiring on an emergency basis; lower salary than colleagues with comparable rank and experience; no voting privileges; must secure salary from research grants; no professorial rank; change of field or specialty.

Illustrations

I am the only person to my knowledge with a Ph.D. who wasn't hired as an assistant professor. I also hold one of the lowest salaries in the department. This is my tenth year of teaching and I am publishing. An instructor with a doctorate always earns more than I do.

Apparently, the rule at _____ is if two members of the family are both employed by the college, nepotism does not apply. But in the summer of '61 there was a resignation and I filled the vacancy for one year. When they had no one for the following year, they asked me to return for another year, but I refused because I am not interested in a job for which I am hired at the last minute.

The ruling at the University of _____ is that no two people from the same family shall be paid by the university. If one member receives his pay from the university, the other member or members must work without salary or be paid from outside funds. At present, I receive my salary from grant funds. But I do not and cannot hold any professorial rank or strive for tenure.

The nepotism rule at the University of _____ was directly responsible for my shifting my focus of interest from experimental child psychology to clinical child psychology in order to acquire service skills to make me employable at institutions near the university where my husband will work. This set back my career, requiring an additional postdoctoral year as a clinical trainee beyond the one already completed in experimental child psychology. Then, I had to work one additional year in a low level staff position usually open to a new clinical Ph.D. . . . The only other choice open to me was to apply for another NIMH postdoctoral fellowship in order to continue working in my original area of interest. But I did not wish to live from year to year on stipends about half as large as the professional salary I could get as a staff person in another setting.

Situation 2

Women say they are excluded from work at the same university where their husbands work. They therefore find employment at another college or university in the same community or area; are unemployed, but seeking work; or are unemployed, but at the present time not particularly interested in finding a position.

Illustrations

Our move to ——— was largely determined by the erroneous judgment of my husband's chairman that I could be employed. When this was ruled out by the President, I found myself another job (a better one, as it turned out) at a college within commuting distance and have been a full-time faculty member ever since.

The college at which my husband teaches has a nepotism rule which prevented my being considered for teaching (even part-time) there. Hence, I am currently commuting twenty-five miles at considerable expense and inconvenience to teach at another institution.

I applied, as accounting professors were needed, hoping that they would not find anyone in the community and then hire me for a quarter or more. But the policy is never to hire anyone from the same family, unless the institution is desperate. They hired a C.P.A.

My husband has recently been appointed to a professorship in the Department of Zoology of ——— University. Unfortunately, I cannot be appointed to any position in this department because of the nepotism rules. This makes it rather difficult for me to pursue my teaching career since this is the main university in ———.

Situation 3

Women claim that their own mobility and that of their husband is severely limited. They cannot consider employment at certain universities that have good departments because of antinepotism rules.

Illustrations

We are affected in this sense—nepotism rules elsewhere limit our chances to make a move. My husband has had invitations to apply for positions elsewhere, but when we are told that nepotism rules were enforced, or feelings were strong against hiring wives, we did not pursue these invitations. I received an invitation to apply at ———; but there is a nepotism rule that would prevent my husband's consideration.

Our home is in Texas. My husband has been offered at least five college teaching jobs, including head of department. He did not take the positions because there was no job available for me because of the nepotism rule.

We are being entertained as potential teachers in a department which needs people of each of our backgrounds, but the chairman is trying to place my husband in another department to escape nepotism rules. If no other department will cooperate, we are out of luck, a shame, as both jobs appear attractive.

Situation 4

Women claim that antinepotism regulations exist at the universities in which they are employed, but that they are not directly affected by them for one of the following reasons: they had tenure before marriage; they have always been employed as a research associate and receive their salary from research grants; they have not sought employment at the same university as their husband because they have a satisfactory position elsewhere; they have not sought employment at the same university as their husband because they do not feel they would qualify.

Illustrations

At the present time I am not affected by a nepotism rule. However, this may only be true because my husband and I write research proposals which are supported by the U.S. government. Thus, I cost the university no money and in fact bring in sufficient funds to support three or four predoctoral students.

I had tenure at the time of my marriage. I retained my tenure. However, if I had not had tenure at that time, I would not have been eligible for it.

The general rule—to which some exceptions have been made—is that members of the same family cannot work in the same department. This is hardly a practical hindrance in my case, since I could never expect to get a teaching appointment at ⎯⎯⎯⎯⎯; their standards are too high.

THE EFFECTS OF ANTINEPOTISM RULES ON WOMEN PH.D.'S

We turn now to our second set of findings concerning the effects of antinepotism regulations on the professional characteristics and productivity of the woman Ph.D. We reported earlier that among the women who claim to be affected by antinepotism rules, 84 percent are employed, 60 percent of those full-time. In Table 1.1 we see how these figures compare against other women Ph.D.'s and men.

Women who are affected by antinepotism rules are just as likely to be employed as other married women (categories 2 and 3) but less likely than unmarried women or men.[5] Almost all of the married women in each of the three categories who are not employed or who are working less than full-time claim that they have not sought employment or that they do not wish to work any more than they do. According to these figures, antinepotism regulations are not effective or important bars to entry into the academic market, although, as the examples

Table 1.1
Percent Employed by Sex and Marital Status

Presently Employed	Women Presently Affected by Anti- Nepotism Rules (1)	Women with Husbands in Academia (2)	Women with Husbands Not in Academia (3)	Single Women (4)	All Men (5)
Yes	84.3	84.4	86.5	98.3	99.0
Full time	59.9	58.5	68.7	95.2	99.0
Part time	24.4	25.9	17.8	3.1	--
Not employed	15.1	15.1	12.6	1.6	0.2
No answer	0.6	0.5	0.6	0.6	0.8
Combined	100(192)	100(325)	100(684)	100(1232)	100(786)

Table 1.2
Type of Employment by Sex and Marital Status

Presently Employed	Women Presently Affected by Anti- Nepotism Rules (1)	Women with Husbands in Academia (2)	Women with Husbands Not in Academia (3)	Single Women (4)	All Men (5)
Teaching	41.6(69)	40.9(115)	39.2(235)	49.1(600)	39.8(312)
Research	24.7(40)	26.3(74)	17.5(105)	10.6(129)	11.6(91)
Both	19.9(33)	21.7(61)	15.2(91)	18.8(299)	21.3(167)
Other	10.2(17)	8.5(24)	26.0(156)	19.2(235)	26.3(206)
No answer	3.6(6)	2.5(7)	2.2(13)	2.3(28)	1.0(8)

in the previous section suggest, they may restrict entry into specific positions at certain institutions.

Table 1.2 describes type of employment among our five categories of Ph.D.'s.[6] Teaching claims the greatest proportion of respondents in all categories. Women

Table 1.3
Professorial Ranks Among Respondents Employed Full Time at Colleges and Universities

Presently Employed	Women Presently Affected by Anti-Nepotism Rules (1)	Women with Husbands in Academia (2)	Women with Husbands Not in Academia (3)	Single Women (4)	All Men (5)
Instructor	9.6	12.4	9.3	2.9	3.1
Lecturer	6.4	2.4	2.4	1.3	1.1
Assistant Professor	37.7	48.4	43.9	36.5	35.1
Associate Professor	20.4	11.6	21.1	30.9	40.9
Professor	4.2	8.6	8.6	20.0	15.7
Research Associate	18.1	14.7	1.7	7.2	4.0
No answer	3.2	1.9	12.6	1.3	0.9

who maintain they are affected by antinepotism rules are no more likely to be represented in the "research" or "other" categories than are other married women with husbands at colleges or universities. The distribution for both groups, however, shows a greater concentration in "research" positions and a lesser concentration in "other" positions than one finds among the unmarried women or men.[7]

Table 1.3 describes the distribution by professorial rank among those respondents who are employed full-time at colleges and universities.[8] We find three items of interest in Table 1.3: (1) married women (those in categories 1, 2, and 3) are more likely to be represented in the lower ranks of instructor and lecturer and less likely to be represented in the associate and full professor ranks than are unmarried women and men; (2) married women are more likely to be employed as research associates; (3) unmarried women are as likely as men to hold full professorships.

As we would have expected on the basis of the results in Table 1.3, married women are also less likely to have tenure than unmarried women or men (see Table 1.4). There is no difference in the percentage of men and women with tenure among the latter two categories.

The findings in Tables 1.3 and 1.4 suggest that married women as a social

Table 1.4
Percent of Respondents with Tenure Among Those Employed Full Time at Colleges and Universities

Tenure	Women Presently Affected by Anti-Nepotism Rules (1)	Women with Husbands in Academia (2)	Women with Husbands Not in Academia (3)	Single Women (4)	All Men (5)
Yes	25.0	24.8	34.4	48.4	48.4
No	75.0	75.2	65.5	51.6	51.6

category are subjected to discriminatory employment practices as manifested by rank and permanence of position; but only some label these practices as "discriminatory" and object to them. In other words, women who claim that their careers have been hurt by antinepotism regulations are in reality treated no differently than other married women.

An important measure of whether people are treated equally is whether they are paid the same amount of money. We have shown thus far that married women who are working full-time, irrespective of where their husbands are employed or whether the institution has an antinepotism rule, hold lower ranks and non-tenured positions. The questions now become, Do married women who claim they are affected by antinepotism rules receive less money than other married women? And do married women in general earn less than unmarried women or men?

SALARIES OF WOMEN PH.D.'S IN ACADEMIC DIVISIONS

Unlike the factors reported in the previous tables, we know that different fields or academic specialties have different salary scales. Thus, we examined the distribution of women who claim to be affected by nepotism against other married women within the same academic divisions, and then compared incomes among our five categories within the same academic divisions. The data in Table 1.5 show that women who claim they are affected by antinepotism rules are more likely to be found in the natural and biological sciences and in the humanities than in education and the social sciences.[9]

Table 1.6 compares mean incomes by divisions, sex, and marital category within the two professorial ranks for which we have large enough N's to make meaningful comparisons. We note that for both ranks and in all divisions men

Table 1.5
Distribution of Women Affected by Nepotism, and Other Married Women by Division

Division	Women Presently Affected by Anti-Nepotism Rules (1)	Women with Husbands in Academia (2)	Women with Husbands Not in Academia (3)	Total Married Women (4)	RATIO: Married Women Affected by Nepotism to All Married Women (5)
Natural and Biological Sciences	6.3	12.4	16.6	35.3%	1:6
Social Sciences	3.9	18.1	17.6	39.6%	1:10
Humanities	5.8	8.0	16.1	29.9%	1:5
Education	2.1	3.0	16.0	21.1%	1:10.5

earn the highest or close to the highest salaries, and that on most of the comparisons unmarried women earn the next highest. Married women in all three categories generally earn less than unmarried women or men, except in the social sciences.

Table 1.7 compares the mean salaries of full-time academics by sex and field. Again, we see that women who claim to be affected by antinepotism rules are not treated differently from other married women—they do not earn less than their married women counterparts in academia. Thus the findings pertaining to income support the interpretation suggested by the data describing rank and tenure: objectively, women who claim their careers have been hurt by antinepotism regulations have been treated no differently than other married women. But married women *in general* have been subjected to discriminatory practices.[10]

PRODUCTIVITY

What, if any, differences exist in the relative productivity among the five groups? We have found no important differences thus far between married women who claim that their careers have been hampered by antinepotism regulations and other married women. But the data in Tables 1.1 through 1.7 suggest that married women as a whole, including those who do and those who do not see themselves as victims of nepotism rules, receive lower salaries and lower professorial ranks and are less likely to be granted tenure than are unmarried women

Table 1.6
Mean Salary by Division and Rank Among Respondents Employed Full Time

Division	Women Presently Affected by Anti-Nepotism Rules (1)	Women with Husbands in Academia (2)	Women with Husbands Not in Academia (3)	Combined Married Women	Single Women (4)	All Men (5)
		Assistant Professors				
Natural and Biological Sciences	8,656	9,206	9,400	9,039	9,277	9,188
Social Sciences	9,271	9,065	8,977	9,060	9,334	9,336
Humanities	7,427	7,655	8,352	7,988	8,263	8,615
Education	9,250	8,143	8,954	8,856	9,131	10,007
		Associate Professors				
Natural and Biological Sciences	---	---	---	8,928	8,990	10,381
Social Sciences	10,893	9,200	10,179	10,184	10,006	10,712
Humanities	---	8,143	9,333	8,838	9,384	9,903
Education	10,050	---	9,883	9,988	10,224	10,888

or men. The question to ask now is, Are married women who have received their Ph.D.'s at the same time as their unmarried colleagues, and who are working full-time, less productive than unmarried women or men? The two basic measures of productivity that we used are number of professional articles and number of books or monographs published. Table 1.8 describes the percentage of respondents in each category who have not published at all and the mean number of publications among those who have published.[11]

Table 1.8 tells us three things: (1) the percentage who have not published (books or articles) is relatively constant among the five categories; (2) the differences in the mean number of books published are negligible; (3) the differences in the mean number of articles published are larger, and the order is interesting. Married women who claim they are affected by antinepotism rules published more than respondents in any other group (although the difference between them and men is slight).[12] The fact that the women who claim they are victims of discrimination in employment practices are more productive than other women may explain why they are willing to speak out. That is, we do not know whether the category 2 respondents (women with husbands employed at academic insti-

Table 1.7
Mean Salary by Division Among Those Employed Full Time

Division	Women Presently Affected by Anti- Nepotism Rules (1)	Women with Husbands in Academia (2)	Women with Husbands Not in Academia (3)	Combined Married Women	Single Women (4)	All Men (5)
Natural and Biological Sciences	8,343	8,599	9,159	8,700	9,337	9,788
Social Sciences	9,773	8,798	9,412	9,328	9,638	10,140
Humanities	7,259	7,290	8,093	7,547	8,781	8,725
Education	8,950	9,643	9,686	9,426	9,821	10,783
Combined Means	8,581	8,582	9,088	8,750	9,396	9,859

tutions who do not complain of antinepotism regulations) are also victims of discriminatory practices. We only know that, unlike the women in category 1, they *do not claim* to be affected by antinepotism regulations. The figures in Table 1.8 offer a plausible interpretation, namely, that although the women in category 2 work under the same conditions as those in category 1, their levels of expectation or aspiration are not as high, and for reasons that are quite realistic. They are not as productive as the group against which they cannot help but compare themselves, their male colleagues. But the women in category 1 who work full-time are as productive as their male colleagues. Yet they receive lower salaries, hold lower ranks, and are denied tenure. Hence they complain.

SUMMARY AND CONCLUDING REMARKS

Antinepotism rules that were originally enacted in order to protect colleges and universities from the political pressures of having to hire incompetent people with influential connections have largely been used, in recent years, to prevent women who have husbands on the faculty from receiving positions and rewards comparable to those awarded unmarried females and male colleagues with similar qualifications. Our data, which represent the responses of about 60 percent of the women who have received their Ph.D.'s in the past half-dozen years, report that about 15 percent of the married women believe that their careers have been hurt by antinepotism regulations. These regulations do not appear to be barriers to entry into the academic market, but they impose restrictions on conditions of

Table 1.8
Mean Number of Articles and Books by Respondents Employed Full Time at Academic Institutions*

Publications	Women Presently Affected by Anti-Nepotism Rules (1)	Women with Husbands in Academia (2)	Women with Husbands Not in Academia (3)	Single Women (4)	All Men (5)
Percent with no published articles	26.5	29.0	29.2	36.0	32.4
Mean number of articles published	7.1	5.0	4.8	4.3	6.5
Percent with no published books	69.3	74.8	71.1	69.7	73.2
Mean number of books published	1.7	1.5	1.8	1.6	1.9

* We compared only persons employed at colleges and universities because presumably these respondents are under more pressure to publish than persons employed by the government or private industry. By keeping place of employment uniform we also assume that the extent of the pressure is distributed evenly among the five categories. Inspection of the mean number of publications (articles or books) by persons in other institutions confirmed our guess that those employed at colleges and universities would be higher.

employment such as the securing of permanent positions, the likelihood of advancement, and salaries. In describing how antinepotism rules have affected their careers, women are most likely to mention restrictions on mobility, having to change their areas of interest or specialization, having to accept lower professorial ranks, denial of tenure, and lower salaries.

The major finding that emerges from this inquiry into the effects of antinepotism rules on the employment of women with Ph.D.'s is that the objective conditions of employment among women who claim their careers are interfered with because of antinepotism rules appear no different from those of other women whose husbands are, or are not, employed at academic institutions. A comparison of the ranks, salaries, permanence of positions, and types and places of employment among women who complain of antinepotism rules shows that they produce significantly more than other women, married or unmarried, and as much as men.

Thus, while the employment situation of the women who complain of antinepotism rules is in fact no worse than that of women at universities that do not have antinepotism regulations, or of women at universities that have such regulations but do not feel their effects, the productivity of the former is greater. They are, therefore, less willing to accept the lower rewards and lesser recognition that the majority of married women who are employed at colleges and universities have come to accept as a basic feature of their employment. The fundamental problem, then, of unfair treatment of full-time professionals who are also married women would not be wholly resolved by the removal of discriminatory legislation from the books. As we have observed in the area of race relations and other social problems, the elimination of discriminatory legislation and the passage of laws prescribing equality comprise but one step, although certainly a large and crucial one, toward the attainment of complete equality.

NOTES

1. Malcolm Moos and Francis E. Rourke, *The Campus and the State* (Baltimore: Johns Hopkins University Press, 1959), pp. 148–149.

2. Eleanor F. Dolan and Margaret P. Davis, "Anti-nepotism Rules in Colleges and Universities: Their Effect on Faculty Employment of Women," *Education Record* 41 (1960): 285–291. Two earlier studies were done by Dr. George H. Huff, who dealt with small institutions, and by the College and University Personnel Association. Unpublished study by George H. Huff reported in Dolan and Davis, pp. 286–287. William E. Poore, *Personnel in Colleges and Universities* (Champaign, Ill.: College and University Personnel Association, 1958).

3. Dolan and Davis, "Anti-nepotism Rules in Colleges and Universities," pp. 286–287.

4. Funds for the Research on "Productivity and Professional Contributions of the Woman Ph.D." came from the U.S. Office of Education Cooperative Research Project S-049.

5. The proportion of married women who have children is similar among the three categories. The percentages range from 68 to 71.

6. The figures in parentheses represent those respondents who are employed (part- or full-time).

7. The distributions of responses of the women with husbands not employed at academic institutions show that they fall between the responses of persons in categories 1 and 2 and those in categories 4 and 5.

8. We also compared respondents by the mean length of time they have held their current job and found no noticeable differences among our five categories.

9. These ratios are based on married women who are employed full time. The ratio does not change significantly when married women who are employed part time are included.

10. Table 1.7 describes the mean incomes by division among respondents holding different ranks. In general, the figures in Table 1.7 are consistent with those described

in Table 1.6. Married women earn less than unmarried women and unmarried women earn less than men.

11. We first compared each of these figures by division and when we found that the rank order and the size of the differences were relatively similar within each division, we decided to present only the combined figures.

12. We ran ''t'' tests between women in category 1 and respondents in categories 2, 3, 4, and 5. Between groups 1 and 2, $t = 2.4 < .05$; 1 and 3, $t = .90 > .05$; 1 and 4, $t = 3.9 < .05$; 1 and 5, $t = 1.2 > .05$.

2

The Productivity of Female Scholars

Beginning with the study published in 1966 on nepotism rules and the productivity of women Ph.D.'s, this chapter reports the results of work done in the 1970s and 1980s on the relative scholarly productivity of single and married women with and without children as opposed to male Ph.D.'s in the same disciplines. It asks and answers questions about the enhancing or inhibiting influence of marriage and motherhood on female scholarship.

In the early 1960s, I reported the results of a study that measured the productivity of women Ph.D.'s. I embarked on the study because I wanted to find out the extent to which women with Ph.D.'s were in the labor force working as professionals, and whether nepotism rules disadvantaged women more than men.

One of the pieces emanating from that study, "The Woman Ph.D.: A Recent Profile" (Simon, Clark, and Galway, 1967), compared the professional characteristics and contributions of women and men who received their doctorates between 1958 and 1963 in four disciplines: the natural and physical sciences, the social sciences, the humanities, and education.[1] That article reported on answers to two questions: Are women who have doctorates as productive as men with Ph.D.'s (holding year and field constant); and are married women (with and without children) as productive as unmarried women? This chapter compares the findings of that study against subsequent research conducted from the 1970s to 1990.

To answer the questions posed above, we tried to contact the universe of women who received their doctorates between 1958 and 1963 in the natural and physical sciences, the social sciences, the humanities, and education. Of the 5,370 women involved, we could mail questionnaires to 93 percent of them; and 60 percent who received the questionnaires filled them out and returned them. We then drew a sample of male Ph.D.'s that was one-third the size of

Table 2.1
Tenure by Field, Sex, and Marital Status

Sex and Marital Status	Field				
	Social Sciences	Sciences	Humanities	Education	Combined
	(percent)				
Women					
Unmarried	28.3	34.0	36.5	61.1	44.2 (670)
Married	1.9	12.2	26.7	57.9	21.8 (148)
Married with Children	16.3	19.5	25.6	46.7	25.6 (234)
Men	31.5	46.8	45.6	53.9	46.3 (354)

* The percentages in Table 2.1 are based on the numbers of respondents who are employed at academic institutions.

the female list and that maintained the same proportions by academic field. From a sample of 1,787 men we were able to mail questionnaires to 1,700 and received returns from 60 percent.

We found that 99.2 percent of the men, 96.3 percent of the single women, 87.2 percent of the married women without children, and 59.3 percent of the married women with children were employed full-time in their professional capacities. An additional 3.5 percent of the married women without children and 24.5 percent of the women with children worked part-time in their fields. A much higher percentage of the men were married (95 percent) as opposed to the women (50 percent). And among the married respondents, over 90 percent of the men, as opposed to 70 percent of the women, had at least one child.

On the whole, men were more likely than women to have tenure, but there were differences by discipline and marital status, as shown in Table 2.1. Women in schools of education were more likely to have tenure, save for the married ones with children, than were men.

The major indices of productivity examined were the number of articles and books published by men and women, and the number of research grants men and women received. The results by field and marital status are shown in Table 2.2.

The one anti-intuitive result in Table 2.2 was the productivity of the married women as opposed to the single women; and, in the sciences, of the married women with children as opposed to the men. On the average, married women produced more books and articles than unmarried women and men.

On the likelihood of receiving research grants, we noted that men were more likely to receive research grants than women (married and unmarried) in the social sciences and the humanities. In education there was no difference by

Table 2.2
Productivity Measures: Article and Book Publication, Research Grants, and Consulting, by Field, Sex, and Marital Status

Field, Sex, and Marital Status	Percent Published at Least One Article (1)	Mean Number of Articles (2)	Percent Published at Least One Book (3)	Mean Number of Books (4)	Percent Received at Least One Grant (5)	Percent Consult (6)
Sciences						
Women						
Unmarried	83.5	5.8	10.1	1.1	35.9	14.2
Married	75.4	6.3	6.2	2.6	30.4	7.8
Married with children	91.9	7.8	9.5	1.7	25.6	7.9
Men	88.8	6.1	10.2	1.5	36.7	15.5
Social Sciences						
Women						
Unmarried	59.3	4.0	23.1	1.8	23.4	34.1
Married	61.5	4.2	20.9	2.1	22.2	27.2
Married with children	66.9	3.9	19.9	1.5	24.9	33.6
Men	55.9	4.6	30.3	1.8	35.4	31.5
Humanities						
Women						
Unmarried	47.0	2.8	22.6	1.3	21.0	15.2
Married	69.7	3.7	22.9	1.6	28.2	10.3
Married with children	69.7	3.4	32.8	1.6	18.6	14.4
Men	50.0	4.3	27.7	1.6	32.9	26.8
Education						
Women						
Unmarried	51.2	3.5	23.5	1.6	15.3	42.6
Married	57.4	5.4	35.3	1.7	15.3	50.9
Married with children	39.6	3.9	26.0	2.0	14.2	41.5
Men	44.2	5.1	22.2	1.8	14.2	44.4
Combined						
Women						
Unmarried	57.9	4.1	21.1	1.6	21.9	30.6
Married	66.2	5.3	20.2	1.9	24.0	24.0
Married with children	63.9	4.3	21.8	1.7	21.9	27.7
Men	57.5	5.2	23.1	1.7	28.2	32.2

gender or marital status, and in the natural sciences the proportions were about the same for unmarried women and men. Married women were less likely to receive grants. We had no measure of the proportions of men and women who applied for research grants, so we cannot say whether the lower percentage of women who received grants in the social sciences and humanities was due to a higher rate of turn-down than their male colleagues or to lower productivity.

Neither gender nor marital status turned out to be a significant factor in explaining the likelihood of working as a consultant, except in the humanities, where men did better. The main finding was that male and female respondents in education were more likely to serve as consultants than were respondents in other fields.

To summarize: of the four measures of productivity, in the two most direct ones—numbers of articles and books published—married women published as much, or more, than men, and unmarried women published slightly less than men. The differences on the whole were not great. Of the proportion receiving research grants, men in two of the four disciplines were more likely to have received a grant. The likelihood of doing consulting work did not appear to be affected by gender except among respondents in the humanities.

The most anti-intuitive finding to emerge from our 1967 study was the relatively high scholarly productivity, as measured by article and book publications, of married women across all fields. In the review conducted for this chapter about what has happened over the last twenty years, we have had an opportunity to determine whether our results were anomalous or whether they were the forerunners of what was to become a general pattern. We turn next to those studies.

The Ferber and Loeb (1973) survey of 186 female and male faculty at the University of Illinois found no relationship between marital status or parenthood and publications.[2] They concluded that married women with or without children were no less productive than single women, yet they experienced less success in academic life. The relative lack of success was measured by professorial rank, salary levels, and honors. As shown in Table 2.3, on each of those measures, single women did better than married women.

The authors commented that married women were more inclined to believe that they did not enjoy equal opportunities with men and that they were generally more aware of discriminatory treatment than were the single women.

In a 1977 article, "Children and the Productivity of Academic Women," based on a Carnegie-American Council on Education survey of male and female Ph.D.'s under forty years of age representing all major academic disciplines, the authors reported no significant relationships between marital status or parenthood and publications.[3] There are differences in productivity by field, with male and female scholars in the laboratory sciences publishing more articles than scholars in the social sciences and the humanities. The findings in Tables 2.4 and 2.5 show that women in all categories (single, married, married with children) published less than men. The authors go on to suggest that women are less productive because they are less competitive and less ambitious—factors that they claim stem from their upbringing and societal expectations. On the other hand, women with children may be more highly motivated and more capable. In other words, a selectivity factor is apparent: those women who continue to work in their fields after becoming mothers are special.

A 1978 national study of male and female chemists who received their Ph.D.'s between 1955 and 1961 showed that men published more than women.[4] No data were reported by marital status or parenthood.

A 1985 study of 300 faculty in forty-four graduate schools of social work

Table 2.3
Relation of Marital Status and Parental Responsibility to Performance and Rewards

	Marital Status (a)				Parental Responsibility (b)			
	Women		Men		Women		Men	
	N	r	N	r	N	r	N	r
Books	144	-.047	134	.128	143	.097	133	.162
Books edited	144	-.025	134	.105	143	.062	133	.149
Bulletins	144	-.039	134	.087	143	-.145	133	.009
Reviews	144	.016	134	.040	143	.113	133	.032
Papers read	144	-.054	134	.206*	143	-.040	133	.190*
Articles	144	.059	134	.167	143	.022	133	.038
Other publications	144	-.042	134	-.120	143	.099	133	-.059
Current salary	139	-.333*	127	.228*	139	-.114	126	.292*
	(139)	(-.275)c						
Honors	144	-.194*	134	.150	143	-.117	133	.145
	(139)	(-.191)c						
Rank (d)	143	-.243*	133	.157	142	-.085	132	.228*
	(139)	(-.152)c						
Age	142	-.229	132	.010	142	.010	131	.148

	Combined		Combined	
	N	r	N	r
Sex (e)	278	.394*	276	.397*

(a) 2 = married; 1 = single
(b) 1 = children; 0 = no children
(c) Partial r with age partialed out
(d) 4 = full professor; 3 = associate professor; 2 = assistant professor; 1 = instructor
(e) 2 = male; 1 = female
* Significant at .05 level

found that men were more productive than women and that marital status was not a significant factor; .but having children was positively and significantly related to women's productivity.[5] These authors relied on the selectivity factor for part of their explanation (''women with children'' may have greater health, energy, and stamina than ''women without children''), but also suggested that women may delay childbearing and caring until they are established in their careers, until they have ''established a pattern of publication productivity'' (see Table 2.6).

As part of each of their long-term interests in the performance of academics, Cole and Zuckerman reported in *Scientific American* (1987) that ''women publish

Table 2.4
Regression Results: Carnegie–American Council on Education Data (Dependent Variable: Number of Articles)

	All Men and Women (9,174)
Independent Variables	Regression Coefficient/Standard Error
Years since Ph.D.	.97 (.02)*
Number of hours teaching	-.26 (.02)*
Teaching undergraduates	-1.25 (.18)*
First teaching job in top 12 universities	1.19 (.21)*
Currently teaching at a university	1.22 (.20)*
Humanities	-1.80 (.20)*
Physical sciences	1.49 (.18)*
Biology	2.58 (.24)*
Single	-.94 (.25)
Sex	-1.38 (.30)*
Number of children	.07 (.07)
Constant term	3.65
R^2	.40

* Asterisk indicates coefficient is significantly different from zero at 99 percent confidence level.

Table 2.5
Regression Results: Carnegie–American Council on Education Data (Dependent Variable: Number of Articles)

Independent Variables	All Women (596) Regression Coefficient/ Standard Error	Married Women (344) Regression Coefficient/ Standard Error
Years since Ph.D.	.46 (.07)*	.51 (.07)*
Number of hours teaching	-.14 (.07)**	-.14 (.07)**
Teaching undergraduates	-1.46 (.56)**	-1.43 (.56)**
Physical sciences	1.78 (.78)**	1.96 (.80)**
Biology	2.72 (.77)*	2.92 (.78)*
Number of children	.08 (.27)	***
Constant term	-2.04	-2.51
R^2	.32	.33

* Asterisk indicates coefficient is significantly different from zero at 99 percent confidence level.
** Asterisk indicates coefficient is significantly different from zero at 95 percent confidence level.
*** F-level or Tolerance-level insufficient for computation.

less than men, but marriage and family obligations do not generally account for the gender difference."[6] Married women with children publish as much as their single female colleagues do. Their study examined the productivity of seventy-three female and forty-seven male scientists who received their doctorates between 1920 and 1959, 1960 and 1969, and 1970 and 1979 in the physical and biological sciences, mathematics, economics, and psychology. They divided their female subjects into "eminent" and "rank and file" and found that the "eminent" married women (and "eminent" women were just as likely to marry and have children as "rank and file" women) published slightly more papers than did the single "eminent" women. Married women with children were slightly less productive than childless women, but they reported no drop in women's publications after childbirth and no relationship between the number of children the "eminent" woman has and her productivity. Among the "rank and file" women, no relationship was found among

Table 2.6
Multiple Regressions of Publication on Variables at Steps I, II, III by Sex

	Step I Coefficients		Step II Coefficients		Step III Coefficients	
	Male	Female	Male	Female	Male	Female
Subordinate to Work	.078	-.101	-.289	-.217	-.409	.167
Nonseparation Work-Leisure	.577	.459	.683	.243	.843	-.255
Definition as Researcher	.504	.663	.460	.534	.449	.485
Dedication	.661	.952*	.676	1.165***	.642	1.075***
Time in Research	.206*	.385***	.150	.315*	.136	.291*
Professor	.272	-.308	.055	-.294	.087	-.286
Associate	-.013	-.087	.163	-.054	.185	-.262
Tenure	1.182***	1.465***	.761	1.546***	.880	1.753***
Doctorate	.699	.481	.499	.456	.356	.295
Years Academic	-.088***	-.075*	-.085***	-.067	-.065	-.053
Research Important			.632	.517	.449	.670
Publication Quality Important			-.711	-.305	-.582	-.523
Number of Publications Important			.139	.142	.265	.187
Doctoral Program			.099	.077	-.065	.007
Faculty Size			.026	-.019	.023	-.014
National Officer			.200	-1.283***	.265	-1.077***
Editorial Board			1.134***	1.265***	1.242***	1.253***
Preschool Children					.649	1.938***
Children age 5-13					.561	1.205***
Children age 14-18					-.048	.587
Married					-.355	-.503
Constant	.164	-.559	.337	.333	-.509	-.554
R²	.190	.267	.274	.357	.292	.416
R² (adjusted)	.132	.198	.180	.247	.176	.287
S E	2.156	2.019	2.095	1.958	2.100	1.904
N	150	117	150	117	150	117

* $\leq$ .10
** $\leq$ .05
*** $\leq$ .01
sex difference $\leq$ .10
sex difference $\leq$ .05

marital status, presence of and number of children, and publications. Cole and Zuckerman concluded:

Our study shows . . . that for most of these women science and motherhood do mix. Women scientists who marry and have families publish as many papers per year, on the average, as single women.

The results of this study should not be interpreted as meaning that marriage and children have no effect on the careers of women scientists. They do, but they generally do not take their toll on women's research performance. How then can the persistent disparity in rate of publication between men and women scientists be explained? Why do men publish substantially more papers over the course of their careers than women with comparable backgrounds? The difference is evidently not explained by marriage and motherhood. It remains a puzzle requiring further comparative inquiry into the research careers of men and women scientists.[7]

One of the pieces of the puzzle suggested by the authors is, again, a selectivity measuring factor. Cole and Zuckerman report that close to four-fifths of the married women were married to scientists. "Women scientists married to scientists publish on the average 40 percent more than women who are married to men in other occupations." The difference in publication rate, the authors suggest, may result from "self selection, congruence of values or the flexibility of academic schedule."[8]

The most recently published study (June 1990) to examine male and female differences in scholarly productivity reported the results of a national survey of male biochemists who received their Ph.D.'s between 1956 and 1958 and between 1961 and 1963, and of female biochemists who received their Ph.D.'s between 1950 and 1967.[9] Examining scholarly productivity at different stages in the respondents' careers showed that, as students, childless married men and women were more productive than single respondents and respondents with children. Overall, men were more productive than women. Note in Table 2.7 that six years after obtaining their Ph.D.'s, childless married men and women were still the most productive, and single women were least productive. But overall, at each time period, men were more productive than women.

CONCLUDING REMARKS

In the quarter-century since the publication of "The Woman Ph.D.," with its surprising finding of higher productivity among married women than single women, many other studies on the productivity of female scholars have been conducted. Some of those subsequent studies have found positive relationships between publication rates and marital status and parenthood among women (Fox and Faver; Cole and Zuckerman). But almost all the more recent studies have also shown lower productivity among women as a whole compared to men. Simon et al.'s 1967 study found that on some measures, for example, mean numbers of articles and books, childless married women had higher publication rates than did men. None of the later studies supported that pattern. Overall, the data suggest that marriage and children are not impediments to women's scholarly productivity, but that gender, per se, seems to impede productivity.

Why does this pattern prevail? The most frequently offered explanation is a selectivity factor. Married women, and especially married women who have children, are special. They have more drive, more stamina, more ability, greater capacity to organize their multiple roles and responsibilities, and maybe, according to Cole and Zuckerman, more support from their mates, than other women. No explanations are offered for why single women are less productive

Table 2.7
Publications by Sex, Marital Status, and Number of Young Children

PANEL A: Publications in the Three-Year Period Ending Year Six

	Single	Married			
		No Children	One Child	Two Children	Three Children
Males					
Mean	3.15	4.16	3.69	3.45	4.71
Standard Deviation	3.42	5.48	3.94	2.98	3.99
N	142	87	102	60	7
Females					
Mean	1.86	2.54	1.95	2.11	0.00
Standard Deviation	2.24	2.96	2.19	2.30	0.00
N	309	107	41	18	1

PANEL B: Publications in the Three-Year Period Ending Year Eleven

	Single	Married			
		No Children	One Child	Two Children	Three Children
Males					
Mean	4.37	4.51	4.91	4.12	5.86
Standard Deviation	4.98	5.24	5.31	4.43	5.64
N	142	87	102	60	7
Females					
Mean	1.76	3.18	3.78	3.17	0.00
Standard Deviation	2.50	3.24	3.82	3.31	0.00
N	309	107	41	18	1

than men. Are they less able, less competitive, less driven than women who are married and have children? Or are they more likely to be the victims of discriminatory practices? After more than twenty-five years of study, the jury still seems to be out.

NOTES

1. Rita J. Simon, Shirley M. Clark, and Kathleen Galway, "The Woman Ph.D.: A Recent Profile," *Social Problems* 15, 2 (1967): 221–236.

2. M. S. Ferber and J. W. Loeb, "Performance, Rewards, and Perceptions of Sex Discrimination Among Male and Female Faculty," *American Journal of Sociology* 78 (1973): 995–1002.

3. W. Hamovitch and R. D. Morgenstern, "Children and the Productivity of Academic Women," *Journal of Higher Education* 48, 6 (1977): 663–645.

4. B. F. Reskin, "Scientific Productivity, Sex, and Location in the Institution of Science," *American Journal of Sociology* 83 (1978): 1235–1243.

5. M. F. Fox and C. A. Faver, "Men, Women, and Publication Productivity: Patterns Among Social Work Academics," *Sociological Quarterly* 26, 4 (1985): 437–549.

6. J. R. Cole and H. Zuckerman, "Marriage, Motherhood and Research Performance in Science," *Scientific American* 256, 2 (1987): 119–125.

7. Ibid., p. 125.

8. Ibid.

9. J. S. Long, "The Origins of Sex Differences in Science," *Social Forces* 68, 4 (1990): 1297–1315.

3

Career Patterns Among Women Law Graduates

This chapter compares the professional experiences of women and men who graduated from the College of Law at the University of Illinois from its founding in 1897 until the study was conducted in 1978. The year 1971 marked the beginning of a new era—one in which women formed sizable minorities in law school classes. The study found that, like their male counterparts, the large majority of women practiced law on a regular and continuous basis; but the women were more likely to work for public institutions and to earn less money. The "best" of the graduates were more likely to feel that their careers had been hurt by the fact that they were women.

The College of Law at the University of Illinois was founded in 1897. Three years later, in 1900, it graduated its first woman. Between 1900 and 1978, 300 women attended the College of Law, representing 5 percent of all students in the college from its founding through 1978. Between 1900 and 1941, forty-seven women graduated from the law school. During none of those years did women comprise more than 5 percent of the graduating class. The percentages, although not the absolute numbers of women in the college, increased dramatically from 1942 through 1945, when the United States was at war. During those years, women comprised 10, 22, 38, and 31 percent, respectively, of the graduating class, even though there were never more than six women in each of the graduating classes.[1] Between 1946 and 1970, fifty-seven women were graduated from the college. In each of those years there were never more than seven women in a graduating class; and women never comprised more than 7 percent of the graduates in a single year.

The graduating class of 1971 marked the beginning of change, signalling an upward trend that has continued until the present. The year 1978 witnessed the largest number (forty-one) of women ever to graduate from the College of Law in the 109 years of its existence. In the eight years from 1971 through 1978, 188 women, representing 62 percent of the total number of women, graduated from the College of Law.

The Illinois experience generalizes to other major law schools throughout the country. Earlier studies by White (April 1967) of 108 law schools and by Glancy (1970) of women at Harvard Law School confirm the upward trend.[2] Also, American Bar Association (ABA) statistics show that the number of women law students in all ABA-approved law schools increased from 7,031 in 1970 to 32,934 in 1977.[3]

The purpose of our study was to find out what Illinois women law students have done with their legal training after graduation. How many of them have pursued full-time legal careers? How many chose alternative careers? How many opted to become full-time wives, homemakers, and mothers? For those who have done or who are currently engaged in law work, to what extent have their careers been similar to or different from those of their male colleagues as measured by type of practice, size of firm, earnings, and so on? How did their performance as students affect their careers? And how many of them believe that they have been discriminated against because they are women?

RESEARCH DESIGN

A list of the alumni of the College of Law was compiled. Questionnaires were sent to all women graduates for whom we had addresses (284 out of 300). We then organized a male sample frame of the same size by selecting the first male name that appeared either directly above or below that of every female respondent in the alumni directory and mailed questionnaires to the same number of male graduates. Of the 568 questionnaires that we sent, 6 were returned "addressee unknown." From the remaining 562 we obtained filled-out questionnaires from 161 women and 164 men, for a return rate of 57 percent.[4]

The figures below describe the percentages of male and female respondents by their employment status.

Currently Employed	Men	Women
	(in percent)	
Full-time legal work	85(139)	73(117)
Part-time legal work	2(4)	8(12)
Full-time nonlegal work	10(16)	6(10)
Retired	2(3)	4(7)
Not employed	1(2)	9(15)*
Total	100(164)	100(161)

* We asked these women: If you are not presently employed because of your responsibilities to your family and if a law firm or business offered to hire you on a part-time basis, would you accept employment? Six women answered that they would.

Ninety-five percent of the men work full-time as opposed to 79 percent of the women. Over 90 percent of both sexes who work full-time are engaged in legal work. An additional 8 percent of the women pursue part-time legal careers. Only 9 percent of the women respondents (compared to 1 percent of the men) are not employed, or have not pursued a legal career in the past. Further analysis of the relationship between employment and personal status revealed that practically all of the women who are employed part-time have children.

While we cannot be certain that the women who did not respond to our survey have professional experiences similar to those who did, we did find that our results were remarkably similar to those reported by White and Glancy, who had higher return rates because they were able to recontact respondents several times. For example, the survey of women graduates from Harvard Law School conducted in 1970 revealed that 84 percent of the unmarried and 65 percent of the married women were working full-time.

MALE AND FEMALE CAREER PATTERNS

More Illinois law graduates (53 percent of the men and 38 percent of the women) are engaged in private practice than any other type of practice. As shown by the following figures, the biggest difference between the sexes is that women are more likely to work for federal and state governments (35 versus 21 percent) and men are more likely to have a private practice or work for a corporation (72 versus 50 percent):

Work Setting Current Position	Women	Men
	(percent)	
Private practice	38	53
Corporation	12	19
Federal government	11	9
State government	24	12
Public interest	3	1
Academic	5	3
Clerk	2	2
No answer	5	1
Total	100	100

A woman's marital or parental status has no major effect on the setting in which she works. For example, 37 percent of the never married, 42 percent of the married without children, 43 percent of the married with children, and 40 percent of the separated/divorced or widowed are employed in private practice. The types of practice that the men and women engage in are described below.

Type of Practice	Men	Women
	(percent)	
General	33	26
Trusts and estates	3	7
Litigation	11	7
Corporate	15	7
Tax	5	4
Criminal	6	12
Real estate	4	4
Other*	23	33
Total	100	100

* Includes family, labor, divorce, environmental, and poverty law practices.

Aside from "other," general practice is the largest category for both men and women. Men are somewhat more likely to specialize in corporate law and litigation, and women in criminal law.

The titles held by men are more impressive than those held by women. Thirty percent of the men as opposed to 15 percent of the women are either partners, advisers or counselors, or officers of a firm (presidents or vice presidents). Surprisingly, among those men and women in private practice, almost 25 percent of the women as opposed to 13 percent of the men are in firms with more than fifty attorneys.

Thirty percent of the respondents would not say how much they earned. Among those who were willing to reveal their incomes, 16 percent of the men earned $60,000 or more, compared to 3 percent of the women. The mean annual salary among all the women who worked full-time was $20,860; for the men it was $30,900.[5] When we divided respondents by sex and year of graduation, the following income picture emerged.

Year of Graduation

	Mean Income Before 1971	Mean Income 1971-1975	Mean Income 1976-1978
Female	$29,000	$24,480	$19,380
Male	40,980	35,290	19,615

These findings support those reported by White, who noted that the longer the time since graduation, the bigger the income gap between men and women.[6] As more and more women enter the legal profession, the long-term gaps in income are likely to decline.

On none of the characteristics we examined—work setting, type of practice, size of firm, or annual income—did a woman's marital or parental status make a difference so long as she was practicing law full-time.[7]

One major similarity among the women graduates from Illinois, Harvard, and the hundred or so other law schools that participated in the White survey is that a very large percentage of women have full-time legal careers. The White study found, as we did, that women were more likely to work for federal and state governments than were men (33 percent as opposed to 16 percent). White also reported that men earned more money than women, and with the passage of each year, men increased their lead over women. All three surveys discredited the myth that women are undependable associates because they are likely to leave their practice for marriage, motherhood, or other nonprofessional reasons. The Harvard study found that women changed jobs or dropped out of the labor force less frequently than did men. The White study reported that 55 percent of the women, compared to 39 percent of the men, made no more than one job change; and 34 percent of the men, compared to 24 percent of the women, changed jobs more than three times. The median number of jobs held by women since their graduation was 1.2, as compared to 1.3 for men; 15 percent of the women and 24 percent of the men had been working in the same firm or agency for more than ten years.

PERFORMANCE IN LAW SCHOOL

Respondents were asked to recall their academic performance, as measured by their senior class standing and whether they served on the Law Forum; these criteria were used to compare their subsequent careers.

Thus, when we asked about class rank on graduation from law school, the responses were as follows:

Class Rank	Women	Men
	(percent)	
Upper 10th percentile	20	17
Top quartile, but below upper 10th percentile	24	27
Second quartile	23	31
Third quartile	14	17
Fourth quartile	10	6
Don't remember	4	1
No answer	5	1
Total	100 (161)	100 (164)

Twenty percent of the women and 17 percent of the men said they ranked in the upper tenth percentile, and 67 percent of the women and 75 percent of the men said they ranked in the top half of their class. Twenty-three percent of the women and 20 percent of the men said they served on the Law Forum.

The shape of the response distributions to both of the items may be a function of "rose colored" memories or the greater willingness of "successful" graduates to fill out and return questionnaires. Nevertheless, we compared these responses about class rank and service on the Law Forum against various career characteristics and found that there were strong relationships between both activities and some of the standard measures of success in practice. For example, respondents who said they graduated in the top tenth percentile of their class were more likely to work in large firms and to specialize in corporate practice. As the figures below show, this pattern holds for women as well as men.

Women and Men in Top 10 Percent of Class by Size of Firm

Size of Firm	Women	Men
	(percent)	
Solo	16	5
2-10	26	27
11-25	11	9
26-50	5	32
Over 50	42	27
Total	100	100

Women and Men in Top 10 Percent of Class by Specialization

	Women	Men
	(percent)	
Trusts-Estates	11	0
Real Estate	4	4
General	21	23
Litigation	7	19
Corporate	25	27
Tax	7	19
Criminal	4	0
Other	21	8
Total	100	100

We also found that men and women who ranked high and who served on the Law Forum earned considerably more money than classmates who said they did not rank as high or did not serve on the Law Forum. But the sex differential remains quite stable when class rank or service on the Law Forum and year of graduation are controlled. For example, the current annual incomes of men and women who graduated in the top quartile of their class in the three time periods discussed earlier are as follows:

Year of Graduation	Men	Women	Difference
Before 1971	$48,000	$38,570	$ 9,430
1971-1975	43,330	26,470	16,860
1976-1978	19,335	20,000	+665

The income distributions for men and women who graduated below the top quartile look like this:

Year of Graduation	Men	Women	Difference
Before 1971	$36,000	$24,550	$11,450
1971-1975	26,250	21,670	4,580
1976-1978	16,725	16,000	725

The only deviation occurs among men and women who graduated in the top quartile of their class between 1971 and 1975: these women seem to be discriminated against more heavily than are their older or younger female colleagues.[8]

In one section of the questionnaire, we asked the women to tell us more about their experiences in the profession. For example, we asked them: "Think back to the time you graduated from law school up to the present and describe what (if any) effect the fact that you are a woman had on your career as a lawyer." When we compared the responses to this item by class rank, we found that those women who said they graduated in the top tenth percentile of their class were most likely to feel that they had been discriminated against.[9]

Perceptions of Discrimination by Class Rank

Fact of Being a Woman	Top 10%	All Others
	(percent)	
Little, if any, effect	27	25
Advantage	9	21
Disadvantage/discriminated against	43	25
Had to prove myself more than men	6	4
Less flexibility because of family responsibilities	0	5
Other	12	7
No answer	3	13
Total	100	100

One woman who graduated in the top tenth percentile of her class over thirty years ago and who today earns $100,000 a year wrote, "As the saying goes, you had to be twice as good to go half as far—but it was true."

A recent graduate who served on the Law Forum and who was in the top tenth percentile observed: "I believe that professional discrimination exists but is subtle. Partners are more likely to look over my work more carefully and critically than they would a male counterpart. Even liberated men seem to expect you to fulfill all traditional roles. This need to be a 'super woman' is tiresome." Another woman who graduated within the last two years and was in the upper quarter of her class and on the Law Forum wrote: "I feel that I have had to work harder in my career because of my sex. I have not been hampered within my firm, which has two senior women partners, but as a trial attorney I have encountered, on a daily basis, prejudices against women lawyers from judges, clerks, bailiffs, other lawyers, and even clients."

BIOGRAPHICAL DATA

One big difference between the men and women is that 77 percent of the men were married at the time of the survey compared to 46 percent of the women. Thirty-eight percent of the women have never been married, as opposed to 16 percent of the men. Forty percent of the women who are or have been married do not have children, as opposed to 17 percent of the men. The differences between male and female lawyers are comparable to those between men and women who have doctorates. For example, in a national survey of women Ph.D.'s conducted by the senior author in 1967, 95 percent of the men were married compared to 50 percent of the women.[10]

Among those women who are married, 41 percent are married to attorneys, 35 percent to other professionals (such as doctors and engineers), 10 percent to academics, and 14 percent to businessmen. Among the men, almost half (44 percent) of their spouses are homemakers, 6 percent are attorneys, and 13 percent are other professionals or in academia. The rest are teachers, secretaries, or salespersons.[11]

CONCLUDING REMARKS

The major findings of this survey are that the large majority of women who invested three years attending law school at the University of Illinois went on to practice law on a regular and continuous basis. But their careers have been different from those of men. Women are more likely to work for public institutions, their jobs are less likely to have prestigious-sounding titles, and their annual incomes are, on average, $10,000 lower. At the time of the survey many fewer women were married than men: 46 compared to 77 percent. Among those who are married, the husbands tend to be attorneys, doctors, and professors; the wives are most likely to be full-time homemakers.

Thirty-one percent of the women reported that they have been the targets of discrimination because they are women. Those who said they graduated at the top of their class were more likely than other women to report that they have been treated unfairly, although their salaries do not show that they have been discriminated against more heavily than women who were not at the top.

There is at least one encouraging postscript to this study. The women's belief that they have been or are being treated unfairly does not seem to have embittered them. All but 4 percent of the women urged prospective female law students to go to law school and to pursue careers in the law. They believe that the future for women lawyers will be brighter than the past or the present, and will afford opportunities for a wide variety of legal careers.

NOTES

1. The period in which the United States was involved in World War I did not affect the percentage or number of women in the College of Law. From 1909 until 1921 there were no women graduates.

2. Dorothy Glancy, "Women in Law," *Harvard Law School Bulletin* 21, 5 (1970): 22–23; James J. White, "Women in the Law," *Michigan Law Review* 65 (1967): 1051–1122.

3. *Prelaw Handbook 1977–1978* (San Francisco: Association of American Law Schools and the Law School Admission Council, 1977), p. 23. Between 1964 and 1970, the number of women law students jumped from 2,183 to 7,031.

4. We checked to see if there was any systematic bias in the rate of responses by year of graduation.

5. Based on data collected in 1965, White, "Women in the Law," reported that 9 percent of the men and 1 percent of the women earned more than $20,000 per year (p. 1057).

6. Ibid., p. 1059.

7. When we examined the previous position held by the respondents (62 percent of the women and 67 percent of the men described at least one other job), we found a pattern similar to that which we have described for their current position.

8. In general the same pattern emerged when we substituted service on the Law Forum for class rank. The average difference in income was about the same for women who served and for those who did not serve.

9. White reported that nearly half of the women believed that they had certainly or almost certainly been the object of discrimination because of sex by their present, former, or potential employer ("Women in the Law," p. 1068).

10. R. J. Simon, S. M. Clark, and K. Galway, "The Woman Ph.D.: A Recent Profile," *Social Problems* 15, 2 (1967): 221–236.

11. Two-thirds of the women's mothers and three-quarters of the men's mothers were homemakers. None were lawyers.

4

A Survey of Gender Bias Among Corporate/Securities Lawyers: Does It Exist?

Following publication of the American Bar Association's 1984 survey on the relative satisfaction of men and women with their chosen careers, and the hearings held in 1988 by the ABA's Commission on Women in the Profession, we decided to survey men's and women's beliefs about gender bias in one of the most prestigious legal specialties, and one that has been characterized as a male-dominated bastion of power—securities law. The survey found that both male and female respondents reported little in the way of bias or discrimination vis-à-vis women in the pursuit of their careers. At least in this specialized field, most women believe they are being treated fairly save for one area: the likelihood of making partner, especially a managing partner.

As recently as 1970, only 3 percent of all lawyers in the United States were women.[1] Since 1970, however, the number of women lawyers has increased exponentially, and women now represent 20 percent of the legal profession.[2] Recent surveys and commissions have addressed this influx in an effort to determine the effect of gender bias on the ability of women to advance in the legal profession while balancing that goal with marriage and family.[3]

In 1984 the American Bar Association Young Lawyers Division undertook the first in-depth survey to study the conditions for men and women in the legal profession and to measure their satisfaction with law as a career.[4] The National Survey of Career Satisfaction/Dissatisfaction (ABA Young Lawyers Survey) found that although "among both men and women, the vast majority were satisfied,"[5] twice as many women as men were dissatisfied in the legal profession.[6] Furthermore, the survey confirmed the difficulty women faced in making partner: only 13 percent of women were partners compared with 44 percent of men.[7] These professional barriers were mirrored in the lack of personal fulfillment: "Far more women lawyers [were] divorced, separated or single (45 percent v. 27 percent); more women lawyers [had] no children than their male colleagues (56 percent v. 40 percent)."[8]

To address these inequalities within the legal profession, the American Bar Association Commission on Women in the Profession (Commission) held hearings in 1988.[9] The Commission's Report (ABA Report)[10] concluded, first, that "although the profession has made room for women at an entry level, certain attitudinal and structural barriers exist which subtly limit women's opportunities for advancement";[11] second, that "women are not rising to 'upper' levels of the profession in appropriate numbers";[12] and third, that "sheer numbers of women entering the profession will [not] eliminate barriers to their advancement."[13] These conclusions, combined with current statistics indicating that "94 percent of all partners are men while only 6 percent are women,"[14] point to the existence of a "glass ceiling"[15] where women attorneys "can see but not reach the top."[16]

Even women attorneys who managed to penetrate this glass ceiling did so at great personal expense. Successful witnesses testified to partnership achieved "at the expense of not having a spouse and children."[17] Thus, it is not surprising that "data showed that significantly more men lawyers than women lawyers are married with children."[18]

Witnesses who chose to combine marriage and children with a law career found themselves on the "mommy track,"[19] not the partnership track.[20] Both women and men testified that because they requested part-time work arrangements to care for children, they were regarded as less dedicated to their careers.[21] Moreover, part-time work arrangements subjected these lawyers, male and female alike, to resentment from their peers.[22]

While both of these studies report on important data concerning the legal profession, neither takes into account the relationship of a legal specialty to gender bias. The purpose of this survey is to compare gender bias within one legal specialty with the findings of the ABA Report and the ABA Young Lawyers Survey. The specialty chosen was corporate/securities law because, for women lawyers, the business law firms that practice this specialty have always represented "male-dominated . . . bastions of power within the legal profession."[23] Moreover, securities law is ranked by other lawyers as the most prestigious of all legal specialties, as well as one of the most intellectually challenging.[24] This chapter discusses the results of a survey directed to the men and women in the Corporation, Finance and Securities Law Section of the District of Columbia Bar Association (Corporate/Securities Bar).[25]

RESEARCH DESIGN

The survey instrument was a self-administered questionnaire consisting of two sections. The first section asked respondents for basic demographic data (i.e., age, sex, marital status), law school education, and present employment information. The second section was designed to probe respondents' beliefs and opinions about issues relating to gender in their place of work and in the legal profession generally. In addition, several questions were either modeled on or duplicated from surveys from recent national polls in order to compare the attitudes of the present sample of District of Columbia attorneys against those of a national sample of the general population.[26]

An official membership list (excluding judges and inactive members) of the Corporate/Securities Bar was obtained from the District of Columbia Bar through their "Direct Mail with D.C. Bar Lists" service. Of a 1,438 attorney universe (the number of section members as of March 1, 1989), 1,055 were men and 383 were women. Questionnaires were sent to a random sample of 192 men and 192 women.[27] Thirty percent of the men and 49 percent of the women returned their questionnaires. Since no telephone or letter follow-up was made requesting participation, the 40 percent response rate was quite respectable. We attribute the high response rate to the issues addressed and to the nature of the questionnaire.[28]

SURVEY RESULTS

The respondents were 37.5 percent male and 62.5 percent female. Forty-seven percent graduated from the top twenty law schools in the United States.[29] There was no significant variation in law school attended by gender. The mean year of graduation from law school was 1980. Women were significantly more likely to have graduated from 1980 through 1988; 66 percent of the women surveyed graduated in this period, whereas 54 percent of the men graduated in the period ranging from 1959 through 1979.[30]

Sixty-eight percent of the respondents reported that their place of employment was a private firm; 16 percent were employed by the government, and 16 percent worked in corporations or trade associations or as solo practitioners. Respondents who reported that they were employed in a private firm were asked to state the number of attorneys in the firm. Forty-one percent replied that their firm size was ten attorneys or less. Firm sizes of eleven through fifty attorneys were reported by 12 percent of respondents; 8 percent identified their firm size as fifty-one through ninety-nine attorneys; and 39 percent of respondents reported that they worked in firms employing over one hundred attorneys. There were no significant differences between men and women regarding employment in a private firm or in the size of the firm in which they were employed.

Fifty-three percent of the attorneys in private firms were associates; 43 percent were partners. A higher proportion of men (53 percent) than women (40 percent) said they were partners. Four respondents were managing partners; none were women. Our survey also indicated that the male respondents entered the work force earlier. These results suggest that women corporate/securities lawyers face less gender bias in becoming partner than do women lawyers in general.

All respondents were asked about the number of hours they worked during the week, weekend work, and the amount of time spent on business travel. Law firm respondents reported that they averaged forty-two billable hours per week. Attorneys employed by a government or a corporation reported that they worked a mean of fifty hours per week. All respondents stated that they worked a median of twelve Saturdays and eight Sundays during 1988, and travelled an average of two days. We found no significant differences in the amount of travel or of work time between men and women.

In addition to information about law school education and employment, we asked respondents about their personal lives. The age range of the respondents was twenty-five to fifty-nine, and the mean was thirty-five years of age. Sixty percent of the respondents were married; 28 percent were single and have never been married; and the remainder (12 percent) were divorced or separated. There was a statistically significant difference in marital status between men and women.[31] Nearly three-fourths (72 percent) of the men, but only about half (53 percent) of the women, were married. More women (32 percent) than men (23 percent) were single; more women were also divorced or separated than men (15 percent of the women; 5 percent of the men). These 1989 statistics coincide with the disparities found by the 1984 ABA Young Lawyers Survey and the 1988 ABA Report.

Those attorneys who were married also reported on the employment of their spouse. Seventy-two percent of the spouses were employed full-time, 13 percent were employed part-time, and 15 percent were not employed. As might be expected, there was a difference between men and women regarding the employment status of their spouse. Only half of the men reported that their spouse was employed full-time, in contrast to 90 percent of the women.[32] Twenty-two percent of the attorneys who reported their spouse's occupation stated that their spouse is also an attorney.

Respondents were asked to state the number of children they had and, if they had no children, whether they planned to have any in the future. Forty-one percent of the respondents reported that they had one to seven children, with a mean of three. Fifty-six percent of the respondents stated that they did not have children. There was a significant difference between men and women on this question. While 64 percent of the men had children, 71 percent of the women did not have children.[33] Of those respondents who did not have children, more men (61 percent) than women (55 percent) planned to have them, and more women (23 percent) than men (11 percent) reported no plans to have children.

THE ROLE OF GENDER IN THE WORKPLACE

Respondents were asked if men and women in their place of work were treated equally on matters pertaining to salaries, responsibilities, promotions, and (for those employed in a private firm) becoming a partner and becoming a managing partner. As shown in Table 4.1, men responded positively to each of these questions more often than women.

The differences were statistically significant in three areas: responsibilities,

Table 4.1
Beliefs About Equality of Work Experiences by Gender, and Comparison of Present Study with National Poll*

	Attorneys, 1989		National Poll, 1985	
	Women	Men	Working Women	Men
Salary				
Equal chance	79**	93	57	48
Not equal	14	4	33	46
Don't know	6	4	10	6
N	95	57	1560	1000
Responsibility				
Equal chance	72	95	73	61
Not equal	26	5	18	33
Don't know	2	0	9	6
N	95	57	1560	1000
significance 0.002				
Promotion				
Equal chance	52	81	53	45
Not equal	26	5	35	49
Don't know	22	14	12	7
N	90	57	1560	1000
significance 0.001				
Becoming a Partner/Executive				
Equal chance	55	76	38	37
Not equal	17	7	45	54
Don't know	28	17	17	9
N	60	46	1560	1000
Becoming a Managing Partner				
Equal chance	11	33		
Not equal	30	19		
Don't know	60	49		
N	57	43		
significance 0.02				

* The exact questions are as follows: (1) in the present study, "Specifically, do you believe that men and women in your place of work are treated equally in the following areas."; (2) in the Roper study, "Do you believe women stand an equal chance with men they work with in the following areas?"

** Numbers are percentages. N is the actual number of respondents.

Source: The Roper Organization, reported in Simon and Danziger, Women's Movements in America (NY: Praeger, 1991), p. 87.

promotions, and managing partner potential. It appeared that men were more likely than women to believe that men and women have equal opportunity for advancement in their work environment. While most of the women believed that they had equal opportunities in the salary and responsibility areas, only slightly more than half thought that the same held true in the promotion and partnership areas, and only 11 percent felt that they had the same chances as men to become a managing partner. These percentages tend to reinforce the findings in the ABA Report of the existence of a glass ceiling.

Table 4.1 also shows the responses given to those items by a cross section of the American public in 1985. Note that women lawyers and working women in the population generally shared similar beliefs on the responsibility and pro- motion issues. Women lawyers were more likely than working women in the general population to believe they had the same chances as men to achieve a certain salary level or to become partner (in the case of working women, to become executives). There were, however, large differences between the re- sponses of the male lawyers and men in the general population. The male lawyers were much more likely to perceive equality between themselves and their female colleagues than were men in the general population.

In the next part of the survey, respondents expressed no significant gender variance in working with, supervising, being supervised by, being interviewed by, or entrusting a ''big case/deal'' to either a man or woman. Preferences were also solicited as to mentoring or being mentored by a man or woman.[34] The proportion of respondents who felt there was ''no difference'' ranged from 74 percent for whom they would rather be mentored, to 97 percent for whom they would entrust the ''big case/deal.'' Seven percent of the respondents stated they would rather be supervised by a man, while 4 percent said they would rather be supervised by a woman; and 9 percent reported that they would rather be inter- viewed by a woman as opposed to 5 percent by a man.

As shown in Table 4.2, statistically significant differences were apparent in the two situations related to mentoring. When asked whom they would rather mentor, 93 percent of the men said ''no difference,'' while 33 percent of the women preferred to mentor a woman. When asked whom they would rather be mentored by, 20 percent of the men answered a man and 4 percent said a woman. Seventeen percent of the women would rather be mentored by a woman, and 11 percent preferred a man. But over 70 percent of the men and women said they had no preference. Most of the gender preferences expressed tended to support current opinion that ''men are still generally more comfortable with other men''[35] and women ''can act as role models and mentors to younger women.''[36]

A portion of the questionnaire included items that had been asked in recent national surveys.[37] Table 4.3 shows responses to hypothetical questions about a husband or wife receiving a good job offer and what the couple should do.

In the national surveys a large majority of respondents stated that the wife should quit her job and relocate with the husband. When the hypothetical situation was changed so that the wife received the job offer, a smaller majority of

Table 4.2
Mentoring Preferences by Gender

	Respondents	
	Women	Men
I would rather mentor a:		
Man	1[*]	4
Woman	33	4
No difference	66	93
N	94	56
significance 0.0001		
I would rather be mentored by a:		
Man	11	20
Woman	17	4
No difference	72	77
N	63	56
significance 0.02		

[*] Numbers are percentages. N is the actual number of respondents.

respondents stated that the wife should turn down the job. In our survey, the majority of respondents checked more than one option in ways that could not be coded, and wrote comments. In fact, these questions elicited more write-in comments than any other items on the survey. The main points emphasized were the rejection of split or commuter marriages, and that consideration be given to the non-offeree spouse's personal and professional preferences in moving to a new location. In summary, there were no significant differences between men and women in our survey on these two questions, thus indicating an absence of gender bias on this issue.

The data in Table 4.4 compare the present survey with an item that appeared on a national survey directed only at women. It asked for respondents' preferences combining marriage, children, and career in order to provide "the most satisfying and interesting life." A large majority of the men and women attorneys in our survey wanted it all. Eighty-three percent of the women attorneys and 89 percent of the men attorneys wanted to combine marriage, children, and a career. In fact, women attorneys favored this goal even more than women in the national survey. Yet only 3 percent of the women lawyers would give up a career for marriage and children, as opposed to 26 percent of women in the general population. This appears to indicate that women attorneys value their law career highly. Consistent with this finding, we see that a certain contingent of women attorneys (12 percent), as compared with the women in the national survey (7 percent), also favored careers over children.

The last part of the questionnaire probed respondents' attitudes on the "mommy track" debate. Specifically, we asked if respondents believed that their place of work "should grant greater flexibility to employees with young children," and if these employees should expect fewer promotions (including making

Table 4.3
Opinions on Which Spouse in Childless Couples Should Move for a Better Job*

| | Attorneys, 1989 | | National Poll, 1985 | |
	Women	Men	Women	Men
Husband should turn down the job	5**	11	10	19
Wife should quit and relocate with husband	23	13	72	62
Husband should take new job and move, and wife should keep her job and stay	7	2	6	5
Other	65	74	12	14
N	82	46	3000	1000

If the wife is offered a very good job in another city?

| | Attorneys, 1989 | | General Public, 1985 | |
| | Women | Men | Women | Men |
	(percentages)		(percentages)	
Wife should turn down the job	4	13	55	58
Husband should quit and relocate with wife	23	9	20	22
Wife should take new job and move, and husband should keep his job and stay	9	0	8	6
Other	65	78	17	14
N	82	45	3000	1000
Significance	0.009			

* The exact question is: Suppose both a husband and wife work at good and interesting jobs and the husband is offered a very good job in another city. Assuming they have no children, which one of these solutions do you think they should seriously consider?

** Numbers are percentages. N is the actual number of respondents.

Source: The Roper Organization, reported in Simon & Danziger, Women's Movements in America (NY: Praeger, 1991), p. 122.

partner) and salary opportunities as a result of this greater flexibility. We asked this question of both women and men. The results are shown in Table 4.5, which consolidates the responses of male and female respondents because of their similarity.

Although over 80 percent of male and female respondents believed that their place of work should provide greater flexibility to employees with young children, more than 50 percent of both men and women also believed that these employees (both male and female) should expect fewer promotions and salary opportunities.

Table 4.4
Women's Choices for a Most Satisfying Life

	Women Attorneys	Women 1985
Combining marriage, children, and career	83[**]	63
Marriage, children, no career	3	26
Career, marriage, no children	11	4
Career, no marriage, no children	1	3
Marriage, no children, no career	0	1
Don't know	2	2
N	94	

[*] Exact question: Considering the possibilities for combining or not combining marriage, children, and a career, and assuming you had a choice, which one of these possibilities do you think would offer you the most satisfying and interesting life?

[**] Numbers are percentages. N is the actual number of respondents.

Source: The Roper Organization for Virginia Slims, reported in Wilkins and Miller, "Working Women: How It's Working Out," _Public Opinion_, Oct/Nov 1985, p. 45.

These responses tended to be in accord with the mommy track construct that those who work part-time receive less pay and advance more slowly than full-time attorneys.

Furthermore, the male and female respondents' attitudes reflected what the ABA Report found: "The assumption is that lawyers who ask for an extended leave or part-time work arrangement display a reduced professional commitment and want to receive 'special treatment.' This 'special treatment' subjects these lawyers to resentment from both male and female coworkers."[38]

CONCLUSIONS

On the one hand, our survey showed the District of Columbia Corporate/ Securities Bar to be without gender bias in many respects, especially when compared to the general population. On the other hand, gender bias does exist, as indicated by the responses of women lawyers to our survey's questions regarding the possibility of making partner or managing partner.

While the large majority of both men and women attorneys believed that they had equal opportunities in the areas of salaries and promotions, only slightly more than half of the women believed they had an equal chance with men of becoming a partner, and only 11 percent believed they had an equal chance of becoming a managing partner. In reality, among the respondents to our survey, only 40 percent of the women were partners, while 53 percent of the men were partners. Our survey also indicated that male respondents entered the work force

Table 4.5
Opinions Regarding Flexibility for Employees with Young Children, and Related Promotion and Salary Opportunities*

		For Women Employees	For Men Employees
Do you believe your firm/place of work should grant greater flexibility (e.g., in fewer hours per week and less travel) to women/men with young children?	% Yes % No N	83 17 145	81 19 144
If these female/male employees receive greater flexibility, do you believe that they should expect:			
Fewer promotions (including making partner)?	% Yes % No N	54 46 133	55 45 132
Fewer salary opportunities?	% Yes % No N	63 37 127	65 35 127

* Male and female respondents were consolidated because of the similarity of their responses.

earlier. These results suggest that women corporate/securities lawyers face less gender bias in becoming partner than do women lawyers in general.

In examining aspects of their personal lives, we found that while women lawyers overwhelmingly preferred the combination of marriage, children, and career, the majority were in fact single or divorced, and childless. As the ABA Report pointed out, women attorneys have given up many personal aspirations in order to achieve professional advancement. While survey respondents endorsed mommy track job flexibility for male and female attorneys alike, these same respondents felt that job flexibility should result in fewer promotions (including making partner). This statistic underlies the mommy track debate: once women attorneys get on the mommy track, can they ever get back on the partnership track? And will job flexibility be used to reinforce the glass ceiling, thereby resulting in a new lower-paying job classification for women only? Perhaps the answer to this debate lies in an awareness of the hazards of the mommy track, and a reexamination of the value our society places on the care and nurturing of future generations.

NOTES

1. See *Women in Law* (available from the American Bar Association).
Throughout U.S. history, until the 1970s, women have made up a very small proportion

of the lawyer population. The percentage varied only slightly between 1948 and 1970, from 1.8 percent to 2.8 percent, respectively. From 1963 through 1970, the percentage remained at or near the 2.8 percent mark.

See Jason, Moody, & Schuerger, Woman Law Student: The View from the Front of the Classroom, 24 *Clev. St. L. Rev.*, 223 (1975).

Prior to 1970, it was commonly believed that women would never be interested in law as a profession. See White, Women in the Law, 65 *Mich. L. Rev.*, 1051 (1967).

2. See *Women in Law*, supra note 1. Over 80 percent of women lawyers have entered the legal profession since 1970. Id.

This increase is also reflected in law school enrollment. Id. In 1966, 4 percent of all law students were women. Id. By 1986 women comprised 40 percent of law school graduates. Id.

3. The prevalence of gender bias is well documented. For a discussion of the gender bias women face in the courtroom, see W. Hepperle & L. Crites, *Women, the Courts, and Equality* (1987); D. Kirp, M. Yudof, & M. Franks, *Gender Justice* (1986); C. Lefcourt, *Women and the Law* (1984); K. Decrow, *Sexist Justice* (1974); Schafran, Women in the Courts Today: How Much Has Changed, 6 *Law & Inequality* 27 (1988); Cole, Gender Bias in the Courts, 13 *Vt. B.J. & L. Dig.* 5 (1987); Copleman, Sexism in the Courtroom: Report from a "Little Girl Lawyer," 9 *Women's Rts. L. Rep.* 107 (1986); Eich, Gender Bias in the Courtroom: Some Participants Are More Equal than Others, 68 *Judicature* 339 (1986); Discipline Caselaw Reflects Gender Bias in the Justice System, 7 *Jud. Conduct Rep.* 1 (1985); Frank, Sex Bias in Culprits: Women Suffer, 70 *A.B.A. J.* 36 (1984); Sex Bias in the Courtroom: Women Are Fighting Back, 69 *A.B.A. J.* 1017 (1983).

For a discussion of gender bias in selection of women judges, see Martin, Gender and Judicial Selection: A Comparison of the Reagan and Carter Administrations, 71 *Judicature* 136 (1987); Slotnick, Gender, Affirmative Action, and Recruitment to the Federal Bench, 14 *Golden Gate U.L. Rev.* 519 (1984); Federal Judges: Fewer Women, Blacks Today, 11 *Hum. Rts.* 3 (1983); Cohen, Is the Judicial Selection System Fair to Women and Minorities? Project Charges Discrimination, 4 *Pa. L.J. Rep.* 6 (1981).

For a discussion of gender bias commissions, see Fallon, Joint BenchBar Task Force on Gender Bias in the Legal System: A Challenge for the Future, *Vt. B.J. & L. Dig.* 3 (1988); Wakeen, Illinois' Gender Bias Task Force, *Chi. B.A., Rec.* 15; McLaughlin, Report of the New York Task Force on Women in the Courts, 15 *Fordham Urb. L.J.* 11 (1987); Schafran, Documenting Gender Bias in the Courts: The Task Force Approach, 70 *Judicature* 280 (1987); Blodgett, Gender Bias Studied in Tucson Area Courts, 12 *B. Leader* 14 (1986); Establishing a Gender Bias Task Force, 4 *Law & Inequality* (1986); Task Force Finds "Pervasive" Sexism in New York Courts, 17 *Crim. Just. Newsl.* 6 (1986); Caputo, Status of Women: A Review of Gender Bias in the Courts, 22 *Ct. Rev.* 16 (1985); Frank, Woman Power: N.Y. Panel to Dig Out Sex Bias, 70 *A.B.A. J.* 33 (1984).

4. See Hirsch, Will Women Leave the Law? 16 *Barrister Mag.* 22 (1989). The survey was based on a random probability sample of 3,000 lawyers of all ages drawn from both ABA member and nonmember lists totalling 596,706 lawyers (roughly 90 percent of the estimated number of lawyers at that time). The sampled individuals were sent lengthy surveys covering many aspects of their work environment, job histories, educational backgrounds, health and psychological profiles, and basic demographics. A total of 76.9 percent responded to a combination of the mailed survey and telephone follow-up survey.

5. Id. at 25.

6. Id. at 22.

7. Id.

8. Id.

9. The ABA created the Commission on Women in the Profession (Commission) in August 1987. See Siegel, Presumed Equal, 17 *Student Law*. 22, 26 (1988). Prior to that, the ABA Commission on Minorities addressed women's issues; however, the influx of women into the legal profession exacerbated gender issues and led to a widespread movement for a separate commission. Id.

The Commission's goals are "to improve women's status within the legal profession; identify the barriers women face; develop educational programs and other projects to resolve the difficulties; and recommend effective action for the ABA to take against inequities." Id.

10. See American Bar Association Commission on Women in the Profession, Report to the House of Delegates, ABA Commission on Women in the Profession (1988), based upon open hearings at the 1988 Midyear Meeting and from written testimony reports, surveys, and articles. Id. at 2.

11. Id. at 3–4.

12. Id. at 7.

13. Id.

14. Id. at 5. In addition, the Commission found that 75 percent of all associates in private practice are men, while only 25 percent are women. Id. The Commission further noted that "[a]ccording to a recent National Law Journal survey of the nations' 250 largest law firms, women are 33 percent of the associates but less than 8 percent of the partners. Women have been increasing their representation among partnerships at a rate of only 1 percent a year." Id.

Ironically, gender bias is prevalent even against women graduates of Harvard Law School. A 1984 study of the Harvard Law School class of 1974 found that less than a quarter of women class members who enter private practice were partners (23 percent). See J. Abrahamson & B. Franklin, *Where They Are Now: The Story of the Women of Harvard Law 1974*, at 201 (1986). Well over half (59 percent) of the men were partners. Id.

15. For the majority of women lawyers, the phrase "glass ceiling" connotes that the positions of greatest power, prestige, and economic reward are seemingly within their grasp, yet are unattainable. See Kaye, Women Lawyers in Big Firms: A Study in Progress Toward Gender Equality, 57 *Fordham L. Rev*. 111, 119–20 (1988).

A glass ceiling pervades law schools, the judiciary, and the government as well as private law firms. See ABA Report, supra note 10, at 6–7. In government, "women lawyers are concentrated in midlevel positions and underrepresented in positions with supervisory and decision-making responsibility." Jost, The Women at Justice, 75 *A.B.A. J*. 54 (1989).

16. See Kaye, supra note 15, at 120.

17. See ABA Report, supra note 10, at 7. One successful witness testified that "she found herself to be, '43, single, childless and typical.' " Id.

18. Id. at 16. The same statistics are amplified in the corporate sector, where "some 90 percent of executive men but only 35 percent of executive women have children by the age of 40." See Schwartz, Management Women and the New Facts of Life, *Harv. Bus. Rev*., Jan.–Feb. 1989, at 65–69.

19. See Schwartz, supra note 18, at 70–71.

Schwartz advises corporations to divide women into two separate and unequal classes: the career-primary women, who remain single or at least childless, and the career-and-family women, who mix children with the job. Id. at 70. The first group should be encouraged to pursue the fast track and aim for the A-Team in corporate management. Id. at 69–70. But most women, she writes, "are willing to trade some career growth and compensation for freedom from the constant pressure to work long hours and weekends." Id. at 70. This second track, derogatorily named the "mommy track," has sparked vociferous debate among members of the legal and business sectors alike. See Ehrlich, The Mommy Track, *Bus. Wk.*, Mar. 20, 1989, at 126; Skrzycki, "Mommy Track" Author Answers Her Many Critics, *Wash. Post*, Mar. 19, 1989, at 1, col. 1; Trafford, Mommy Track—Right to the Top, *Wash. Post*, Mar. 19, 1989, at C1, col. 1.

20. See ABA Report, supra note 10, at 14–16. Witnesses warned that "part-time arrangements must be structured so that they do not become another source of professional disadvantage to women, relegating them to lower-paid, lower-status jobs within the profession." Id. at 15. This lower-status job is already a reality. See Kingson, Women in the Law Say Path Is Limited by "Mommy Track," *N.Y. Times*, Aug. 8, 1988, at A1, col. 5.

21. See ABA Report, supra note 10, at 15. In particular, mothers who insist on part-time work often pay a price. See Rubin, Whose Job Is Child Care? *Ms*, Mar. 1987, at 32, 35.

22. See ABA Report, supra note 10, at 15.

23. See Kaye, supra note 15, at 112.

24. See Laumann & Heinz, Specialization and Prestige in the Legal Profession: The Structure of Deference, 73 *Am. B. Found. Res. J.* 155, 166, 178–179 (1977). Other lawyers view "securities law [as] the province of the specialist, if not the shaman. The financial activities regulated by the securities laws are incomprehensible to the uninitiated, and the federal securities laws themselves are an amalgam of seemingly oracular statutes, intensely detailed rules, and, in the anti-fraud area, a lively tradition of federal common law." Sargent & Greenberg, Research in Securities Regulation: Access to the Sources of the Law, 15 *Law Libr. J.* 98 (1982). Indeed, securities lawyers even tend to view themselves in the same manner. In one fable, a securities lawyer says to his partner, a tax attorney, "I'm a securities expert, and you're a tax wizard. We've mastered our respective fields of gimmickry." Id. (quoting L. Auchincloss, Powers of Attorney 71 [1963]). Securities and corporate lawyers tend to "band together" in what have become some of the world's largest law firms. They never travel alone as sole practitioners. See Laumann & Heinz, supra, at 187.

25. The Corporate/Securities Bar focuses on issues that arise under federal securities laws, including capital formation, enforcement, broker-dealer regulation, and the management of publicly held companies. It also addresses issues that concern federal and local regulation of banks, savings and loans, and other financial institutions and the management of publicly held companies.

26. See Simon & Landis, The Polls—A Report: Women's and Men's Attitudes About a Woman's Place and Role, 53 *Pub. Opinion Q.* 265 (1989).

27. The survey randomly sampled one out of every two women and two out of every eleven men. The questionnaire-cover letter packets were mailed April 5–7, 1989, with a return date of April 15, 1989.

28. The questionnaire design and response method were kept simple to encourage

attorneys to respond. We recognized that corporate/securities lawyers "bill" from $100 per hour for associates to $200–$300 for partners. Thus, a twelve- to fifteen-minute survey for an attorney billing by the quarter hour represents a substantial investment in money as well as time. Given this consideration, the high response rate indicates that the issues are important to attorneys, especially women attorneys.

29. The top twenty United States law schools are Harvard University; Yale University; University of Michigan; Columbia University; Stanford University; University of Chicago; University of California, Berkeley; University of Virginia; New York University; University of Pennsylvania; University of Texas, Austin; Duke University; Georgetown University; University of California, Los Angeles; Cornell University; Northwestern University; University of Illinois, Urbana-Champaign; University of Southern California; University of Minnesota, Twin Cities; and University of Wisconsin, Madison. See Brains for the Bar, *U.S. News & World Report*, Nov. 2, 1987, at 72, 73.

30. Significance < .05. Throughout this chapter "statistical significance" refers to the probability that the observed relationship is due to chance alone (i.e., due to sampling error). For example, a significance at .05 means that the observed relationship between the two variables could be found by chance alone in only 5 out of 100 samples drawn.

31. Significance < .05.

32. Significance < .0001.

33. Significance < .0001.

34. For purposes of our survey and this chapter, *mentor* is used as a verb.

35. Schwartz, supra note 18, at 70.

36. Id. The ABA Report found male attorneys unwilling to serve as mentors for women lawyers. See ABA Report, supra note 10, at 11–12.

37. See Simon & Landis, supra note 27.

38. ABA Report, supra note 10, at 15.

5

Women Corrections Officers in Men's Prisons

In addition to briefly reviewing the literature on women who serve as corrections officers in men's prisons, this chapter reports the results of a study that tests the legitimacy of women's authority to enforce prison rules, and offers a first-person account of what it feels like for a woman to serve as a guard in a medium security men's prison. The autobiographical data originate in my daughter's experiences as a prison guard. The chapter probes the relationships that are formed between male and female guards and between female officers and male inmates.

Women began working as guards in men's prisons in the early 1970s. Before 1972 Virginia and Idaho were the only two states that hired women as guards in men's prisons. According to Lynn E. Zimmer:

The job of prison guard is an extremely nontraditional occupation for women. Because the literature on occupational choice suggests, first, that people choose careers that match their personality and areas of expertise and, second, that women who choose nontraditional occupations tend to have nontraditional sex-role attitudes, one might expect female prison guards to espouse rather "liberated" attitudes concerning male and female roles in society. This is not the case. Female guards are a diverse group, especially with regard to sex-role attitudes. Only a small minority defined themselves as "liberated" or claimed to favor major changes in sex-role patterns. Many have extremely conservative views about sex roles; a few even suggested that guard jobs in men's prisons should not be open to women. If there is one generalization to be made about these women, it is that they become guards primarily because of extrinsic rewards—money, security, and fringe benefits. In this respect, the women are probably quite similar to their male counterparts.[1]

Male guards and male administrators of men's prisons were openly and strongly opposed to the presence of women or, at the very least, concerned about the consequences of their presence in the institutions. Male guards were not simply concerned about the threat to their own safety and the security of the institution posed by the presence of women guards. They were also resentful of the intrusion by women into their all-male world, the interruption of the camaraderie between the male workers. As Zimmer points out, not only did the introduction of women guards require the men to act differently on the job, but it also called into question their assumptions about the nature of their work.

Some inmates, on the other hand, reacted favorably to the presence of women guards, claiming that they treated them better and were more compassionate than male guards. But even these inmates expressed reservations about the ability of female guards to protect them in the event of an attack by another prisoner. Other complaints by inmates, as Zimmer observed, included the following: women guards invade their privacy, and women belong either in the home or in traditionally female occupations.

THE LEGITIMACY OF WOMEN PRISON GUARDS' AUTHORITY

An important question raised by Zimmer toward the end of her monograph is whether women guards "have the authority to enforce the rules and regulations against recalcitrant inmates." In 1987 we sought to answer that question by doing an empirical test of the legitimacy of women's authority to enforce prison rules.

The setting for the study was a medium security state institution in the Midwest that housed some 650 male prisoners and had a staff of 160 corrections officers.[2] The inmates had been convicted of crimes that included murder, rape, armed robbery, assault, and a wide range of property- and drug-related offenses.

The data collected for testing the legitimacy of the female officers' authority were the reports or tickets that were filed by the officers against inmates whom they claimed had violated a prison rule, and the consequences of such reports.[3] The reports were reviewed by prison officials (reviewing officers), who then determined whether a hearing should be conducted. Their decision to destroy the ticket or to go ahead with the hearing was based on substantive considerations (e.g., the information on the ticket did not substantiate the charges made by the corrections officer; or the ticket referred to physical evidence such as contraband and the evidence was not provided) as well as procedural considerations (e.g., the prisoner's identification number on the ticket had not been reviewed within twenty-four hours after being issued). During the hearing the inmate had the opportunity to present his case and to provide written testimonials obtained from witnesses. The hearing officer, an attorney employed by the state, acted as a judge and decided both the validity of the charges and, if the charges were upheld, the appropriate punishment.

The study design involved comparing the total number of tickets filed by all of the male and female corrections officers, the charges on the tickets, the pleas

Table 5.1
Violations for Which Tickets Were Written by Sex of Corrections Officers

Violations	Males	Females
	(percent)	
Physical attack with weapon	3.0	4.1
Physical attack without weapon	10.6	6.4
Insolence	7.1	12.2
Refused to obey orders	23.2	25.5
Alcohol and drugs	4.2	3.7
Disturbance	1.3	2.0
Wrong place	31.9	29.0
Threatening behavior	4.9	6.4
Sexual misconduct	0.8	4.7
Other	13.0	6.0
Total	100.0	100.0

the inmates made at the time of the incident, and whether the tickets were eventually upheld or denied by the hearing officers. Tickets written by civilians and supervisory personnel with the rank of sergeant and higher were excluded. Each of those groups contributed less than 7 percent of the total number of tickets.

The information collected was expected to indicate (1) whether women corrections officers filed as many tickets as male officers, and (2) whether the female officers' tickets were as likely to be upheld at the hearing as those filed by the male officers. If there was little or no difference in the number of tickets filed and in the rate at which they were upheld, then, we would argue, the female corrections officer's authority was as legitimate as that of her male counterpart.

In total we examined 1,170 tickets written by 45 female officers and 115 male officers. Women officers accounted for 28 percent of the corrections officer staff, and they wrote 24 percent (275) of the tickets. The difference in mean number of tickets by gender, 6.1 for women and 7.8 for men, was not significant.[4]

Men and women wrote tickets for the same types of violations, as Table 5.1 describes in detail. "Being in the wrong place" and "refusing to obey a direct order" accounted for 55.1 percent of the men's tickets and 54.5 percent of the women's tickets. The only behaviors for which women seemed to write more tickets than men were "insolence" and "sexual conduct" (e.g., reaching out to touch, or verbal misconduct). But even for those behaviors, the differences between men and women did not reach statistical significance. More tickets were written in the dormitories (59 percent) than anywhere else by both male and female officers: 72 and 56 percent, respectively. The school and the dining room were the next most frequent places in which violations occurred.

Eighty-six percent of the prisoners entered pleas of not guilty to the violations for which they were charged, with no difference by the gender of the officers writing the tickets.

The crucial question for establishing the legitimacy of the women's authority is what percentage of the prisoners were *found guilty* by the hearing officers after they stated their case. The results shown below clearly indicate that there was no difference in the likelihood of female as opposed to male guards' tickets being upheld or rejected.

Corrections Officers	Of Those Prisoners Who Pleaded Not Guilty Percent Found Guilty
Female	73.6
Male	74.5

The sanctions following the guilty verdicts also showed no clear differences on the basis of the guard's gender. Loss of privileges was the most frequently applied sanction, received by 70 percent of the prisoners who received tickets from male officers, and by 81 percent for tickets written by female officers.

Finally, we also compared the decisions made by the three male hearing officers as opposed to the three female hearing officers for tickets that were written by male and female corrections officers. Again, only the tickets of prisoners who pled not guilty were included. The figures in the cells are the "Percent Found Guilty," that is, the percentage of tickets that were upheld.

Hearing Officers	Corrections Officers Percent found guilty	
	Male	Female
Male	75.1	74.3
Female	75.2	70.6

Clearly, gender makes no difference. The three male hearing officers were just as likely to uphold the female corrections officers' tickets as the male officers' tickets, and the three female hearing officers also made no distinction in upholding the tickets written by male and female guards. On the basis of the data collected in this study, the answer to the concern raised by Lynn Zimmer is that the authority of the women corrections officers is as legitimate as that of their male colleagues.

A FIRSTHAND ACCOUNT BY A FEMALE PRISON GUARD

In this section we provide a first-person account of a young, middle-class white female guard's experiences in a men's prison.[5] The interview focuses on two controversial issues concerning female roles in the criminal justice system: (1) the quality of the interaction between the male and female corrections officers, and (2) the relationships between the inmates and the female officers. The controversy surrounding both these issues is developed in the course of the interview.

Biographical Statement

At twenty years old, I was the second youngest officer and the youngest female corrections officer assigned to the men's prison that housed 650 inmates. Four weeks into the four-month training program, I was still finishing my bachelor's degree in sociology at the University of Wisconsin in Madison. My last eight credits were independent study in which I wrote a paper describing the training program. Prior to this experience I had never seen the inside of a prison. My closest experience was doing volunteer work in Madison with delinquent adolescents.

I am 5'3'' and weigh 100 pounds. Although I was twenty years old when I started working in the prison, I heard later that when the Assistant Deputy Warden saw me enter the facility with other newly hired officers, he commented, "Here comes trouble." He said later that I looked more like sixteen than twenty, and the fact that I was "pretty," white, and female all added up in his mind to a complicated and troublesome situation. I left my job as a corrections officer thirteen months later to go to law school. During my stay at the prison, I received a letter of commendation from my shift commander for my role in a practice emergency mobilization; I graduated in the top 10 percent of the officer's training class of 240; and I believe I gained the respect of my supervisors and of the administrators at the prison.

The Prison Staff and the Size and Composition of the Inmates

When I started working at the prison, there were 150 corrections officers, about 40 of whom were women. I was the second youngest officer and one of two white female guards. The administrative staff consisted of the warden, two assistant deputy wardens, the inspector, three captains, six lieutenants, and ten sergeants. All of them were men except for two female lieutenants and one sergeant. The first woman corrections officer was hired about a decade earlier, in the late 1970s. Prior to that, women had worked in the prison as teachers, secretaries, [and] nurses, and in a social service capacity.

The inmate population in the fall of 1986 was 650; a year later the number had been reduced to 500, the maximum permitted under state regulations. Under the state classification system, the facility was a medium security prison specializing in parole violators. That meant that most of the inmates had served time earlier and were somewhat older than the typical state prisoner. The offenses for which they had violated their parole were primarily drug-related property crimes. There was also a fairly large group of violent offenders who had been found guilty of murder, manslaughter, rape, armed robbery, and aggravated assault. At least 80 percent of the inmates were black; there was a small group of Hispanics, and all the others were white males.

Duties and Responsibilities of Male and Female Officers and Guards

There was no difference between the duties and responsibilities of the male and female commanding officers. They included scheduling the custody staff, reviewing and updating employee personnel files, insuring that the daily operations of the prison ran smoothly, and filing reports on all critical incidents. Additionally, the commanders reviewed disciplinary "tickets" (reports) that officers wrote on the prisoners, occasionally heard prisoners' complaints, and monitored the on-the-job training of new officers. One member of the command staff was required to monitor each meal in the dining hall, and at least once during their eight-hour shift, they made rounds and inspected all the housing units. There was one commander in the control center at all times.

According to Department of Corrections policy, commanding officers were supposed to assign staff to positions without consideration of the officer's sex. The extent to which this policy was followed depended on which commander was doing the scheduling. At the beginning of my thirteen months, I noticed that women were always assigned to the information desk, the control center, and the front gate, and men were always assigned to the arsenal, the alert response vehicles, and the yard. But after a few months, I noticed a change. Men as well as women were regularly assigned to the information desk and the control center, and women were just as likely as men to be assigned to the arsenal and to the alert response vehicles. This change was the result, I think, of an influx of new officers and changes in the command staff.

Attitudes of Male Guards Toward Female Colleagues

I found that there was a dramatic difference between the attitudes of the men who had recently completed the training academy and those who had worked for either the state or the city for many years. The men who were newer to the system generally accepted women as equals and respected the women officers and commanders. There was a sense of camaraderie and teamwork among the new officers who completed the academy. But since the academy had only been in existence for a few years, there were a limited number of officers who shared this experience.

The male guards who had either worked for the city previously or had worked for the state for many years, by contrast, were more likely to resent women generally, and many of these officers indicated that they would have preferred that women not work inside the prison at all. For example, many of the women were housing unit officers. They were in charge of running a unit of forty to fifty-five men for eight-hour shifts. The yard crew, frequently all male officers, were in charge of relieving these unit officers for their restroom breaks as well as their regular meal breaks. The yard crew would often complain that the women officers demanded many more restroom reliefs than the male officers—even when the women officers did not need to use the restroom.

It is possible that the women did abuse the system. However, it is important to note that the male officers did not need to ask for frequent restroom reliefs because they were able to use the restrooms in the housing units, where there were only men's restrooms. The only women's restrooms were located in the kitchen and in the administration building.

Situations occurred several times a week when an officer would call the control center asking for assistance or complaining that he/she was having difficulty managing the unit. Other times a member of the yard crew who arrived at a housing unit to relieve a regular officer would notify the control center that the unit was out of control. These problems occurred more frequently with male officers than with female officers. There were several men and women who had problems controlling their units on a regular basis, and there seemed to be no solution for these officers other than to assign them to posts with less intimate contact. Additionally, there were some officers who could not carry out their duties properly whatever their assignment. The commanders were well aware of these problems and of the problem officers. But the commanders rarely, to my knowledge, made generalized statements indicating that one gender of officers was more capable than another. The shift commander occasionally remarked that women officers had a better overall record of reporting for work on time than men officers. One explanation offered was that the women officers were less likely "to stay out drinking until late at night." The occasions when women officers failed to report to work were usually because their children were sick or there were other family problems.

Occasionally, there were disturbances in the yard or in the housing units that required several officers to respond immediately. All officers, men and women alike, who were in a position to do so were expected to respond. As a general rule, officers were anxious to come to the aid of their fellow officers and responded quickly. However, there were some men and women officers who were notorious for disappearing during emergencies. There were also men and women officers who their fellow officers preferred not to have on the scene. Generally, the unwelcome male officers were feared because they tended to get the prisoners riled up and to escalate the situation. Certain women officers were not desired on the scene because they were ineffective. The prisoners made fun of these women, and thus it was more difficult to quell the disturbance.

Relations Between Prisoners and Female Guards

In general, the prisoners tended to relate to each officer as an individual. A minority of prisoners resented women in positions of authority. Some thought women officers deliberately teased them, while others believed that the women officers were too "manly."

The inmates tried to play on the officer's weaknesses in the hopes of receiving favorable treatment, or of getting the officer to do favors for them, or of allowing them to get away with prohibited acts. The prisoners would capitalize on women officers' appearance by complimenting them, making suggestive remarks, and asking a lot of personal questions. For example, the inmates frequently made comments about my age and the fact that I was white. They asked a lot of questions about my feelings toward black men, and about my marital status. I was given several letters full of compliments on my appearance, my charm, and my friendliness. I was also given special meals from the kitchen by prisoners who worked in food service.

For the first several weeks the prisoners would pull out all the stops to try and "set up" a new officer, be it a man or a woman. They tried hard to treat the officer as a "special" person. A different approach some prisoners took was to try to make new officers, women officers in particular, feel uncomfortable and frightened, hoping that these feelings would prompt the officer to seek out friendships with the prisoners.

The prisoners' primary concern is their personal safety and the safety of their belongings. Protecting the prisoners does not necessarily involve great physical strength or size; rather, it involves the guard's ability to maintain order and enforce the prison's rules. Initially, prisoners are skeptical of any officer's ability to maintain order. But once an officer proves him or herself, most prisoners are ready to accept that officer.

Not surprisingly, many of the prisoners were pleased to have a woman officer in place of a man as long as she established her competency. They believed that women treated them with more respect and more care than the male guards. They also felt that the women guards did not need to constantly affirm their power over the prisoners, in contrast to the male officers, who saw power and control as symbols of their manhood. Many of the prisoners were also more anxious to talk to women officers about their own personal situations, once they were past their initial "wooing" stage. In general, then, male prisoners like female officers.

Fear and Stress

Working at the prison was always stressful. There was a constant fear that the prisoners would riot and take control of the prison. I became accustomed to this type of fear and stress on a daily basis; but if there was a break in my schedule, such as a vacation, I would suddenly become aware of how different I felt without the fear and stress.

In addition to this constant stress, there were specific nerve-wracking incidents throughout the day. Any confrontation with a prisoner was frightening. Would he "get me" when I turned my back? Would he continue wandering around the cell block and not enter the cell? Would he give me the knife he was holding?

There were two particularly harrowing incidents. The first occurred in the dining hall, in which there were several hundred inmates and ten or fifteen officers monitoring the meal. One prisoner, as he entered the food line, began picking up trays and dropping them on the floor so that they made a loud noise, and continued to do this for several minutes. Many of the other prisoners became angry because of the disturbing noise. Others were clapping and laughing, apparently in support of the prisoner's behavior. It became clear, very quickly, that either the prisoners who were upset were going to put an end to the noise or the other prisoners would begin dropping trays as well. The officers in the dining hall had to remove the tray-throwing prisoner from the dining hall immediately, but they had to do it without the other prisoners becoming involved. If a battle broke out, the outnumbered officers would not have [had] much of a chance.

I was in the control center listening to the action on the radio. The lieutenant, the only commander on duty, and I worked out a plan of action. My role in the "plan" was to operate the video camera in order to make sure there was a record of the incident in case of lawsuits. I was also to be one of two officers responsible for preventing the prisoners in the dining hall from interfering with the officers trying to apprehend the disruptive prisoner.

Just as the prisoner stopped dropping the trays and turned to walk out of the dining hall, five officers and the yard sergeant approached him. The prisoner did not react, and walked with the officers down the walkway toward the cell block. As the prisoner and officers walked past me and the other young officer, we stepped onto the walk in front of a large group of about 100 approaching prisoners. As soon as the prisoners saw me holding the video camera, they were aware that something unusual was taking place and began shouting questions and accusations. As they came closer to where the other officer and I were standing, I wondered how we were going to keep 100 angry prisoners from marching over us into the cell block.

Inside the cell block the officers and sergeant escorting the prisoner grabbed him for the first time. They quickly handcuffed him and marched him off to the control center. He did not resist. I had managed to film the action by running from where I had been standing on the walk into the cell block. Once the prisoner and officers were on their way to the control center, I ran back to help the lone officer restrain the prisoners from coming inside. Two scenarios kept running through my mind: they would grab me and the other officer, carry us to another part of the yard, and kill us; or they would just knock us to the ground and trample over us.

One prisoner began recounting to the others information he had about an incident at another prison where the officers had beaten an inmate to death. Suddenly all the prisoners became convinced that the same thing would happen in our cell block. As loudly and clearly as we could, we tried to convince the prisoners that nothing of the kind was going to happen, that the lieutenant and sergeant had merely handcuffed the prisoner and taken him to the control center to try and find out what inspired the tray throwing.

The incident passed without anyone getting hurt. We were fortunate that the prisoner stopped throwing trays and walked out of the dining hall on his own because we had no plan for getting him to stop. We all knew that if the officers grabbed the prisoner in the dining hall in full view of the other inmates, there could have been a riot. Some of the prisoners would have come to his aid, while others might have tried to help get the disruptive prisoner out of the dining hall.

In retrospect, I can still remember how frightened I felt standing in the yard in front of a hundred angry inmates. But as the incident was occurring, I also knew I had no choice but to stand there and try to dissuade the prisoners from taking any violent action, hoping meanwhile that the sergeant would get the prisoner up to the control center before the prisoners in the yard decided to get me! Both my instincts and my record of behavior with the prisoners worked in our favor. Because I had a reputation of being straightforward with the prisoners, instead of pushing toward me, many of them stood still and asked me a lot of questions that I must have answered to their satisfaction. Perhaps the fact that I was a woman, and a woman for whom they had some respect, helped defuse the situation.

The second particularly frightening experience occurred late one night in the segregation unit. I found working the midnight shift more frightening than either of the other two shifts because usually I worked alone and, except for dim safety lights, the cell block was dark. There were far fewer officers assigned to midnight shifts because there were no prisoner activities or movement during the night.

On this particular night, I was making my rounds through the segregation unit to which I had been assigned. As I walked past each cell, I pulled on the bars to make sure the cell door was securely locked. Just as I reached the last cell, one of the prisoners called my name. I was startled because I thought they were all sleeping. I turned around quickly and saw a prisoner standing in the middle of the cell walkway, the cell door wide open. I knew I did not have time to run out of the cell block, open the lock box, close the cell gate behind me, and lock it. The prisoner could jump on me before I ever made it out of the gate.

I looked at the prisoner and calmly asked him to step back into the cell. He did not move. I decided I had better get closer to him if I was going to speak, as several prisoners had already been awakened by our exchange. When I got within several feet of the prisoner, but not, I hoped, within arm's reach, I again asked him to step back into his cell and shut the door. He began to chuckle, but he did not move. We both stood there looking at each other. Finally, the prisoner slowly walked into his cell and pulled the door shut. There was one more thing I had to do: check that the prisoner's cell was, in fact, locked so that he could not step out of it again. With great apprehension I walked up to his cell door and pulled on it. It did not open.

I said goodnight and walked down the long walkway and out of the gate. It seemed as if it took me twice as long as usual to get to the gate and lock it. When I finally made my way back to the officers' station, I was shaking so hard I could not write.

In retrospect, I have a positive overall assessment of women corrections officers' ability to exercise authority in a men's prison and of their acceptance by male colleagues. I never saw a male officer threatened or endangered by having to work alongside a female officer. Female officers were as likely as male officers to assume their responsibilities, stand up to the prisoners, and enforce the rules—a fact that was recognized, for the most part, by both male and female officers. As for the prisoners themselves, most of them liked women corrections officers, viewing their presence as a humanizing influence in the prison environment.

NOTES

1. Lynn E. Zimmer, *Women Guarding Men* (Chicago: University of Chicago Press, 1986), p. 50.

2. Judith Simon was employed as a corrections officer at the prison and collected the data described in this chapter during her period of employment from July 1986 to August 1987. This section appeared in Rita J. Simon and Judith D. Simon, "Female COs: Legitimate Authority," *Corrections Today*, August 1988, pp. 124–132.

3. Prison personnel other than corrections officers may write tickets. We found that counselors and other civilian employees, along with sergeants, lieutenants, and captains, did exercise that prerogative, but that over 71 percent of the tickets were written by the corrections officers.

4. One of the women guards wrote more tickets (twenty) than anyone else. Before coming to work at the prison described in this study, she had worked at a maximum security men's prison in the same state, where she had been badly beaten by inmates who used bricks.

5. A shortened and edited version of this section appeared in Judith Simon and Rita J. Simon, "Some Observations on the Status and Performance of Female Correction Officers in Men's Prisons," *Issues in Justice* (Bristol, Indiana: Wyndham Hall Press, 1990), pp. 140–148.

6

Rabbis and Ministers: Women of the Book and the Cloth

This study compares the backgrounds, motivations, and experiences of female rabbis against those of female ministers. It specifically describes and contrasts the findings from our study of women in the rabbinate against findings from our study of women clergy in selective Protestant denominations.[1] The findings indicate that rabbis are more likely to emphasize the secular aspects of their work, while ministers, many of whom feel they were "called" to the ministry, first identify spiritual roles. Women from both traditions believe they are more approachable and less formal than their male counterparts. They also believe they are more likely to "personalize" religious ceremonies, and that their preaching is more emotional and more relational than that of their male colleagues.

In 1972, at Reform Judaism's Hebrew Union College in Cincinnati, Ohio, the first woman rabbi was ordained in the United States. Today more than 150 women rabbis have been ordained through Reform Judaism, and since then, by the Reconstructionist (1974) and Conservative (1985) movements. Women rabbis represent about 5 percent of the approximately 3,500 rabbis in the United States.

Although several Protestant denominations were ordaining women by the 1880s, it was not until the 1970s that Protestant women clergy began to appear in large numbers. Today they represent between 10 and 12 percent of all Protestant ministers, recognized and ordained by almost all of the mainstream Protestant denominations, with the exception of the Mormons.

There is no social science literature comparing the experiences and role performances of female rabbis and ministers. While there is substantial literature on female ministers, much of it consists of personal accounts and essays,[2] impressionistic and journalistic works,[3] or scholarly and passionate essays about the debate over women's ordination.[4]

In the social science literature, significant studies explore the experiences of female seminarians;[5] the reactions of lay leaders to the idea of women in the ministry and how actual encounters with these women have lessened their resistance;[6] the commonalities of the spiritual life stories of female Pentecostal preachers in central Missouri;[7] and the experiences of seventeen clergywomen and their commitment to responsible caring for others, rooted in their normative female orientation to life.[8] The most extensive study to date interviewed nearly 1,500 male and female ministers and lay leaders about their education, ministries, and role performance.[9]

The literature on women rabbis falls into the same genres as that on women ministers. Hundreds of articles have appeared in the popular, and especially the Jewish, press. In the beginning, they covered the debates about female rabbinic ordination.[10] Since then, they have included scores of interviews with these women and offered impressionistic accounts of the ways in which they are reshaping the rabbinate.[11] The few social science works surveying female rabbis and their career paths, aspirations, and performances have been largely unpublished papers and theses.[12] The few published studies explored the questions of male and female role performance and lay receptivity evident in the social science literature on female ministers.[13]

DATA COLLECTION

We conducted in-depth interviews with thirty-five female rabbis and twenty-seven female ministers. Eighteen of the rabbis were interviewed during a biennial meeting of the Women's (Reform) Rabbinic Network in Boston in April 1989. Most of the others were interviewed in the Washington, D.C., metropolitan area. They included nearly all female rabbis working or living in Washington ordained before 1988 and several of the rabbis who attended the 1989 annual meeting of Conservative Judaism's Rabbinical Assembly, which was held in Washington. Working from denominational church directories, we randomly selected the names of female ministers living in the Washington metropolitan area. All of the women contacted agreed to be interviewed.

Each interview consisted of three major sections. In the first, the respondent told her story—why and how she chose to become a rabbi or a minister. The second part addressed the religious training she had pursued as well as her job history since ordination. In the third section, the respondent had an opportunity to explain how she performs and interprets her role as a minister or rabbi as compared with her male counterparts.

COLLECTIVE PROFILE

Of the thirty-five rabbis interviewed for this study, twenty-five have pulpits, two are Hillel directors, and three work as educators and counselors in Jewish schools or community centers. Of the remaining five, one is a faculty member at an urban university, two are graduate students, and two are not employed outside their homes. Their geographic locations range from Toronto to Florida, from Boston to California. Sixty percent of the respondents are located in communities in New York, Pennsylvania, New Jersey, Maryland, and Washington, D.C.

Among the rabbis who have pulpits, six are assistant rabbis, three are associates, and sixteen are solo rabbis whose congregations range in size from 55 to 350 families. Those who are associates or assistants often serve congregations with 1,000 families or more.

The Protestant ministers include six Presbyterians, five Episcopalians, five Unitarian Universalists, five United Methodists, four Lutherans, one Southern Baptist, and one African Methodist Episcopal. Fourteen of them work as assistants or associates in large churches headed by male ministers. Six are solo pastors in their own, generally smaller, churches. A seventh woman is the senior pastor in her church, supervising a younger female minister.

The other six are not involved in parish ministry. One is on leave to pursue a doctoral degree. Another is at home to raise her children. Two are adjunct professors at seminaries, and two are chaplains, one in a part-time position at a retirement home, the other at a large medical center.

The rabbis are generally younger than the ministers, most likely because of the more recent dates of the ordination of the first woman rabbi in the various denominations: all but four are in their thirties, two are younger than thirty, and two are in their forties. Ten of the ministers are in their thirties, nine in their forties, and seven in their fifties, and one is sixty-five years old. Twenty-seven of the rabbis and twenty of the ministers were ordained between 1980 and 1988. Five ministers and eight rabbis were ordained in the 1970s. One minister has been working as a religious educator since 1960.

All but three of the rabbis were ordained at Hebrew Union college; one is a graduate of Conservative Judaism's Jewish Theological Seminary; and two were ordained by the Reconstructionist Rabbinical College. Since Reform Judaism has been ordaining women for the longest period of time, the bulk of the female rabbis graduated from its seminary. In fact, until Conservative Judaism's leaders admitted women to its Rabbinical School in 1984, several women who were raised within the Conservative movement entered the rabbinate via Hebrew Union College. All but three of the congregational rabbis lead Reform temples, two are assistant rabbis at Conservative synagogues, and one has her own Conservative pulpit.

The Protestant ministers attended a wide variety of theological seminaries in preparation for their religious careers. For many, the decision involved choosing a conveniently located seminary that was affiliated with their church. Others said that they specifically sought out seminaries that would be ethnically or theologically diverse, or that offered stringent academic challenges. Several second-career women said that they wanted to attend a seminary where they would be treated as adults, where their age, past experience, and education would be taken into consideration. For women with families, geographical considerations were important because they did not want to uproot or be separated from their families.

The ministry was a second—and sometimes third—career for sixteen of the Protestant women. Their previous careers included art editor, store manager, counselor, writer, professional bowler, teacher, college professor, business management executive, and nurse. While many of the women were at least peripherally involved in their churches while they worked at other careers, only four mentioned holding lay positions in the church for any extended period of time prior to attending seminary.

Seven of the rabbis have graduate degrees in social work, law, Hebrew literature, and other fields, which they completed either before or after ordination. Fourteen of the Protestant ministers hold academic degrees beyond Master of Divinity, in part because the ministers were more likely to have entered the ministry from other careers.

Most of the ministers and rabbis come from middle-class families. The rabbis' fathers are lawyers, engineers, and businessmen; one is a rabbi. Their mothers are either homemakers or work in predominantly women's professions, such as social work, nursing, and teaching. Five of the ministers have fathers who are or were ministers. Others are daughters of professionals, businessmen, government workers, and farmers. Their mothers are homemakers, clerical workers, teachers or professors, clerks, artists, and writers.

Of the eighteen rabbis who are currently married (four are divorced), six are married to practicing rabbis, three to professors of religion. The others are married to lawyers, engineers, and businessmen. Seventeen of the twenty-two who are or have been married have at least one child.

Seventeen of the Protestant ministers are currently married. Five are single, three divorced, one widowed, and one separated. Four are married to ministers. The husband of one is recently retired and currently attending seminary. Five are married to attorneys. The occupations of the other spouses include physician, chemist, mathematician, writer, backhoe operator, fundraiser, health physicist, and government worker. Seventeen have at least one child.

WHY THEY OPTED TO BECOME RABBIS AND MINISTERS

The rabbis and ministers were asked to describe the ideal role or roles a minister or rabbi should play in a community, and whether that role applies to men as well as women. Although there was some overlap in the responses of the ministers and rabbis, the ministers were much more likely to identify spiritual roles, while the rabbis tended to mention more secular roles, such as "community leader" and "social justice advocate." Some of the roles most commonly identified by the ministers were "preacher," "teacher," "enabler," "giver of pastoral care," "prophet," "advocate of justice," "priest," "healer," "administrator," and "leader." Many of the ministers emphasized the importance of being able to fill the spiritual needs of the religious community.

Whatever else she said, almost every rabbi included "teacher" in her definition of her role in the community. After that, "counselor," "spiritual advisor," and "leader" were frequently mentioned roles. Some saw the rabbi's role as a "community spokesperson and a leader," as a "resource person," "a moral voice," "a spokesperson for what we want Judaism to stand for," "a person with roots," "someone who cares about Judaism and the Jewish people," "the moral conscience of the Jewish community."

Both groups believed the roles should apply equally to male and female clergy, although a few ministers said that they thought some roles—such as those of "facilitator" and "nurturer"—came more easily to women than to men.

When asked why they decided to enter their present careers, the ministers frequently spoke of being "called" to the ministry, a term absent in the rabbis' responses. In fact, fourteen of the ministers specifically said that they were called to the ministry; several others spoke of being pulled or drawn in that direction. Many of the ministers who spoke of a call said that the only decision they had to make was whether to respond to it. A few said that they first received the call as children; others felt called as adults, but said that they could look back and interpret earlier events as calls. Most often, these women said that the call came gradually and subtly.

Other Protestant women spoke of this process in more pragmatic and rational terms. Entering the ministry, they said, seemed a logical step. The Unitarian ministers especially said that it represented a career where they could best use their talents and interests. Others had found the church a symbol of stability as children, a place where they felt comfortable and welcomed.

The rabbis' responses lacked similar references to "spiritual" reasons. The closest any of them came to such a discussion was a mention of interest in religion expressed by two rabbis. Instead, they said that being a rabbi allowed them to be more involved in Jewish life, with more influence and higher status than are usually afforded by careers in teaching, social work, or counseling. For example: "I wanted the freedom and power that being a rabbi allows one to have in the Jewish community." And "I wanted to be a leader as well as a teacher in the Jewish community." Another gave "no spiritual reason, but felt inadequate working in the Jewish community with [only] an MSW." These aspects involving prestige and status were noticeably absent in the Protestant ministers' responses. In fact, a few ministers spoke of the recent "devaluation" of the church in people's lives.

The rabbis and ministers who were ordained in the 1970s and early 1980s were more likely than those ordained later to tell stories of negative reactions to women in the ministry and of difficult periods of adjustment. The women who were ordained earlier did not have the smooth sailing experienced by those who were ordained from the mid-1980s onward. Their stories had many of the same elements as those told by other women pioneers in the profession.[14] The message had a familiar ring to it: the journey of the pioneer was harder and more uncertain, while those who came later have an easier time because they can walk in the paths forged by their predecessors. Four of the sixteen solo rabbis chose part-time work. For the remaining twelve, their current positions were their second or third rabbinic posts since ordination. Of the nine assistant and associate rabbis, five had held rabbinic positions elsewhere—one as a Hillel director and the others as assistants, associates, or part-time rabbis in smaller congregations.

The solo rabbis were happier and more satisfied, and expressed a greater sense of accomplishment than did the respondents who worked in other capacities. We comment on this even though most of the solos began their job descriptions with the phrase, "I do everything," and went on to describe long hours, involved relationships, complex responsibilities, and the different functions they perform. Nevertheless, on the whole, they claimed to do either what they wanted to do or what they had always envisioned a rabbi should do when they decided on that profession and lifestyle.

Fourteen of the Protestant ministers worked as assistants or associates in multistaff churches headed by men; six were solo pastors in relatively small churches; and one was a senior pastor in a rather large two-pastor church. Like the solo rabbis, the solo ministers seemed, in general, more satisfied with their situations and optimistic about the future. Some went from larger, multistaff churches to small one-pastor churches. Others had their first jobs in small country churches and were able to move up as associates in large multistaff churches. The solo pastors also appeared less bothered by negative reactions to them, more in control, and more confident than the associates and assistants.

ROLE PERFORMANCE AND INTERPRETATION

Almost all of the rabbis and seventeen of the ministers said that they carried out their duties as ministers and rabbis differently from male colleagues of comparable age and background. While these were impressions unsubstantiated by outside observation and analysis, it is significant that both the rabbis and the ministers claimed to differ from their male colleagues in almost identical ways. The women described themselves as "less formal," "more engaging," "more approachable," "more likely to reach out to touch and hug," "less likely to seek center stage," "more people-oriented," "more into pastoral care," "more personal," and "less concerned about power struggles." The respondents believed that they were easier to talk to than their male colleagues. The ministers generally portrayed themselves as being less hierarchical and less likely to stress the power difference between minister and parishioner.

Many of the ministers and rabbis said that they conducted rite of passage ceremonies differently from their male colleagues. They saw themselves expending greater effort to involve the parties in the ceremony as much as possible and to tailor the ceremonies to the personalities of the participants. Both rabbis and ministers emphasized the warmer and more personalized nature of their services. Some of the ministers said that the differences were more likely generational than gender-related.

About half of the ministers, including all five of the Unitarian Universalist ministers, and nearly all of the rabbis believed that their sermons differed significantly from those of their male counterparts. Again, the explanations were similar, in some cases nearly indistinguishable. The ministers considered their sermons "more personal," "more emotional," "conversational," "casual," "more relational," "more spiritual," and seemingly more spontaneous, although they are rarely so in fact. Several mentioned that they were more willing than male ministers to expose themselves emotionally, to deliver sermons in which they "pour everything out." Nine women specifically said that they used "storytelling"—sometimes about their own lives—much more often than men do.

On this question, the rabbis frequently mentioned psychologist Carol Gilligan and the influence of her work on the manner and tone of their sermons.[15] The female rabbis said that male rabbis were much more likely to "pontificate," to "hold forth," "to exhort" their audience. These women, on the other hand, believed that they spoke in more "relational terms." Like the ministers, they considered their style more personal and more conversational. Also like the ministers, they emphasized "inclusivity" and language that is less abstract, more concrete and vivid.

The rabbis were more likely than the ministers to report that their sermons explored social justice issues. In fact, a few ministers said that such topics fell more within the purview of their male counterparts than their own. For the rabbis, the most frequently mentioned topics were abortion, family violence, homelessness, child care, civil rights, and AIDS. Several of the ministers said that while they tackled such topics, they were more likely to approach them from a first-person perspective.

The respondents were asked whether they placed greater emphasis than did male ministers on some aspects of their jobs. Several of the rabbis said that they tended to spend large amounts of time with children and adolescents because their primary responsibilities and assignments—such as religious education—required that they do so. This was also true of the ministers: several said that they spent more time with people, and less on administrative tasks, because time spent with people makes up the "heart" of the ministry. Indeed, the women seemed most reluctant to learn and to participate in those aspects of the rabbinical and ministerial roles that involve supervision of staff, dealing with board members, and the general responsibilities of running a complex organization.

For the rabbis, the most gratifying experiences derived from their roles as teachers and as therapists and counselors. For most of them, these were the roles they performed best and for which they felt most appreciated. In addition, they frequently cited innovations in the life cycle ceremonies as a source of satisfaction. Younger rabbis spoke of the pleasure they received from being role models for young girls in the congregation.

Somewhat similarly, the ministers spoke of "the privilege of being involved in people's lives, from birth to death," and of "navigating life's passages with people." During rite of passage ceremonies, especially dealing with the dying and their funerals, the ministers spoke of how they felt close to God and to the participants, and of their satisfaction that God had used them to comfort those in need.

Toward the end of the interview, the respondents were asked to look ten years into the future. The ministers believed that ministers of both sexes will be more alike in the way they approach their work. The rabbis, on the other hand, thought that women will be more likely to forge their own definition of how a rabbi should relate to and interact with her congregants, a role that male rabbis will not emulate.

CONCLUDING REMARKS

Like law, the ministry has become a recent avenue of opportunity for women desiring a professional career. Where the rabbis and ministers differ is in how they expect to perform in those careers. The rabbis see their roles in much more secular terms. They want to change the world, especially on matters affecting women. Hence, they champion social justice causes and perceive their new status as enhancing their effectiveness in bringing about these changes. While the ministers care about these issues, they also stress spiritual matters, God, and the belief that they were "called" to their new role.

NOTES

1. Rita J. Simon and Pamela S. Nadell, "Teachers, Preachers and Feminists in America: Women Rabbis," *Shofar* 10, 1 (Fall 1991): 2–10.

2. Joy Charlton, "Women in Seminary: A Review of Current Social Science Research," *Review of Religious Research* 28 (1987): 305–318.

3. Priscilla Proctor and William Proctor, *Women in the Pulpit: Is God an Equal Opportunity Employer?* (New York: Doubleday, 1976).

4. Emily C. Hewitt and Suzanne R. Hiatt, *Women Priests: Yes or No* (New York: Seabury Press, 1973); and H. Wayne House, *The Role of Women in Ministry Today* (Nashville: Thomas Nelson, 1990).

5. Sherryl Kleinman, *Equals Before God: Seminarians as Humanist Professionals* (Chicago: University of Chicago Press, 1984).

6. Edward C. Lehman, Jr., *Women Clergy: Breaking Through Gender Barriers* (New Brunswick, NJ: Transaction, 1985).

7. Elaine J. Lawless, *Handmaidens of the Lord: Pentecostal Women Preachers and Traditional Religion* (Philadelphia: University of Pennsylvania Press, 1988).

8. Martha Long Ice, *Clergy Women and Their Worldviews: Calling for a New Age* (New York: Praeger, 1987).

9. Jackson W. Carroll, Barbara Hargrove, and Adair T. Lummis, *Women of the Cloth: A New Opportunity for the Churches* (San Francisco: Harper and Row, 1983).

10. Simon Greenberg, ed., *The Ordination of Women as Rabbis: Studies and Responses* (New York: Jewish Theological Seminary of America, 1988).

11. Janet Marder, "How Women Are Changing the Rabbinate," *Reform Judaism*, Summer 1991, pp. 4–8.

12. Judith A. Bluestein, "Women Rabbis: A Study of Advancement," American Jewish Archives, typescript, 1983; and Rachel Susan Frielich, "A Sociological Analysis of the Ordination of Women as Conservative Rabbis," B.A. thesis, Barnard College, 1984.

13. Task Force on the Equality of Women in Judaism, *Choosing a New Rabbi: The Impact of Female Rabbinic Candidates on the Placement Process* (Paramus, NJ: New Jersey-West Hudson Valley Council of the Union of American Hebrew Congregations, 1987); and Elaine Shizhal Cohen, "Rabbis' Roles and Occupational Goals: Men and Women in the Contemporary American Rabbinate," *Conservative Judaism* 42, 1 (1989): 20–30.

14. Penina Megdal Glazer and Miriam Slater, *Unequal Colleagues: The Entrance of Women into the Professions, 1890–1940* (New Brunswick, NJ: Rutgers University Press, 1987).

15. Carol Gilligan, *In a Different Voice* (Cambridge, MA: Harvard University Press, 1982).

PART II

Social and Economic Adjustments and Aspirations of Women Migrants

7

Sociology and Immigrant Women

This chapter provides an overview of the various methods that have been employed, and the data that have been obtained, from sociological studies of female migration. It traces some of the early work that emanated from the "Chicago School" to current labor force and demographic analyses. It notes that from the 1940s to the 1980s more women than men immigrated to the United States; and it examines how immigration, for many women, serves to enhance their public status.

This chapter brings together two topics that are currently the focus of much political, intellectual, and professional attention: immigration and women. Twenty-five years ago, neither subject aroused much interest in the scholarly and professional marketplace. Through different sources and for different reasons, both have become important research and public policy issues. As Nancy Foner observed: "Migrant women have emerged from academic invisibility. . . . Female migrants . . . have become a recognized presence."[1]

Immigration as a topic for research and debate has emerged largely because Congress, after a long hiatus, is debating immigration issues and enacting new standards and policies. Indeed, on October 27, 1990, the U.S. Congress passed the first major immigration bill since 1965. The bill represents the first comprehensive revision of immigration law in sixty-six years. It increases the number of immigrants admitted per year from 540,000 to 700,000 for at least the first three years, and it more than doubles the number of immigrants allowed entry because of their job skills. In addition, more than half of the visas will be set aside for families of U.S. citizens and permanent residents.

HISTORY OF INTELLECTUAL INTEREST IN IMMIGRATION

Social scientists and public policy analysts began focusing on immigration some thirty years ago when the first group of Cuban refugees were admitted to the United States following the Castro takeover in Cuba. The Cubans were the first in a series of refugees to be admitted to the United States in the post–World War II era. Shortly before the Cubans were admitted, 21,000 Hungarians came in under refugee auspices following the 1956 revolt, and prior to that 280,000 displaced persons were admitted in 1948. Subsequent to the entry of the first group of Cuban immigrants, Vietnamese, Soviet Jews, more Cubans, and other Hispanics from Central American countries were admitted as refugees in the 1970s and 1980s. In addition, growing numbers of immigrants have come across the border from Central American countries and Mexico, as well as from the Philippines, Korea, and other Asian countries.

The establishment of a Presidential Commission on Immigration in 1981 to study the social, economic, and cultural impact of immigrants on American society and to make recommendations about numbers and conditions of admission contributed to an intellectual reawakening of interest in the importance of immigrants to American society. Over the past decade, this has resulted in numerous monographs and articles on immigrant entrepreneurs, the adjustment and absorption of refugees, the social mobility of various immigrant groups, language facility, and immigrant children's academic success.

Along with a revitalization of intellectual interest in immigration, there has also been a good deal of ferment at the societal and community action level. Great numbers of organizations concerned with immigration, almost all of which have assumed a restrictive or anti-immigration stance, have appeared on the scene. The major argument made by most of these organizations has been that more people are bad for the country, economically and socially. Also creeping into some of the anti-immigrant rhetoric have been subtle warnings with racist overtones, describing immigration, for example, as "the browning of America." The print and electronic media have also paid far more attention to immigration in recent years, albeit often in negative accounts of illegals crossing the borders, taking away jobs from Americans, carrying diseases, or distributing drugs.

Tracing the development of interest and work on women migrants involves recognition of the importance of the appearance of a women's movement in the late 1960s. In part as a function of that movement's visibility, interest in topics about women and funding for research on women's lives skyrocketed. Any topic concerning women was considered intellectually interesting, important, and highly marketable. The spate of recent work by sociologists on women migrants can be explained easily by the enormous attention that any topic on women receives; but coupled with the renewed interest in immigration, it is all the more obvious why sociologists have been paying so much attention to patterns of female migration.

With these explanations as background, it is important to note that the current sociological studies of immigrants tend to have a somewhat different focus and to employ different methods than the work done during the earlier periods of immigrant research in the 1920s and 1930s. Many of the studies emanating from that period were done by the so-called Chicago School of Sociology, which focused on patterns of adaptation, acculturation, and assimilation by different immigrant communities into the larger American society. The methods for studying the communities were often observational and biographical. Scholars examined life histories in the form of letters, diaries, and other direct first-person accounts that explained transitions and passages in individual lives, in families, and in larger units. Studies reported on conflicts between immigrant parents and their first-generation American-born offspring. Accounts dealt with how quickly and in what form different immigrant communities became Americanized through loss of accent, change of names, style of dress, choice of foods, and movement into "nonethnic" neighborhoods. The unit of analysis was often the family or an entire immigrant community that had recently established itself in an urban neighborhood. Thomas and Znaniecki's *The Polish Peasant in Europe and America* is one of the classics to emerge from that era.[2]

The revival of interest in immigrants in the 1970s and 1980s did not restore the earlier research agenda either substantively or methodologically. The issues today tend to be different than they were sixty and seventy years ago, and the methods have changed as well. Today, economic issues are more likely to be the dependent variables. Thus, data on labor force participation, educational background, job skills, work ethic, income, and mobility are collected through surveys or from archival sources such as the U.S. Census. The focus is more on individual behavior, which is then aggregated, than on families or whole communities. There are fewer observational studies, and researchers are less dependent on subjective accounts.

When women are the focus, economic variables still play an important role. But fertility patterns and changing roles within the family and vis-à-vis the host country society are special topics in the area of female migrants. The methods employed are usually the same whether the target population is male or female, and the unit of analysis also tends to be the individual, irrespective of gender.

FEMALE IMMIGRATION DURING THE PAST TWO DECADES

One fact that often goes unnoticed or unreported is that more women than men have immigrated to the United States over the past sixty years. This predominance of female migrants is a phenomenon unique to the United States (see Table 7.1). The predominance ranges from 51.4 percent to 74.9 percent. The latter occurred in 1947 and is attributable largely to the migration of "war brides," that is, wives of U.S. servicemen stationed overseas following World War II. From January 1946 through December 1948, 112,882 war brides were

Table 7.1
Immigration to the United States, by Sex, 1930–1979

	Both Sexes	Males	Females	Percent Female
1930–39	699,375	312,716	386,659	55.3
1930	241,700	117,026	124,674	51.6
1931	97,139	40,621	56,518	58.2
1932	35,576	13,917	21,659	60.9
1933	23,068	9,219	13,849	60.0
1934	29,470	12,101	17,369	58.9
1935	34,956	14,010	20,946	59.9
1936	36,329	14,775	21,553	59.3
1937	50,244	21,664	28,580	56.9
1938	67,895	29,959	37,936	55.9
1939	82,998	39,432	43,575	52.5
1940–49	856,608	332,317	524,291	61.2
1940	70,756	33,460	37,296	52.7
1941	51,776	23,519	28,257	54.6
1942	28,781	12,008	16,773	58.3
1943	23,725	9,825	13,900	58.6
1944	28,551	11,410	17,141	60.0
1945	38,119	13,389	24,730	64.9
1946	108,721	27,275	81,446	74.9
1947	147,292	53,769	93,523	63.5
1948	170,570	67,322	103,248	60.5
1949	188,317	80,340	107,977	57.3
1950–59	2,499,268	1,157,864	1,341,404	53.7
1950	249,187	119,130	130,057	52.2
1951	205,717	99,327	106,390	51.7
1952	265,520	123,609	141,911	53.4
1953	170,434	73,073	97,361	57.1
1954	208,177	95,594	112,583	54.1
1955	237,790	112,032	125,758	52.9
1956	321,625	156,410	165,215	51.4
1957	326,867	155,201	171,666	52.5
1958	253,265	109,121	144,144	56.9
1959	260,686	114,367	146,319	56.1
1960–69	3,213,749	1,427,308	1,786,441	55.6
1960	265,398	116,687	148,711	56.0
1961	271,344	121,380	149,964	55.3
1962	283,763	131,575	152,188	53.6
1963	306,260	139,297	166,963	54.5
1964	292,248	126,214	166,034	56.8
1965	296,697	127,171	169,526	57.1
1966	323,040	141,456	181,584	56.2
1967	361,972	158,324	203,648	56.3
1968	454,448	199,732	254,716	56.0
1969	358,579	165,472	193,107	53.9
1970–79	4,336,001	2,036,292	2,299,709	53.0
1970	373,326	176,990	196,336	52.6
1971	370,478	172,528	197,950	53.4

Table 7.1 (continued)

	Both Sexes	Males	Females	Percent Female
1972	384,685	179,715	204,970	53.3
1973	400,063	186,320	213,743	53.4
1974	394,861	184,518	210,343	53.3
1975	386,194	180,741	205,453	53.2
1976	398,613	184,863	213,750	53.6
1977	462,315	216,424	245,891	53.2
1978	601,442	286,374	315,068	52.4
1979	460,348	219,536	240,812	52.3

Sources: 1911-32: U.S. Department of Labor, Annual Reports of the Commissioner General of Immigration (Washington, DC: U.S. Government Printing Office, 1911-32). 1933-77: U.S. Immigration and Naturalization Service, Annual Reports of the Immigration and Naturalization Service (Washington, DC: U.S. Government Printing Office, 1941-77). 1978-79: U.S. Immigration and Naturalization Service, Statistical Yearbooks of the Immigration and Naturalization Service (Washington, DC: U.S. Government Printing Office, 1978-79).

admitted to the United States. They accounted for almost 25 percent of all immigration for these three years.

But the countries from which over 50 percent of the migrants entering the United States are women are not limited to a small sample or a short period of time. As shown in Table 7.2, over seventy countries are represented, ranging over many parts of the world, including Europe, Asia, and Latin America. The countries that fall below 50 percent are more likely to be in Africa and the Middle East. Indeed, the countries sending the largest number of female immigrants also tend to be among those from which the largest numbers of male immigrants come as well: Mexico, the Philippines, and Korea are cases in point.

Like their male counterparts, most female migrants are under thirty-five years of age. Between the ages of fifteen and twenty-nine, female migrants tend to outnumber males, especially within the twenty to twenty-four age category. A higher percentage of female than male migrants tend to be married: 71 percent as opposed to 66.4 percent.

Although at the time of arrival a much smaller percentage of female than male migrants are likely to report an occupation or labor market experience (77.4 percent for men compared to 34 percent for women), once they are in the United States, female immigrant participation in the labor force increases dramatically. Immigrant women are almost twice as likely to report professional occupations as are native women. Table 7.3 compares immigrant and native women by specific occupational categories.

Note that immigrant women are more likely to be represented than are native women in the highest and lowest occupational categories. For example, 29.1

Table 7.2

Distribution of Countries of Origin of Immigrants to the United States by Percent of Female Immigrants, Fiscal Years 1972–1979

	Percent Female	Total Immigration
Finland	72.4	2,638
Germany	72.1	51,878
Thailand	68.7	37,025
Japan	66.8	38,363
Panama	64.3	17,619
Pacific Islands Trust Territories	64.2	1,551
Iceland	62.6	1,093
Sweden	62.4	4,914
Korea	60.8	225,339
Nicaragua	60.8	10,101
Honduras	60.5	13,537
Philippines	59.9	289,429
Belgium	59.7	3,133
Brazil	59.7	10,675
Singapore	59.4	1,964
Australia	59.0	11,417
El Salvador	59.0	26,490
Denmark	58.5	3,509
Malaysia	58.0	3,494
Costa Rica	57.9	9,607
France	57.7	13,851
New Zealand	56.9	4,148
Netherlands	56.6	8,385
Colombia	56.2	59,829
Paraguay	56.2	1,206
Guatemala	55.7	19,629
United Kingdom	55.6	97,274
Canada	55.5	88,108
Belize	55.3	5,797
Montserrat	54.9	1,575
Cuba	54.8	140,119
Grenada	54.8	6,206
Poland	54.6	35,910
Ireland	54.5	11,510
Austria	54.4	3,635
Norway	54.0	3,175
Bermuda	53.9	1,596
Indonesia	53.8	4,831
Bolivia	53.0	5,062
Ecuador	53.0	5,062
China (Taiwan and Mainland)	52.8	160,454
Barbados	52.7	16,550
Trinidad and Tobago	52.7	49,492
Dominican Republic	52.5	118,147
Switzerland	52.5	5,066
Venezuela	52.4	5,544
Guyana	52.3	30,035
Peru	52.3	23,991
Haiti	52.3	44,721
Macau	52.2	1,810
Hong Kong	52.0	40,438
Jamaica	51.8	108,454
Burma	51.6	7,570
Cape Verde	51.6	4,560
Chile	51.4	14,078

Table 7.2 (continued)

	Percent Female	Total Immigration
USSR	51.4	31,951
St. Kitts-Nevis	51.3	5,229
Anguilla	51.1	1,045
St. Vincent and Grenadines	51.1	3,678
Antigua-Barbados	50.8	4,803
Kenya	50.8	3,582
Bahamas	50.5	3,447
Czechoslovakia	50.5	7,304
Netherlands/Antilles	50.5	2,202
Vietnam	50.4	134,160
Zimbabwe	50.4	1,018
British Virgin Islands	50.2	2,561
Dominica	50.1	3,519
Tanzania	50.0	2,467
Turkey	50.0	14,599
Uruguay	49.9	6,487
Fiji	49.7	5,299
Spain	49.7	23,962
Yugoslavia	49.6	33,952
Argentina	49.5	20,321
Portugal	49.5	84,394
Sri Lanka	49.5	3,230
Western Samoa	49.4	3,097
Malta	49.3	2,010
St. Lucia	49.2	3,512
South Africa	49.2	9,124
Cyprus	49.0	3,610
Mexico	49.0	530,378
Zambia	49.0	1,127
Italy	48.7	102,528
Uganda	48.3	2,930
India	48.0	139,834
Hungary	48.0	9,213
Romania	47.8	13,924
Angola	47.7	1,229
Egypt	47.7	19,019
Laos	47.3	8,572
Morocco	47.0	3,575
Tonga	46.0	4,371
Greece	45.9	73,104
Kuwait	45.4	1,234
Israel	45.2	21,343
Syria	45.1	10,730
Iraq	44.6	19,515
Ethiopia	44.4	2,774
Kampuchea	44.1	5,604
Jordan	43.1	23,668
Lebanon	43.1	27,843
Pakistan	42.5	24,857
Bangladesh	42.0	3,322
Iran	41.0	33,331
Bulgaria	40.5	1,854
Liberia	40.0	1,858
Afghanistan	34.4	1,258
Ghana	34.1	3,854

Table 7.2 (continued)

	Percent Female	Total Immigration
Nigeria	32.3	6,420
Yemen (Sanaa)	13.2	4,446

Note: Data are by country of birth. Table includes all countries with 100 or more immigrants admitted to the United States during the period.

Source: Unpublished tabulations based on Immigration and Naturalization Service's Public Use Tapes for Immigrants (complete enumeration) for fiscal years 1972-1979.

percent of the immigrant women were employed as professionals compared to 16.1 percent of the native female labor force, and 13.9 percent of the immigrant women worked as domestics as opposed to 2.6 of native women. The same pattern, although not as dramatic, appears when comparisons are made between male immigrants and natives. For example, we see that 22.4 percent of the male immigrants work in professional positions as opposed to 15.1 percent of the natives, and 12 percent of the male immigrants are employed as laborers as opposed to 7.3 percent of male natives. The greater concentration of both female and male immigrants at the extremes of the occupational hierarchy is a reflection of the immigrants' educational backgrounds. Like their occupational distributions, male and female immigrants are more likely than natives to be represented at the extremes of high and low years of schooling (see Table 7.4).

While much sociological discussion of female immigrants in the 1970s and 1980s has centered around demographic and labor force characteristics, data on fertility patterns of immigrant versus native women have been examined largely as one indication of the importance of culture as a differential characteristic among immigrant cohorts. The argument is usually phrased as follows: Women in less developed countries give birth to more children than women in Western European countries and the United States. For how long after female immigrants arrive in the United States are the differences in fertility patterns between foreign-born and native women likely to continue? To the extent that they exist throughout the subject's childbearing years and are passed on to future generations of daughters, cultural traits would be deemed important. But suppose the gap between the immigrant women's birth rates and those of natives grows increasingly smaller, and suppose it is nonexistent in the next generation. Such a trend would diminish the importance or persistence of cultural differences. The data in Tables

Table 7.3
Percent Distribution of Occupations of 1979 Employed U.S. Workers and
Reported at-Entry Occupations of Fiscal Years 1972–1979 Immigrants, by Sex

	Percent Employed in U.S.			Percent Females in Occup.
	Both Sexes	Males	Females	
White Collar	50.9	41.2	64.4	52.7
Professional, technical, and kindred workers	15.5	15.1	16.1	43.3
Managers and administrators	10.8	14.0	6.4	24.7
Sales workers	6.4	6.0	6.9	45.1
Clerical and kindred	18.2	6.1	35.0	80.3
Blue Collar	33.1	46.3	14.6	18.4
Craft and kindred	13.3	21.5	1.8	5.7
Operatives	11.3	11.6	10.8	39.9
Transport operatives	3.7	5.9	0.7	0.7
Nonfarm laborers	4.8	7.3	1.3	11.3
Service	13.2	8.5	19.8	62.3
Service, except private household	12.1	8.5	17.2	59.1
Private household	1.1	--	2.6	97.5
Farm workers	2.8	3.9	1.2	18.0
Farmers and managers	1.5	2.3	0.3	9.6
Farm laborers and supervisors	1.3	1.6	0.9	27.5
Total number (in thousands)	98,824	57,607	41,217	41.7

	Percent Immigrants Employed in U.S.			Percent Females in Occup.
	Both Sexes	Males	Females	
White Collar	44.1	40.0	52.0	40.4
Professional, technical, and kindred workers	24.3	22.4	29.1	39.5
Managers and administrators	7.6	9.6	3.7	16.8
Sales workers	2.4	2.5	2.2	31.7
Clerical and kindred	9.8	5.5	18.0	62.9
Blue Collar	36.5	43.4	23.3	21.9
Craft and kindred	12.0	17.2	2.1	5.9
Operatives	13.6	11.4	17.9	45.1
Transport operatives	1.9	2.8	0.2	3.1
Nonfarm laborers	9.0	12.0	3.2	12.2
Service	14.7	10.2	23.4	54.4

Table 7.3 (continued)

	Percent Immigrants Employed in U.S.			Percent Females in Occup.
	Both Sexes	Males	Females	
Service, except private household	9.8	10.0	9.5	33.2
Private household	4.9	0.2	13.9	96.7
Farm workers	4.6	6.3	1.3	9.8
Farmers and managers	0.3	0.4	1.3	14.2
Farm laborers and supervisors	4.3	5.9	0.1	9.5
Total number (in thousands)	1,432	941	491	34.3

Note: Percentages may not add up to 100 due to rounding.

Sources: U.S. Department of Labor, 1983, Tables 16 and 26. Unpublished tabulations based on the U.S. Immigration and Naturalization Service's Public Use Tapes for Immigrants (complete enumeration) for fiscal years 1972-1979.

7.5 and 7.6 show that foreign-born women between twenty-five and forty-four have fewer children than native women and that native women of mixed or foreign-born parentage in all other age categories have fewer children than foreign-born or native women. Cultural differences thus do not seem to persist and are thus not likely to have long-term implications.

To review the picture that has begun to form of immigrant women in the United States, we have found that most of them arrive when they are between fifteen and twenty-nine years of age. They have a bimodal educational distribution, more of them being found at the higher and lower educational levels than are native women. Once they have migrated to the United States, they are more likely to work outside their homes than are native women. Over 70 percent are married at the time of arrival. They have about the same number of children as native women.

THE PUBLIC STATUS OF WOMEN MIGRANTS

A theme distinctive to work done on female migrants concerns the basis for the "double" and "triple" oppression/discrimination models. Briefly, the thesis these models set forth is that as women immigrants move from traditional cultures

Table 7.4
Percentage of the Population (Aged 25 Years or over) with High and Low
Education: U.S. Natives and Immigrants, 1980

Education Attainment	Natives	Immigrants, Arrived 1970-1980
Percentage with 4 year college education	8.7	9.7
Percentage with 5 or more years of college education	7.5	12.5
Percentage with less than 5 years elementary school education	2.9	12.8

Source: Julian Simon, The Economic Consequences of Immigration,
London, Basil Blackwell, 1990, p. 39.

Table 7.5
Children per 1,000 Women in the United States, 1970

Age	Native Women of Native Parentage	Foreign-Born Women	Native Women of Mixed and Foreign Parentage
15-24	364	413	306
25-44	2,565	2,141	2,522
45-64	2,530	2,534	2,177
65-74	2,479	2,518	2,064
75+	2,762	3,284	2,390

Source: U.S. Census.

to modern cultures they are oppressed by virtue of their class, by virtue of their status as foreigners, and by virtue of their gender. They are oppressed by employers and by men. Are there data that bear out or support these assumptions?

A review of the literature indicates a more complex situation. Studies of Muslim female migrants to France, Turkish migrants to Germany, and Mexican, Jamaican, Cuban, and Vietnamese migrants to the United States suggest that women enhance their roles and statuses as a function of their migration. Yolanda Prieto explains Cuban women's high labor force participation as follows:

Table 7.6
Children per 1,000 Women in the United States, 1980

Age	U.S. Total	Native	Foreign-Born	Foreign-Born Immigrated 1970-1980	Foreign-Born Immigrated before 1970
35-44	2,639	2,652	2,509	2,571	2,478

Source: U.S. Census.

The strongest factor behind the intense economic activity of Cuban women (as that of Cubans in general) is the combination of middle-class values and a strong anti-Communist ideology. These strong beliefs, common to refugees from socialist countries, are manifested in a strong work ethic and aspirations for social mobility. Primarily to compensate for the lost rewards in their home country, these migrants justify the massive entrance of women into paid production.[3]

Muslim women take on more visible ceremonial and public roles in their host country than they performed in their country of origin. Sossie Andezian writes:

During immigration, one can observe a redefinition of the traditional roles within Algerian families. In the absence of mothers-in-law and other individuals of the extended female kinship network, Algerian wives assume a greater role in the decision concerning children's education, children's matrimonial choices, relations to the host society, and relations to the home country. The sphere of their activities spreads, and they have access to a public world previously reserved primarily for men. Although few Algerian women work outside the home, they must contend with different services such as schools and health and administrative departments to carry out their roles as wives and mothers. They are the ones who are free, during hours that these institutions are open, to pursue an explanation or express some family need. They quickly learn that in the bureaucratic world of France, they cannot rely on husbands who are often equally illiterate and who have little leisure time. Thus, contrary to the belief that Algerian women in France are increasingly enclosed in the domestic world, immigration has placed them in contact with the exterior world almost of necessity. . . . They become wholly responsible for the tasks of making symbolic life official and legitimate.[4]

In her account of East African Sikh women in London, Parminder Bhachu writes:

A great many are involved in temple activities. At the time of marriages, most of the pre-wedding ceremonies are almost entirely women oriented. . . . Hence, contrary to the stereotype of the submissive and secluded Asian woman, East African Sikh women in particular have considerable amounts of freedom and spend a great deal of their time in women's activities. This is a consequence of the expansion of their contacts as a result of their employment. . . . Although migrant women are mostly in the "dirtiest and lowest paid jobs," this discussion of East African Sikhs in Britain suggests that wage labor has a strong impact on both the negotiation of power within the domestic sphere and on specific traditional patterns. Asian women in Britain have acquired greater control over cash than they ever had in the past, whether in India or East Africa. . . . The women in my study who had entered the wage economy for the first time constantly emphasized their delight at the acquisition of a potent commodity like money, which previously they had to look to their men folk to attain.[5]

Turkish women in Germany become more actively involved in the education their children receive in the German school system than they do in their homeland.[6] Mexican women migrants participate more prominently in immigrant community affairs in the United States than they did in Mexico. Nancy Foner describes the situation of Jamaican women in New York and London as follows:

Outside the workplace, female migrants in New York and London can engage in certain activities that were unacceptable or at least unusual for women at home, and this also contributes to their sense that living abroad offers them a new kind of freedom. . . . A number of white collar women in New York said that life in America allowed them to develop their potential in a way that would not have been possible for them as women at home. They spoke of the new opportunities to expand their cultural horizon through the theater, concerts, and films, and of the opportunities in New York to pursue their interests and lead their lives without the eyes and censure of the local community so closely upon them.[7]

These are some examples of enhanced public status that female migrants achieve as a function of their emigration. Contrary to popular assumptions, many female migrants to more developed countries have worked outside their homes in their country of origin. Nevertheless, the likelihood is that they will join the labor force in their host country in far greater numbers. And while their wages in the first few years of their migration will be lower than those of female natives, there are studies that indicate that women migrants enter the labor force in their host countries sooner than male migrants emigrating from the same country and that the women earn more than the men. Indeed, it is the changes in roles within immigrant families that often provide female migrants with higher status and more visibility in their host community than they achieved in their countries of origin. The enhancement in status that the migrant women obtain reverberates into the next generation.

CONCLUDING REMARKS

While this chapter has focused heavily on the United States, many of the findings about female migrants would generalize to other immigrant-receiving societies such as Canada, Australia, and New Zealand. For example, women immigrants are more likely than native women to be in the labor force in all of those countries. The female migrant is an important research topic because immigration and women are highly marketable as well as intellectually challenging topics for study. Both issues have important and far-ranging public policy implications.

NOTES

1. Nancy Foner, "Sex Roles and Sensibilities: Jamaican Women in New York and London," in *International Migration*, edited by R. J. Simon and C. Brettell. (Totowa, NJ: Rowman and Allanheld, 1986), p. 133.

2. W. L. Thomas and F. Znaniecki, *The Polish Peasant in Europe and America*, edited and abridged by Eli Zertsky (Chicago: University of Illinois Press, 1984).

3. Yolanda Prieto, "Cuban Women in New Jersey," in Simon and Brettell, *International Migration*, p. 231.

4. Sossie Andezian, "Women's Roles in Organizing Symbolic Life: Algerian Female Immigrants in France," in Simon and Brettell, *International Migration*, pp. 257–258, 265.

5. P. K. Bhachu, "Work, Dowry, and Marriage Among East African Sikh Women in the United Kingdom," in Simon and Brettell, *International Migration*, p. 231.

6. F. J. Davis and B. S. Heyl, "Turkish Women and Guestworker Migration to West Germany," in Simon and Brettell, *International Migration*, p. 188.

7. Foner, "Sex Roles and Sensibilities," pp. 145–146.

8

The Social and Economic Adjustment of Soviet Jewish Women in the United States

How well have Soviet Jewish women who were admitted as refugees to the United States from the mid-1970s to the early 1980s—women with considerable human capital in the form of education and occupational skills—adjusted to their new lives? The first section of this chapter describes the roles women play in the Soviet Union from a historical and ideological perspective. The second part focuses on the place of Jews in the Soviet Union and compares various demographic and social characteristics of Jewish and non-Jewish Soviet women. The third part, the heart of the chapter, portrays and compares the social and economic adjustment of Soviet Jewish women (and men) who left the Soviet Union between 1975 and 1981.

WOMEN IN THE SOVIET UNION

The Bolshevik Revolution of 1917 was the first political movement to make an ideological commitment to women's liberation. It sought complete political and sexual equality for women. The 1918 Constitution gave women the right to vote and hold elective office (Article 64), and in 1936 the Stalinist Constitution gave women the right to equal pay (Article 122).

In order to relieve working women of household burdens and facilitate their participation in the work force, early Soviet leaders committed themselves to improving maternal and child health and to establishing support services such as child care, public kitchens, and central laundries. But these public services were short-lived. Starting in the late 1920s, Stalin required extensive capital to develop heavy industry, the funds for which were shifted away from the consumer sector, particularly from the institutions that supported the female work force.

But the commitment to industrial power, coupled with the manpower losses resulting from the Stalinist purges and World War II, left women no option but to work. A decline in the number of service enterprises, however, meant that Soviet women assumed a "double burden": the necessity of working full-time while also holding responsibility for most of the domestic work.

The double role of laborer and housewife increases the average Soviet woman's stress while diminishing her chances for advancement. She rises earlier than her husband to dress and feed her one or two children before escorting them to a nursery or school. Then, unlike the women surveyed for this study, she spends the next seven to eight hours at a boring, low-skilled job that is often physically demanding. After picking up her children, she must spend the next two hours tracking down and waiting in line for food (inadequate refrigeration in stores makes daily shopping a necessity). When she finally comes home, she prepares dinner, cleans the apartment, and starts such other chores as washing clothes, often by hand. Few Soviet husbands assist their wives with what are viewed as "female tasks," so that men have nearly 150 percent more leisure hours than women.[1]

Soviet experiments with shorter work days for women found that women gained no more leisure time. Their extra hours were divided evenly between their children and their household chores. Moreover, a high proportion of the women who participated in the experiment reported that their husbands took advantage of the opportunity to shift additional household duties to their wives.[2]

Why do more than 75 percent of the women of marital age work when their life is so difficult? (In 1980 approximately 90 percent of the women between the ages of twenty and fifty participated in the labor force.)[3] The extent of female employment may be explained by the increasing numbers of families who are deprived of male breadwinners, by the many women unable to marry or remarry,[4] and by the inability of married couples to live on one salary. While the manpower shortage and financial necessity are important explanations for the high level of female labor force participation, they do not provide the complete answer. Propaganda urging women to be productive and contribute to the economy also plays a role.

Although women are equal to men in the workplace, certain regulations protect women from exploitation. Concessions are made to accommodate the extra burdens of women workers, but they often carry financial penalties. Protective legislation forbids women to work underground and in jobs requiring the lifting of more than twenty-five kilos. In principle, women are allowed to work a shortened workday and to be paid only for the hours they have worked. In practice, this is very rare and happens only in offices, never in factories. Women can retire at age fifty-five after twenty years of employment, but "those who fail to satisfy the employment requirement (because part of their adult life was spent bringing up a family) receive only a reduced pension or none at all."[5]

Protective legislation prevents women from occupying higher-paid "heavy" industry jobs, though it does not protect them from holding the lower-paid "lighter," but no less physically demanding, positions. For example, Lotta Lennon relates the story of one Soviet brewery where each woman laborer is required to shovel fifteen to sixteen tons of fermented barley a day. As long as she is not compelled to exceed a single load norm of twenty-five kilograms, there is no norm limiting the total for a given shift.[6]

Pregnant women are also protected by national legislation that allows four months' paid leave from work (two months before and after the birth). In addition, they receive paid breaks for nursing the baby, night shifts are eliminated, and they have the option of a year's leave with a guarantee of their original job when they return.

Despite the extraordinary increase in literacy and educational attainment among Soviet women, few have risen to the top of the professions, in part because the benefits described above make women a less stable part of the work force. Inability to fill the positions of women on maternity leave provides management with an excuse for not promoting women to high-level positions. Consequently, women are generally confined to unskilled, routine, and lower-level professional jobs where they can easily be replaced.

While the rule of equal pay for equal work is generally enforced, women earn on the average one-third less than their husbands, the apparent result of the concentration of women in occupations that pay less.[7] Furthermore, women often settle for poorly paid jobs in order to be near their husbands. As the Soviet saying goes, "Men take their work home with them but women take the home to work with them."

SOVIET JEWISH WOMEN

The Soviet immigrant women interviewed for this study differed in several important ways from the typical Soviet woman described in the previous section. The former's status as a Jew, a professional woman, and an urban resident of a Slavic or Baltic republic provided her with a different family environment, work experiences, and a unique situation in Soviet society. While her professional status would always set her apart from the average Soviet woman, her Jewish identity sometimes had the more profound influence on her existence.

Waves of anti-Semitism during different Soviet periods have limited the strong assimilationist tendencies of Soviet Jews. In the Slavic republics of the Russian Federal Republic (RSFSR) and the Ukraine, where this inclination to assimilate has been strongest, ironically, the force of anti-Semitism has also been greatest. The extent of overt discrimination has sometimes overshadowed all aspects of Jewish existence. The anticosmopolitan campaigns in the final years of Stalin's rule, beginning in 1946, were possibly the most devastating period for Soviet Jewry, after the dark years of the Hitler period. Apart from the devastating attack on Jewish culture wrought by the execution of many of the major Jewish cultural figures, many Jews were removed from their jobs and unable to find alternate work.[8]

The situation of Soviet Jews improved following Stalin's death in 1953, but "by the early 1960's, Soviet Jews began to give up hope for an improvement in their lot.''[9] Jewish disillusionment manifested itself not only in increasing samizdat (unofficial writings illegally circulated) expressing Jewish concerns,[10] but in the disproportionate participation by both Jewish men and women in the Soviet human rights movement. Many Jews' desire to leave the USSR was fueled by increased anti-Semitism following the Israeli-Arab conflicts and systematic educational discrimination. During the 1970s, 250,000 Jews left the USSR as the fear of emigration lessened and the fate of those Jews who decided to stay became more difficult.[11]

Though discrimination and anti-Semitism defined this group's identity as Jews, their way of life also set them apart from the rest of the Soviet population. Jewish families socialize more frequently as a unit than do Slavic households, where men and women often see their friends separately. Friendship is very important and friends have, in part, replaced the extended Jewish family, acting as a buffer against the difficulties of daily life. Alcohol and spouse abuse, frequent problems in Slavic households, are less common in the Soviet Jewish family, where alcohol is consumed at mealtimes and women have a higher status. Divorces are much less common among Jews, as the traditional emphasis on maintaining and educating a family prevails in the face of the hardships of Soviet residential life. But the strains of Soviet life, as well as the professional status of many Soviet Jewish women, have affected the birth rate. The cohesive Jewish family in the western republics typically has either one or two children, a pattern also observed among those in the study.

The high level of educational attainment of the Jewish population is unique. A greater proportion of Jewish men and women have completed "some" or "all" of their higher education than any other major population group in the western republics (see Table 8.1). Jewish women are 1.5 to 6 times more likely than Russian women or native women of the republic to have completed their higher education. The women interviewed reflected this level of educational attainment.

Jewish women are particularly active in law, medicine, teaching, and engineering—fields in which there is a particularly large concentration of Jewish participants. The careers of these Jewish women professionals are often marked by distinction rather than eminence.

Many educated Jews identify themselves as members of the intelligentsia (intellectuals), a term that has a very particular meaning in Russian culture. Originating in late nineteenth-century Russia, the term "came to be associated with a critical approach to the world."[12]

The professional status of the families, while making them more vulnerable to the antipathy of the Soviet government, permitted them to benefit from the personal and material rewards offered to intellectually productive citizens. In the USSR, professors, scientists, creative individuals, and professionals received proportionately better compensation than in many Western societies. The relative affluence of professional Jewish women gave them access to better and more suitable child-care arrangements than those found in the large and impersonal

Table 8.1

Educational Levels of Three Ethnic Groups: Jews, Russians, and the Local National Majority in the Working Population in Five Republics, 1970

Every 1,000 employed persons having education

	Higher	High school vocat.	High school gen.	Total higher and high school	Primary
RSFSR					
Russians:					
Both sexes	65	143	328	663	255
Men	65	133	342	646	294
Women	65	153	313	679	219
Jews:					
Both sexes	468	139	113	934	50
Men	486	123	110	927	57
Women	447	159	115	943	40
Ukraine					
Ukrainians:					
Both sexes	47	182	308	637	253
Men	51	188	331	659	255
Women	43	176	286	614	252
Jews:					
Both sexes	283	236	143	915	64
Men	286	218	148	894	81
Women	279	255	137	937	45
Russians:					
Both Sexes	98	224	294	776	169
Men	100	211	312	769	188
Women	96	238	275	783	149
Byelorussians					
Byelorussians:					
Both sexes	40	143	279	555	326
Men	43	139	315	573	339
Women	36	148	245	537	314
Jews:					
Both sexes	248	208	197	898	84
Men	256	186	200	868	110
Women	240	230	193	928	57
Russians:					
Both sexes	141	227	258	835	131
Men	137	219	282	833	144
Women	145	237	231	837	116
Moldavia					
Moldavians:					
Both sexes	23	76	290	435	315
Men	28	81	318	469	336
Women	19	70	264	404	295
Jews:					
Both sexes	184	233	197	813	143
Men	181	217	208	782	167
Women	186	252	185	850	114
Russians:					
Both sexes	111	203	281	777	159
Men	106	197	312	168	182
Women	115	208	254	784	139

Table 8.1 (continued)

	Every 1,000 employed persons having education				
	Higher	High school vocat.	High school gen.	Total higher and high school	Primary
Latvia					
Latvians:					
Both sexes	59	135	320	658	261
Men	53	103	345	630	289
Women	64	166	295	684	235
Jews:					
Both sexes	285	211	160	881	96
Men	295	190	164	865	109
Women	273	235	155	898	82
Russians:					
Both sexes	77	165	290	681	230
Men	81	149	313	688	244
Women	73	181	268	677	216

Source: Thomas Sawyer, p.265, Table 3.

state-run nurseries. Furthermore, they were able to provide their children with special lessons and intellectual advantages that gave them a competitive advantage in the highly structured school environment. While these Soviet women also suffered from the double burden of full-time jobs and housework, the material comforts available to them and their families alleviated some of the strain on their existence.

The urban existence of the preponderance of Jewish women also served to make their lives easier. In the USSR, food and consumer goods were not equally distributed throughout the country: the best were saved for the major cities of the western republics. Furthermore, desirable goods were often made available through the workplace to employees of professional organizations. The women surveyed, while still saddled with the daily chore of food shopping and preparation, were often spared the long, exhausting search for food that follows the workday because of their proximity and access to desired foodstuffs as well as their financial ability to shop in the plentifully stocked but more costly farmers' markets.

Housing, still the major problem in the USSR, is far superior in cities than in rural areas. The urban women were spared the problem of hauling water to a log cabin, but often shared an apartment with one or several other families.[13] Many professional women, like those included in the study, lived in one-family apartments provided through their employer or purchased from a cooperative association.

While many Soviet Jewish women report that their lives were not easy, most found them emotionally and intellectually fulfilling. As we show later, their departure from the USSR was not motivated by discontent with their personal lives. Rather, the external problems of anti-Semitism and occupational and educational discrimination led the great majority of these women to leave the USSR.

ADJUSTMENTS OF SOVIET IMMIGRANT WOMEN

The data for this section on the socioeconomic adjustment of recent Soviet women immigrants to the United States have been pulled from a larger study of Soviet immigrants who arrived in the United States in the second half of the 1970s. They are based on a survey of 900 Soviet immigrants who were living in fourteen cities in the United States in 1981.[14]

The study had two major purposes: to explore the immigrants' socioeconomic adjustment to their new country, and to describe the nature and strength of their Jewish ties and identities. The focus of this part of the chapter is on the women's experiences, especially on their social and economic adjustments. We compare them against the men's to provide a more complete picture of the women's adjustments to their new lives.

In each of the fourteen cities, the sample frame was obtained from the Jewish resettlement agency, and every Soviet immigrant family that arrived in the United States between 1972 and 1980 whose "head" was between eighteen and fifty-five years of age at the time of arrival had a chance to be included in the survey. The resettlement agency sent letters to persons whose names had been randomly selected, describing the survey and asking their cooperation. Each person was then contacted by phone and asked if he or she would agree to be interviewed. Eighty-seven percent of all the potential respondents agreed to participate. The 30 percent refusal rate in New York City was higher than elsewhere, where the average refusal rate was 8 percent. Sixty-two percent of the interviews were conducted in Russian, 38 percent in English. The interviews lasted about eighty minutes. The sample was designed so that within each of the fourteen cities where we conducted interviews, 25 percent of the respondents had arrived before 1978, and 75 percent in 1978 or thereafter.

Three hundred eighty-two of the respondents were women and 518 were men. The age distributions for the women are shown below, in percentages.

	Age						
	18-24	25-34	35-44	45-54	55-64	NA	Number
Women	4.9	33.7	31.4	21.4	8.4	.2	100(382)
Men	1.3	30.1	32.9	26.3	8.7	.7	100(518)

The bulk of the respondents were between twenty-five and fifty-five years old.

Almost all the women and men were married at the time of the survey: 2.9

Table 8.2
Reasons for Coming to the United States, by Sex of Respondents (in percent)

Reason	Women	Men
Anti-Semitism in Soviet Union	41.4	49.0
Children's education/Future opportunities	32.0	28.3
Educational opportunities/University training	4.9	7.9
Family reunion/Relatives in US	37.2	32.9
Financial/Level of income	12.3	13.0
Jewish identity/Religious freedom	13.9	16.1
Jobs/Career opportunities	13.6	20.4
Spouse's wish	6.1	2.6

Note: The percentages add up to more than 100 because respondents could cite more than one reason.

percent of the women and 6.4 percent of the men had never been married; and 12.7 percent of the women and 6.9 percent of the men were separated, divorced, or widowed. The average number of children per household was 1.4 for both the male and female respondents. Only 3 percent had more than two children.

A large majority of the immigrants arrived from the Ukraine or from the RSFSR, Russia proper. Fifty-eight percent of the women and 56 percent of the men came from the Ukraine; 23 percent of the women and 22 percent of the men came from the RSFSR. The rest came mostly from White Russia (9.2 percent of the women and 6.6 percent of the men) and Latvia (2.6 percent of the women and 5.6 percent of the men). The major cities from which they emigrated were Kiev and Odessa, followed by Leningrad and Moscow—cities with the largest Jewish populations in the country.

When asked why they settled in a particular city in the United States, by far the most frequent response for both men and women was that they already had relatives living in that city. Having friends in the city was the second most frequently cited reason: 58 percent of the women and 57 percent of the men cited relatives, and 25 percent of the women and 23 percent of the men cited friends.

The major reason given for coming to the United States was to escape anti-Semitism. After that, opportunities for their children to receive a better education in the United States, for the respondents to have a better professional future, and for family reunions were cited by both men and women as major considerations. As shown in Table 8.2, there were no major differences between the reasons given by women and men.

Like the refugees who escaped from Nazi Germany in the 1930s, the bulk of the recent Soviet refugees were highly educated and professionally trained. The average number of years of schooling was 14.2 for the women and 14.6 for the men. Sixty-one percent of both men and women had been students at an institute of higher education; 83 percent of the women and 77 percent of the men had

Table 8.3
Percent Holding Jobs in the United States, by Sex and Age, in 1980

Age	Female	Male
18-24	60.6	54.5
25-34	64.0	81.6
35-44	69.3	85.4
45-54	68.6	81.1
55-64	43.5	62.8

Table 8.4
Comparison of Soviet Women Immigrants and U.S. Women Holding Jobs in the United States in 1980

Age	Soviet Immigrant Women	U.S. Women
18-24	60.6	----
25-34	64.0	57.8
35-44	69.3	58.2
45-54	68.6	54.5
55-64	43.5	39.8

received a certificate of general education. Most of the women were trained in technical professions such as engineering, mechanics, computer science, and commerce. Seventy-one percent of them had been in the labor force in the Soviet Union. Seventy-five percent held professional, white-collar, and managerial positions, and 25 percent worked in blue-collar positions. The gross income they received in their last "normal" year of work in the Soviet Union was 1,235 rubles, compared against 2,137 rubles for the men.[15] Net income for both groups was 1,112.7 rubles for the women, 1,896 rubles for the men. The women's salary was thus 58 percent of the men's, typical of the ratios observed in the USSR.

Shifting from the Soviet Union to the United States, we found that, at the time they were surveyed, more than 60 percent of the immigrant women were in the labor force full-time. A breakdown by age and sex and the percent holding full-time jobs is shown in Table 8.3.

Comparing the Soviet women's participation in the labor force against that of American women (see Table 8.4), a higher percentage of Soviet women in each age category work outside their homes than do American women, even among recent immigrants.

Certainly part of the explanation for the difference is cultural. Soviet women have traditionally held jobs outside their homes, while for most American women this is a more recent phenomenon.[16] In addition, immigrants have greater financial needs than do natives, and therefore economic factors play an important role.

Table 8.5
Occupations in the United States, by Sex of Respondent (in percent)

Occupation	Female	Male
Managerial/Executive	4.1	4.2
Professionals	16.1	29.5
Technicians/Mechanics	17.5	35.2
Clerical/Sales	31.2	7.4
Service	16.1	5.7
Laborers	15.0	16.7
Others/No answer	----	1.3
Total	100	100

The types of jobs in which the Soviet women are employed in the United States are shown in Table 8.5. We see that 69 percent of the women were holding managerial, professional, or clerical positions, as compared to 76 percent of the men. For the bulk of the respondents, the positions reported in Table 8.5 were their first jobs, yet already they were occupying positions consistent with their prior training and skills in the Soviet Union.

The annual gross income the women reported earning in the United States in 1980 was $7,627; they reported their net income as $6,501. For the men, the gross income was $14,607 and the net income $11,480.[17] On the average, the Soviet women's earnings in the United States were 57 percent of the Soviet men's, as had been the case in the Soviet Union. Government statistics in 1984 indicate that for "comparable type work," American women's earnings are about 59 percent of American men's.

When asked how satisfied they were with their current positions, 42.5 percent of the women said they were very satisfied, as compared to 35.4 percent of the men; 40.2 percent of the women were somewhat satisfied, compared to 51.1 percent of the men; and 13.7 percent of the women were not at all satisfied, compared to 10.2 percent of the men. None of the differences between the men's and women's responses was statistically significant.

Both men and women cited two major problems they confronted after arriving in the United States: finding a good job and learning English. The full set of responses is shown in Table 8.6. The respondents defined "good jobs" as work consistent with their prior training and educational experiences in a professional, managerial, or white-collar capacity. Thus, when 74 percent of the men and women said that "finding a good job" was their major problem, it has to be examined within this context. Similarly, when 71 percent of the women and 77 percent of the men reported learning English as a major problem, they were not describing a skill that would simply allow them to carry on casual conversations, do their shopping, and conduct other day-to-day business. They had in mind a facility consistent with their educational level and occupational background.

Table 8.6
Major and Minor Problems of Adjustment Reported, by Sex of Respondents (in percent)

Problem	Sex	Major	Minor	No Problem	NA
Finding a good job	F	74.2	9.5	16.1	.2
	M	74.0	11.2	14.8	--
Making new friends	F	27.9	27.1	44.5	.5
	M	28.2	27.6	43.8	.4
Learning English	F	71.1	16.6	11.8	.5
	M	76.8	14.0	9.2	--
Feeling outside Jewish community	F	7.1	17.4	74.7	.8
	M	7.7	21.3	70.3	.7
Earning enough money for family	F	47.1	28.7	22.6	1.6
	M	46.4	25.7	27.3	.6
Giving children a good education	F	30.5	12.1	52.5	4.9
	M	34.7	11.3	48.0	6.0
Indifference of Americans	F	11.3	20.3	67.1	1.3
	M	9.4	22.5	67.6	.5
Finding a good place to live	F	21.8	20.5	57.4	.3
	M	19.4	18.4	61.8	.4
Being separated from family	F	62.4	18.7	18.7	.2
	M	62.2	17.8	20.0	--
Feeling like an outsider	F	17.6	21.6	59.2	1.6
	M	14.0	19.8	65.8	.4

The kinds of issues that the immigrants felt were not major problems were largely of a personal and emotional nature. They did not feel that being outside the Jewish community was a problem. They were not concerned with the attitudes of the larger American public. They were somewhat concerned about getting a good education for their children, but most of them did not view that as a major problem. Nor did they view making new friends as a major problem.[18] The important issues were bread and butter ones: finding a job that corresponded to their training and experience, and learning a level of English that was consistent with their prior status. The responses of the men and women were almost identical in each of the potential and current problem areas. Women did not seem to have distinctive or unique adjustment problems.

The Soviet immigrants were not avid consumers of American culture, automatically assuming or believing that everything was better in the United States. For example, when we asked the respondents to rate their housing, cultural life, standard of living, and so on, we received the responses shown in Table 8.7.

Table 8.7
Comparisons Between Life in the Soviet Union and the United States, by Sex of Respondent (in percent)

Category	Sex	Better in U.S.	Worse in U.S.	Same	Does Not Apply	No Answer
Housing	F	61.6	18.2	19.7	.5	--
	M	65.6	15.8	18.1	.5	--
Cultural life	F	10.5	73.4	13.2	2.6	.3
	M	17.5	64.7	13.8	3.3	.7
Friendships	F	9.2	47.1	41.1	1.8	.8
	M	11.5	50.2	35.4	2.5	.4
Overall standard of living	F	70.8	16.1	10.3	2.6	.2
	M	77.3	10.8	10.4	1.2	.3
Social status or position	F	23.7	49.5	21.3	4.7	.8
	M	27.9	45.2	21.2	4.2	1.5
Life as a Jew	F	88.4	.8	9.5	1.1	.2
	M	88.0	.6	7.9	1.5	.6
Work situation	F	29.6	48.9	13.4	7.1	1.0
	M	40.3	41.5	14.0	4.0	.2
Income	F	74.4	14.2	7.4	3.9	.1
	M	79.6	11.7	3.6	5.1	--
Spouse's work situation	F	35.3	31.4	12.3	21.0	--
	M	28.8	39.3	9.2	22.7	--
Spouse's income	F	61.2	14.6	4.9	19.3	--
	M	53.1	16.6	4.1	26.2	--

We see that on such objective measures as housing, standard of living, and particularly their life as a Jew, both the men and women felt that things are much better in the United States. But on more subjective matters, such as the quality of their cultural life, friendships, and their social status and position, most of them felt that conditions were worse for them in the United States. Responses to the cultural life question become particularly interesting in the context of a survey of Soviet immigrants to Israel in the early 1970s, which included the same item and found a similar range of responses. Soviet immigrants to Israel were as critical of Israeli cultural life as their counterparts in the United States. In addition, when we compared responses to this item among the different cities, we found that immigrants in Boston, San Francisco, and New York were as critical as immigrants living in smaller cities or in cities that had fewer of the cultural opportunities available in the three cities mentioned above.

Friendship is especially important in the Soviet Union. Perhaps because it is difficult to trust many of the people with whom one comes into daily contact, friendship takes on a special significance in that society. Having been in the United States only a short time, the respondents may not have had the opportunity to establish close friends. They also may have observed that friendship was not as crucial to one's life in the United States as it was in the Soviet Union. In response to the survey items about friendship, 74 percent of the women and 71 percent of the men said that all their close friends in the United States were Jews; 56 percent of the women and 55 percent of the men said that all of their close friends were Jews who came from the Soviet Union in the last ten years.

Social status or position is another issue about which the immigrants in both the United States and Israel feel their lives were better in the Soviet Union. Most of them considered themselves to be members of the intelligentsia in the Soviet Union. In the United States they have not, or have not yet, achieved that status, a status that is important to them.

Incomes were viewed as much higher in the United States than in the Soviet Union. But work situation, which is closely related to one's social status and position, was not considered as good in the United States as it was in the Soviet Union. At first glance, the responses in Table 8.7 might suggest that women are more critical than men of various facets of life in the United States. But statistical tests confirm that none of the observed differences between men and women on any of the measured dimensions is significant.

Toward the end of the interview we asked each of the respondents, "If you had it to do over again, would you remain in the Soviet Union?" Eighty-six percent of the women and 84 percent of the men said that they would come to the United States; 7 percent of the women and 4.6 percent of the men said that they would remain in the Soviet Union; 4.8 percent of the women and 4.9 percent of the men said that they would immigrate to some other country, with Israel being the country cited most often. Thus, regardless of their adjustment problems and disappointments, the large majority of both men and women would make the same choice again.

Turning to the future, we asked a series of questions about what they expected their life to be like in five years. We asked how fluent they felt their language skills would be. Using a 5-point scale, where 5 represents complete fluency and 1 means being barely able to make oneself understood or barely able to speak, both the women's and men's mean scores were 4.2. When we asked what they thought their income levels were likely to be—rich, above average, average, below average, or poor—most of the men and women thought that they would be average. The distribution is shown in Table 8.8.

When we asked how satisfied they believed they would be with their likely jobs five years hence, almost all the men and women thought they would be very satisfied or somewhat satisfied. Twenty-seven percent of the women and 22 percent of the men said that they could not imagine how they would feel about a job five years hence. A few (less than 5 percent in both groups) thought they would be retired.

Returning to the present, we asked, "How would you describe your current

Table 8.8
Expectations About Income Level and Job Satisfaction Five Years Hence, by Sex of Respondent (in percent)

Category	Females	Males
Income Level		
Rich	1.9	2.8
Above average	15.9	26.0
Average	62.1	56.6
Below average	6.8	4.3
Poor	3.6	1.8
Don't know	9.7	8.5
Job Satisfaction		
Very satisfied	23.6	30.6
Somewhat satisfied	40.8	41.6
Neither satisfied nor	3.9	1.3
dissatisfied	1.6	2.8
Very dissatisfied	.6	.5
Don't know	27.2	22.0
No answer	2.3	1.0

Table 8.9
Reported Current Happiness, by Sex of Respondent

Happiness Level	Females	Males
Very happy	14.6	17.2
Pretty happy	58.1	63.9
Not too happy	25.3	18.1
No answer	2.0	.8

Note: The same item appeared in the 1982 General Social Survey for the United States as a whole, and the breakdown looked like this:

	Percent
Very happy	33
Pretty happy	54
Not too happy	13

state? Would you say that you are very happy, pretty happy, not happy?'' The responses in Table 8.9 show that most of the men and women see themselves as somewhat happy. Compared to the American responses, the Soviet immigrants are not as happy, but the difference is not striking.

Taken as a whole, all the data show that both the women and the men have made strong and positive adjustments to their new lives. It is noteworthy that the survey was conducted less than two years after the bulk of them had arrived in the United States; even after such a relatively short period, the large majority are already in the labor force full-time, working in professional and skilled occupations, and they believe that by most of the measured criteria they have a better life in the United States than they did in the Soviet Union. The women's experiences do not appear to be distinctive as compared to those of the men.

Many immigrants have described the transition from life in the Soviet Union to the United States as moving from "another planet." Considering the economic, political, and social changes involved in moving from a communist to a capitalist society, the rapid adjustment of these Soviet immigrants to life in the United States testifies to their willingness to build a new life for themselves.

NOTES

1. Michael P. Sacks, *Women's Work in Soviet Russia: Continuity in the Midst of Change* (New York: Praeger, 1976), p. 115.

2. Gail W. Lapidus, *Women in Soviet Society* (Berkeley: University of California Press, 1978), p. 277.

3. Murray Feshbach and Stephen Rapawy, "Soviet Population and Manpower Trends and Policies," in *Soviet Economy in a New Perspective* (Washington, DC: U.S. Government Printing Office, 1967), p. 152.

4. Sacks, *Women's Work*, p. 29.

5. Alistair McAuley, "Welfare and Social Security," in *The Soviet Workers' Illusions and Realities*, edited by Leonard Shapiro and Joseph Godson (New York: St. Martin's Press, 1981), p. 205.

6. Lotta Lennon, "Women in the USSR," in *Problems of Communism*, 1971, p. 53.

7. Sacks, *Women's Work*, p. 91.

8. Robert Conquest, *The Great Terror* (New York: Macmillan, 1968), p. 498; reports on the 1952 execution of Yiddish writers.

9. Maurice Friedberg, *Why They Left: A Survey of Soviet Jewish Emigrants* (New York: Academic Committee on Soviet Jewry, 1972), p. 3.

10. Ibid., p. 4; William Korey, *The Soviet Cage: Anti-Semitism in Russia* (New York: Viking Press, 1973), p. 125.

11. Liudmila Alekseeva, *Istoriia inakomysliia v. SSSR* (Benson, UT: Khronike Press, 1977), p. 157.

12. Nicholas V. Riasanovsky, *A History of Russia* (New York: Oxford University Press, 1969), p. 125.

13. For a fuller discussion see Henry N. Morton, "Housing Problems and Policies of Eastern Europe and the Soviet Union," *Studies in Comparative Communism* 12, 4 (1979): 320–321.

14. The particular cities included in the survey and the sample sizes within each city were chosen with the intention of producing a representative picture of the bulk of Soviet immigrants who live in the larger cities of the United States, but with large enough samples within the cities so that we could explore whether the immigrants' experiences differ from city to city. The fourteen cities are Atlanta, Boston, Chicago, Cleveland, Columbus, Houston, Kansas City, Los Angeles, Milwaukee, New York, Philadelphia, Rochester, San Francisco, and Worcester.

15. The "normal period" is defined as the period before they applied to emigrate.

16. In another survey conducted by R. Simon in 1980 of Soviet and Vietnamese

immigrants and American-born women, 92 percent of the Soviet respondents said that they work full-time and expect that their daughters will work full-time after they are married; only 22 percent of the American-born respondents answered that way. Fifty-two percent of the American-born mothers said, however, that while they are not employed, they expected that their daughters will work outside their homes after they are married.

17. For a rough comparison with American women in the labor force in 1980, the median weekly earnings of full-time female workers twenty-five years and older were $217 (which equals $11,284 for fifty-two weeks; *Statistical Abstract of the United States*, 1981, p. 407).

18. Ninety percent of the men and 87 percent of the women said that they believed there was a significant difference between how children are reared in the United States and the Soviet Union. The specific differences cited most often by both women and men were that children are treated too leniently in the United States, that they are less respectful of parents and adults, and that children in the Soviet Union are expected to work harder in school.

9

The Work and Personal Experiences of Undocumented Mexican Women Migrants

This chapter reports the demographic characteristics, labor force participation, and personal circumstances of undocumented and documented Mexican women immigrants in Los Angeles County. The women were interviewed in their homes, churches, community centers, and places of work, not in detention centers, where other previous studies of illegal migrants were usually conducted.

Mexican immigrants occupy a special status among all immigrant communities in the United States. This uniqueness stems from a variety of factors, the most important of which are their place of origin, the presumed temporary nature of their migration, the large numbers involved, their unusual tenacity in adhering to the language and customs of their country of origin, and the fact that many of them enter the United States illegally. These factors also make them one of the least favored or desirable of the multitude of immigrant groups who seek political and/or economic refuge in the United States. Public opinion surveys reveal that Mexican immigrants have consistently occupied a low position on the "prestige" or "desirability" ladder among a cross section of the American public.

For example, in 1982 the Roper Organization asked this question:

Since the beginning of our country, people of many different religions, races and nationalities have come here and settled. Here is a list of some different groups. Would you read down the list and, thinking both of what they have contributed to this country and have gotten from this country, for each one, tell me whether you think on a balance, they've been a good thing or a bad thing for this country?[1]

The responses looked like this:

Nationality	Good Thing for Country	Bad Thing for Country
English	66%	6%
Irish	62	7
Jews	59	9
Germans	57	11
Italians	56	10
Poles	53	12
Japanese	47	18
Blacks	46	16
Chinese	44	19
Mexicans	25	34
Koreans	24	30
Vietnamese	20	38
Puerto Ricans	17	43
Haitians	10	39
Cubans	9	59

Mexican immigrants, along with other groups from the Caribbean, rank below any European groups, and below Japanese, blacks, and Chinese. Only the Vietnamese were placed among the Caribbean and the Mexican.

BACKGROUND AND DESIGN

The current period of Mexican migration to the United States began during World War II, when thousands of Mexican agricultural workers were imported under the Bracero Program to offset a labor shortage created by the war. The Bracero Program was designed to admit agricultural workers to the United States on a temporary basis. Officially, the program lasted until 1964. During part of that same period, however, the Immigration and Naturalization Service (INS) initiated a series of actions against Mexican migrants who had entered the country illegally (Operation Wetback), which resulted in rounding up over a million illegals and sending them back across the border.

When the Bracero Program was officially ended, hundreds of thousands of Mexican farm workers who had entered the country legally were left without jobs. In 1965, with the passage of the Hart-Cellars Immigration and Naturalization Act, for the first time a quota system was established for migrants from countries in the Western Hemisphere. It established that no more than 120,000 immigrants per year could enter from those countries. In the period between 1961 and 1978, more immigrants came to the United States from Mexico than from any other country in the world. An amendment to the Immigration and

Table 9.1

Sex Distribution of Illegal Migrants to the United States as Reported in Four Studies*

	(1) Census Bureau 1970-1979	(2) Van Arsdol et al., 1972-1975	(3) Maram 1979
Both Sexes	1,250[a]	2,845	645.0
Percent	100.0	100.0	100.0
Male	57.7	64.2	47.3
Female	42.3	35.8	52.7
Sex Ratio	136.3	179.5	89.7

[a] Number in thousands

Sources: D. S. Massey, Migration Today, 11:1 (1983). (1) U.S. Bureau of the Census (1981). Data taken from the November 1979 Current Population Survey. (2) Van Arsdol et al. (1979). Data gathered from clients of the "One Stop" immigrant counseling center in Los Angeles, California. (3) Maram (1980). Data gathered from a nonrandom sample of Hispanic restaurant and garment workers in Los Angeles, California.

Naturalization Act passed in 1976 imposed an annual ceiling of 20,000 immigrants from each Western Hemisphere country.

Currently, the most controversial issue about Mexican migration is that so many of the migrants cross the border without papers and enter the country illegally. Estimates as to the number of illegal Mexican migrants in the United States range from 1 or 2 million to as many as 10 million.

Much of the research on Mexican migrants, documented and undocumented, has focused on men, even though women have comprised a higher proportion than men of all migrants to the United States in the past half-century. In the 1970s, surveys reveal, between 35 and 50 percent of the illegal migrants from Mexico were women. And the number of women migrants has increased in the last decade. In an article in *Migration Today*, Massey and Schnabel compared the sex ratios of undocumented Mexican migrants, based on three surveys.[2] Table 9.1 describes the sex distribution as reported in those studies.

THE WORK EXPERIENCE OF MEXICAN WOMEN MIGRANTS

This study describes the work experience of these Mexican women migrants. By focusing primarily on illegal migrants, it provides a rare opportunity to answer some important questions about their work experiences, personal circumstances, and migration history.

The survey was conducted in the fall and winter of 1981–1982. At the time of the survey, the respondents had not been apprehended by the INS. The interviews did not take place in detention centers or in the offices of the INS, but in the respondents' homes, churches, and neighborhoods. The women willingly agreed to the interviews, which were conducted in Spanish by Chicano students who were enrolled in courses taught by Professor Bert Corona of the Chicano Studies Department at California State University in Los Angeles. Almost all of the respondents knew or had heard of Corona, and trusted him. Only 8 percent of the women who entered illegally refused to be interviewed. In addition to the undocumented immigrants, we also interviewed a subsample of documented Mexican women immigrants currently or formerly employed in the Los Angeles County area.[3] While the thrust of the study was to describe the experiences of the undocumented women, we felt that this account would be enhanced and sharpened if their experiences were compared against those reported by documented women.

Of the 698 completed interviews, 562 were done with undocumented women and 136 with documented women. Among the undocumented respondents, 467 were in the labor force at the time they were interviewed; 95 were not. The latter had either quit or been fired from their last job and were looking for work. Among the 136 women who were in the country legally, 110 were in the labor force at the time of the survey; 26 were not. This chapter describes the responses of those women—the 467 undocumented and 110 documented—currently in the labor force.

The major issues covered in our overall study concern the respondents' work situation, their demographic and social characteristics, their migration patterns, and their acculturation to the host society. Within the context of their work situation, we examine the types of jobs they are likely to occupy, their hourly wages, whether they are paid by check or cash, how long they have been employed at their current job, the amounts and types of deductions that are taken out of their wages, whether their employers knew that they were illegal at the time of hiring, whether they perceive themselves as targets of discrimination by their employers, the ethnic backgrounds or nationalities of their fellow workers, and whether they belong to a labor union. This chapter focuses on the respondents' work situation, and compares the responses of the undocumented women against those made by women who are in the work force legally.

Before reporting the findings, a few comments need to be made about our research design and the generalizability of our results. As Douglas North and Marion Houstoun, Alejandro Portes, Wayne Cornelius, Barry Chiswick, and others who have done field research with illegal immigrants emphasize, it is not possible to obtain representative samples of such respondents because the number, distribution, and characteristics of the universe are not known.

For our survey, we opted to locate and interview illegal women immigrants in their "natural habitats," and our sample was largely a "convenience" one. Taking advantage of the wide network of contacts that Professor Corona had in the Mexican community in Los Angeles, we contacted leaders and directors of clinics, churches, neighborhood associations, and social and fraternal organizations in Mexican neighborhoods and asked them to publicize the forthcoming survey. Interviewers were also sent door-to-door in neighborhoods in which a high proportion of immigrants were known to be living, to solicit interviews directly. Their identification as students of Professor Corona in Chicano Studies, their language facility, and their appearance, coupled with the unofficial endorsements from the groups mentioned above, all contributed to the very high response rate. We think the experiences reported in our survey should generalize to illegal Mexican women in the Los Angeles area and probably to most large cities in the United States.

DEMOGRAPHIC CHARACTERISTICS

Briefly, demographic profiles of the undocumented and documented women contain the following characteristics. The average age of the undocumented woman was thirty; the average age of the documented was thirty-four. Forty percent of the undocumented women were twenty-five and younger, as opposed to 26 percent of the documented women; and 4 percent of the undocumented women were between fifty and sixty years old (sixty was the oldest), as were 6 percent of the documented. Of the undocumented women, 34 percent reported that they were married and 26 percent said that they were living with a companion; of the documented women, 61 percent reported that they were married and 30 percent said they were living with a companion at the time of the survey. Forty-seven percent of the undocumented women said they had given birth to at least one child (the average number is three), and 71 percent of the documented women reported giving birth to at least one child (the average number is 3.5). Forty-four percent of the undocumented women and 69 percent of the documented women have at least one child living with them; the average numbers are 2.7 and 2.9 for the two categories of women. Fifty percent of the undocumented and 30 percent of the documented women have children who are less than six years old. Only 4 percent of the undocumented women send their children to a day-care center or employ a "professional baby-sitter," while 15 percent of the documented women do so. More of the undocumented than the documented women rely on relatives, neighbors, and friends.

Table 9.2 compares the years of schooling the undocumented and documented respondents reported. Among the documented women there are fewer illiterates and over four times as many who attended a university. But even among the undocumented only 7 percent had no schooling; most had a few years of elementary school or completed the elementary level.

Seven percent of the undocumented women said that they attended school in the United States, most of them for one or two years. In contrast, one-third of the documented women said that some of their schooling took place in the United States, and almost all of those who reported attending college and university did so in the United States. Ten percent of the undocumented women and 24 percent

Table 9.2
Years of Schooling by Legal Status

Years of Schooling	Undocumented	Documented
	(Percent)	
None	7.2	2.7
Few Years--elementary	28.8	15.5
Completed--elementary	28.8	29.1
Few Years--secondary	16.0	14.5
Completed--secondary	15.0	20.0
University--1-2 years	2.6	9.1
University--3-4 years	1.6	9.1
Total	100(110)	100(463)

of the documented women reported receiving some type of vocational education (most often in clerical/secretarial skills).[4]

As one might expect, there was a strong relationship between the amount of education respondents reported and their English language facility. Only a small percentage (12 percent or less of the undocumented women) rated their facility in English as very good. On the reading and writing dimension, most of them evaluated it as ''not serviceable.'' On the speaking and understanding dimension, almost half rated their facility as ''serviceable.'' The large majority of the documented women rated their facility in English (speaking, understanding, etc.) as ''very good'' or ''serviceable.''

Seventy-one percent of the undocumented women reported that they speak only Spanish at their place of work, as opposed to 37 percent of the documented workers. Twenty-six percent of the latter work in situations in which they speak only English. Nine percent of the undocumented women work under such conditions.[5]

We asked the respondents whether they were currently studying English. Fifty-four percent of the undocumented and 27 percent of the documented said yes. When we probed further, it turned out that most of the undocumented who said they were studying English were devoting less than one hour a week to their studies, and only 17 percent were studying at school.

Forty percent of the undocumented and 28 percent of the documented women said that they had held jobs outside their homes in Mexico before they came to the United States. Of those who were in the work force, 43 percent of the undocumented women held clerical and sales positions, 24 percent worked as laborers in factories, 3 percent were farm laborers, and the other 30 percent worked in service capacities in commercial establishments or private homes. About half of the documented women said they were employed in clerical and sales positions. The others worked as laborers in factories or as domestics in

Table 9.3
Mean Hourly Wages, by Respondents' Legal Status

Hours Worked per Week	N	Undocumented	Documented	Difference in Rates of Pay
		(Mean Hourly Wages)		
Less than 14	(29)	3.89 (19)	7.83 (10)	-3.94
15-24	(47)	3.52 (37)	4.19 (10)	- .67
25-34	(317)	3.84(258)	5.03 (59)	-1.19
35-40	(136)	3.50(114)	5.84 (22)	-2.34
40+	(13)	5.66 (6)	4.05 (7)	+1.61
Combined x^*	(542)	3.75(434)	5.32(108)	-1.57

* Thirty-three of the undocumented women and two of the documented women did not answer the income question.

private homes. In the main, these data support those reported by Portes for Mexican male immigrants. They show that even among the illegal women immigrants, most of them are not landless peasants, and many of them bring skills and work experience with them that should be useful in an urban environment.

WORK AND ECONOMIC SITUATION

Most of the women—55 percent of the undocumented and 49 percent of the documented—were working in factories at the time of the survey. The respondents in the two categories differ in that more of the documented than the undocumented women are likely to work in offices and public institutions (37 percent versus 11 percent). The undocumented women are more likely to work in restaurants, small retail stores, and private homes (28 percent versus 10 percent).

Most of the women—50 percent of the undocumented and 50 percent of the documented—work as unskilled or semiskilled laborers. For the undocumented women, the next highest category is service workers in private homes or business establishments (26 percent). The major difference between the two categories of women is that the documented women are more likely to hold white-collar, especially clerical, jobs (32 percent versus 12 percent). Almost all of the women in both categories (88 percent and 87 percent) report that their current jobs are permanent or year-round, not seasonal or temporary.

The number of work hours per week and their hourly rate of pay is shown in Table 9.3. Among those who work fewer than thirty-five hours per week, 78 percent of the undocumented and 80 percent of the documented attributed it to the fact that their boss would not provide them with more hours. On average, the undocumented workers earn 40 cents more per hour than minimum wage;

Table 9.4

Mean Hourly Wages by Type of Jobs, by Respondents' Legal Status

Job Classification	N	Undocumented	Documented	Differences in Rates of Pay
		(Mean Hourly Wages)		
Professionals, proprietors, clerical sales, skilled, craft	(105)	4.17 (69)	6.38 (36)	-2.21
Operatives	(303)	3.83(249)	4.78 (54)	- .95
Service, nondomestic	(86)	3.53 (71)	4.94 (15)	-1.41
Service, domestic	(45)	2.98 (42)	4.06 (3)	-1.08
Combined x*	(539)	3.75(431)	5.32(108)	-1.57

* Thirty-three of the undocumented and two of the documented women did not answer the income question. Three of the undocumented women did not answer the occupation item.

the documented women earn almost $2.00 an hour more. These data seem to be consistent with the observation of John Crewdson, then of the *New York Times*, who wrote that more than three-quarters of the female illegal Mexican aliens earn more than the minimum wage.[6]

We also computed the mean hourly rate of pay by occupational categories and years of schooling. These findings are reported in Tables 9.4 and 9.5. As the figures in these tables indicate, in each occupational and educational category the undocumented workers receive less pay than the documented ones. The biggest differences between documented and undocumented women are found in the white-collar occupations and in years of education. Undocumented women who work in white-collar jobs earn less money than documented women who work as operatives in factories and in service capacities; and undocumented women who have completed high school earn less per hour than documented women who had no schooling or a few years of elementary school. In a regression equation, we found that respondents' legal status was the most important factor in predicting hourly rate of pay. Next was education, followed by year of arrival and age. But only legal status (−.22) and years of schooling (.13) proved significant.

Seventy-six percent of the undocumented and 94 percent of the documented women said that they are paid by check, not in cash. Further analysis of respondents who are paid in cash revealed that they are mostly undocumented women who work as domestics in private homes.

Part of the debate about the impact of the illegal workers on the American economy is that they are "freeloaders." The argument is that they do not pay their fair share of taxes, and they avail themselves of facilities and services that

Table 9.5
Mean Hourly Wages by Years of Schooling, by Legal Status

Years of Schooling	N	Undocumented	Documented	Differences in Rates of Pay
		(Mean Hourly Wages)		
None or few years, elementary school	(170)	3.55(150)	4.62 (20)	-1.07
Completed elementary school	(149)	3.70(118)	4.21 (31)	- .51
Few years secondary school	(87)	3.95 (72)	4.48 (15)	- .53
Completed secondary school	(94)	3.81 (72)	6.05 (22)	-2.24
College/University	(38)	4.85 (18)	7.55 (22)	-2.70
Combined $\bar{x}$*	(539)	3.75(431)	5.32(108)	-1.57

* Thirty-three of the undocumented and two of the documented women did not answer the income question. Four of the undocumented women did not answer the education item.

are paid for by American workers' tax contributions. When we asked respondents about the deductions from their wages, 73 percent reported that income tax is deducted and 71 percent that Social Security is deducted from their wages.[7] These figures match, within three percentage points, the number of undocumented women who said they are paid by check, and support the finding that the large majority of undocumented women pay taxes and contribute toward Social Security benefits that they themselves are not likely to receive in their old age.

Rather surprisingly, when respondents were asked, "Have you ever felt that you have been discriminated against while working in your current job?," only 19 percent of the undocumented workers and 20 percent of the documented workers answered that they had. The basis for the discriminatory treatment, as they saw it, was nationality or legal status. For example, although the large majority of women in both categories (80 percent and 82 percent) believed that the undocumented and documented workers were treated equally, when the undocumented women were asked directly, "Do you believe your employer is paying you less than he or she is paying documented employees for doing the same job?," 23 percent said yes and 30 percent said they did not know.

Forty-three percent of the undocumented women said their bosses knew they did not have papers at the time they were hired. Twenty-seven percent said they did not know what the boss's knowledge of their legal status was; 25 percent said their boss did not know that they were undocumented; and 5 percent did not answer. Of those who said the boss knew they did not have papers, two-thirds also said they believed they were hired because they were illegals.

Perhaps the absence of discrimination, or the perception that they are not the targets of discrimination, can be partially explained because for 60 percent of the women (undocumented and documented), all or almost all of their fellow workers are Mexican, and that 30 percent of undocumented workers and 35 percent of documented workers have an immediate supervisor who is also Mexican.[8] The undocumented women who reported discrimination almost always said that they received less pay than women doing the same job and working as long as they were. Some claimed that their boss made them work harder because he knew they did not have papers. For example, "He made me punch the card for only four days, but I worked five days," or "They shouted at us as if we were animals," or "If any of us [undocumented] complains, he fires us."

Seventy-three percent of the undocumented and 77 percent of the documented workers never asked for a pay raise in their current job. Of those who did ask, 17 percent of the women in both categories reported receiving at least one raise. Ninety percent of the undocumented and 80 percent of the documented workers never asked for a promotion (a job with a higher salary or with more prestige). Thirty percent of the documented but only 11 percent of the undocumented belonged to a union. In response to several questions about their perceptions of the effectiveness of unions, 16 percent of the undocumented and 15 percent of the documented said that they thought unions helped a lot to raise the wages of workers from Mexico. Almost all of the women reported that they have not found any organizations to be particularly helpful with job-related problems.

The last question we asked the women about their current job was, "Do you enjoy working for your current employer?" Eighty percent of the undocumented and 85 percent of the documented answered yes. The reason most often given was, "My boss is a good person."

Among those respondents who held more than one job in the United States (38 percent of the undocumented and 69 percent of the documented), we found that there was little change in job classification between previous and current occupations for either the undocumented or documented women. Among both categories, there was a slight increase in the percentage who worked in white-collar occupations between their first and current jobs. Among the undocumented women there was a decrease in the percentage who worked as domestics in private homes in their first jobs and then shifted, primarily to factory jobs or to service jobs in commercial establishments. Working in a private home, on the other hand, may be the "safest" and least complicated job for a newly arrived undocumented woman.

WHY MEXICAN WOMEN MIGRANTS COME TO THE UNITED STATES

The most important reason Mexican male immigrants (documented and undocumented) gave for why they came to the United States was to find work and to earn more money than they could in Mexico, according to North and

Table 9.6
Reasons for Coming to the United States, by Legal Status

Reasons for Coming to the United States	Legal Status	Very Import.	Of Some Import.	Of Little Import.	Not Import.	NA	Total
Family unity: to accompany or join another member of my family	Doc.	66.4	10.0	4.5	13.6	5.5	100
	Undoc.	45.8	16.7	10.3	20.1	7.1	100
Economic reasons: to earn more money than I could in Mexico	Doc.	59.1	8.2	8.2	5.5	20.9	100
	Undoc.	70.1	12.8	5.1	6.6	5.3	100
Personal benefit: to see and do things and have a better life for myself	Doc.	51.8	11.8	9.1	19.1	8.2	100
	Undoc.	64.0	16.5	5.1	6.6	7.7	100
Children: to offer my children more opportunities for a better life	Doc.	43.6	8.2	3.6	30.9	13.7	100
	Undoc.	39.6	6.6	1.7	34.0	18.0	100

Houstoun, and Portes.[9] Do the Mexican women migrants share these views to the same extent? We asked the women two questions about their reasons for coming to the United States. The first was, "Did you come to the United States with the intention of working?" Sixty-nine percent of the undocumented and 44 percent of the documented answered yes. The second question was, "The following are the most common reasons which people give for coming to the United States. Please tell me whether each reason is 'very important,' 'of some importance,' or 'not very important.'" The distribution of responses is shown in Table 9.6.

Seventy percent of the undocumented women rated economic reasons first, as very important, followed by "personal benefits." More documented women rated "family unity" very important over any other consideration. Economic reasons ranked second. Responses to these two items, as well as some of the biographical data (e.g., 91 percent of the documented and 60 percent of the undocumented are living with a husband or companion), lead us to conclude that the undocumented women have greater economic independence and fewer external supports than do the documented women migrants.

Almost all of the women in both categories said that at the time they came to the United States, they intended to remain "as long as possible." Only 12 percent of the undocumented and 5 percent of the documented women indicated a specific length of time they planned to stay (e.g., one to two years).[10] Altogether, the documented women have been in the United States about ten years longer than the undocumented. These responses contrast sharply with the commonly held view that Mexican migrants come to the United States for a relatively short period of time and then return to their country of origin.

At the close of the interview, we asked the women, "What aspects of working in this country are of most concern to you?" For the undocumented women, their "illegal" status and the fear that they might be sent back to Mexico were cited most often (by 31 percent). These reasons were followed by the low rate of pay they receive for their work (14 percent), fear of losing their job (12 percent), their lack of facility in English, which they view as a handicap on the job (7 percent), a feeling that they are being exploited because they are Mexican (6 percent), and the scarcity of jobs (6 percent). No other reasons were cited by more than 5 percent of the workers. Among the documented women, the low rate of pay they receive for their work was cited most often (by 21 percent), fear of losing their job by 14 percent, not enough jobs to go around by 10 percent, and the sense that they are being exploited because they are Mexican by 10 percent.

CONCLUDING REMARKS

We return to our initial questions about the personal circumstances and labor force participation of the undocumented Mexican women immigrants. How many of the popular impressions have been substantiated by the data collected in this survey?

One of the big surprises of our study is how the undocumented women evaluate their work situation. Only 19 percent say that they have ever been discriminated against on their current job; 80 percent believe they are treated in the same fashion as other workers and enjoy working for their current employer. The personality profile that emerges from these responses is not that of an angry, embittered work force, but rather a timid group of workers who believe they have no real work options and who are relatively satisfied with what they have.

Most of the women, the undocumented as well as the documented, work in factories as laborers. The popular impression that undocumented Mexican women immigrants in urban areas work mainly in private homes as domestics, cleaning houses, babysitting, and so on, has not been substantiated—only 10 percent of the undocumented women are so employed in our survey, although 19 percent held such jobs when they first came to the United States. While the respondents showed some mobility out of domestic employment, on the whole the occupational mobility patterns of both categories of women did not indicate much change between first jobs in the United States and current jobs. On the average, the hourly rate of pay for undocumented women was 40 cents higher than the minimum wage, and $1.57 lower than the average documented woman's rate of pay. We saw that within the same occupational categories, the undocumented women earned less money per hour, the smallest difference occurring in the "laborer" category.

A popular impression not substantiated by our data was the method of payment for the undocumented women. Seventy-six percent of them were paid by check rather than in cash. While that figure is not as high as the 94 percent of the documented women who are paid by check, it is nevertheless much higher than common belief would have it. The respondents who are paid in cash are most likely to work in private homes as domestics. Given the form of payment for all but a small proportion of the women, it follows that most of the undocumented women have income tax and Social Security payments deducted from their wages. This was reflected in our survey responses, but again, not quite to the same extent as the documented women (73 percent and 71 percent versus 89 percent and 83 percent, respectively).

Contrary to popular impression, almost all of the women say they came to the United States with the intention of remaining here permanently (or as long as "MIGRA" does not catch and deport them). The most important reasons for coming to the United States for the large majority are economic factors: better jobs and better pay. Their biggest fear is that they might be caught and sent back to Mexico.

As long as they are not caught, even if they are laid off from work, they will probably opt to remain in the United States because the future is brighter for them here than in Mexico. Even when they are temporarily unemployed, they have enough of a support network to tide them over; and the prospect of obtaining work at the minimum wage level is better in the United States than in Mexico. Like undocumented Mexican men working in the United States, the work they can get and the wages they earn are most important in determining the undocumented women's behavior.

NOTES

1. E. Harwood, "Alienation: American Attitude Toward Immigration," *Public Opinion*, June/July 1983.

2. D. S. Massey and K. M. Schnabel, "Background and Characteristics of Undocumented Hispanic Migrants to the United States," *Migration Today* 11, 1 (1983): 4–12.

3. Three percent of the "documented" immigrants refused to be interviewed.

4. Douglas North and Marion Houstoun's study of "green card commuters" across the Mexican-U.S. border in Texas reported educational levels among Mexican men and women with "green cards." They found that "80 percent of them (there were no differences by sex) did not have more than eight years of school; and nearly 69 percent of them ended their education at or before the sixth grade, which is the last year of primary school in the Mexican educational system." The mean years of schooling were 5.8. Among illegals who were interviewed at the border, the mean years of schooling were 4.7. D. S. North and M. F. Houstoun, *The Characteristics and Role of Illegal Aliens in the U.S. Labor Market: An Exploratory Study* (Washington, DC: Linton, 1976), p. 73.

5. At home, 94 percent of the undocumented women speak only Spanish, as opposed to 73 percent of the documented. The others speak Spanish and English.

6. John Crewdson, "Illegal Aliens Found Work in Better Paying Jobs," *New York Times*, November 10, 1980, p. 1.

7. As expected, a higher percentage of the documented women reported income tax and Social Security deductions: 89 percent and 82.7 percent, respectively.

8. We also asked, "How many of the Mexicans where you work are undocumented?" Seventy-seven percent of the documented women answered the question, in contrast to 37 percent of the undocumented women. Among those who did answer, 60 percent of the undocumented said "many, nearly all, or all"; only 3 percent said "none." Among the documented, 26 percent said "many, nearly all, or all," and 43 percent said "none." To the extent that we can assume the respondents' answers are accurate, they suggest that the documented and undocumented women work in different factories or other business establishments.

9. Alejandro Portes, "Illegal Immigration and the International System: Lessons for Recent Legal Mexican Immigrants to the United States," *Social Problems* 26 (April 1979): 426–438.

10. Our findings are supported by sociologists Herman Baca and M. Bryan's research on single illegal Mexican women, whom they claim "do aspire to stay here permanently." These women are escaping not only an economic situation in Mexico, but also social problems of their own. "They may, in fact, not be able to go back; there may be an illegitimate birth or maybe there is a bad marriage, but they cannot get a divorce in Mexico. So they resolve the matter by truly separating, by coming north" ("Illegal Aliens' Plans for Staying in the U.S.," *Los Angeles Times*, July 16, 1980, p. 22).

10

Refugee Women and Their Daughters: A Comparison of Soviet, Vietnamese, and Native-Born American Families

---

This chapter takes a closer look at refugee women, mothers and daughters, who participated in a larger study that examined areas of likely conflict between mothers and adolescent daughters. It presents a comparison of the responses of 200 Vietnamese and Soviet refugee mothers and adolescent daughters to questions about the daughter's educational and occupational aspirations, plans for marriage and number of children, and the relationships of mothers and daughters. The refugee families' responses were also compared against a subsample of American-born mothers and adolescent daughters.

This chapter focuses on the career expectations and aspirations that refugee parents have for their children and the plans and hopes that the children have about their own futures; on the quality of the relationships between parents and adolescents; and on the expectations that both parents and adolescents have concerning their social and economic adjustment five and ten years hence. The survey also includes 100 American-born families, each of which has children within the same age range as the refugee families.

The Soviet and Vietnamese respondents in the study arrived in the United States during the same five-year period, between 1975 and 1980. In fact, over 70 percent in both groups arrived between 1978 and 1980. Since members of both communities were designated refugees, they came under the jurisdiction of a consortium of agencies in Chicago which helped to resettle them. These agencies procured housing, helped them find employment, introduced them to vocational training programs, and provided them with English classes, medical care, and a variety of other services.

The Soviet Jewish families lived in a section of Chicago where a much older Eastern European Jewish community had resided for more than half a century.

The Vietnamese families lived in a neighborhood that had housed other Asians (Filipinos and Koreans) and some Mexicans for about two decades.

This chapter takes a closer look at the refugee women, mothers and daughters, who participated in that larger study.[1] We examine areas of likely conflict between mothers and adolescent daughters (e.g., choice of friends, style of dress, time devoted to schooling versus other activities). We compare the responses of 200 Vietnamese and Soviet refugee mothers and adolescent daughters concerning the daughter's educational and occupational aspirations, plans about marriage and number of children, and the relationships between the mothers and daughters. The refugee families' responses are then compared against a subsample of American-born mothers and adolescent daughters who were also living in Chicago. All of the Soviet families and 80 percent of the Vietnamese families were intact, with both parents living at home.

While we anticipated that the Soviet and Vietnamese mothers would make quite different short-run adjustments to their new environment because of their disparate experiences in their countries of origin and because of their different skills, we wanted to see how similar or different the Soviet and Vietnamese adolescent daughters would be in their social adjustments and in their expectations about education, jobs, marriage, and children. The specific questions are: How are adolescent girls in the two refugee communities likely to adjust to their new environments? What hopes and expectations do their mothers have for them? And how do the mothers and daughters relate to each other on matters concerning the daughters' behavior in their new environment?

Our samples for the Soviet and Vietnamese families came from the consortium of Chicago agencies that helped resettle them. In each community, we conducted personal interviews with fifty mothers and fifty adolescent daughters between the ages of fifteen and twenty from the same families. The interviews were conducted in Russian or Vietnamese. Each lasted about forty-five minutes. The American sample of fifty mothers and fifty daughters was based on random digit dialing within the city of Chicago. The two clearing questions we employed were (1) Did the respondent have a daughter between the ages of fifteen and twenty, and (2) Were the parents born in the United States? The American respondents were interviewed by phone.

The first section provides some background on the demographic characteristics of the Soviet and Vietnamese refugees and brief profiles of the mothers and the adolescent daughters in each community. The second part compares mothers' and daughters' responses to a series of items pertaining primarily to the future socioeconomic status of the daughters. It also compares levels of disagreement between mothers and daughters in each community and assesses the extent to which the daughters are likely to follow in their mothers' footsteps or instead to pursue a lifestyle antithetical to their mothers', with or without their mothers' approval.

SOVIET AND VIETNAMESE REFUGEES

Between 1966 and 1975, some 125,000 Jews emigrated from the Soviet Union. About 110,000 of them settled in Israel; approximately another 11,000 came to the United States; and practically all of the others immigrated to Canada, Australia, and New Zealand.[2] Since 1975, an increasing number of Soviet Jews have opted to come to the United States rather than settle in Israel. Whereas earlier in the decade over 75 percent went directly from Vienna to Israel, 65 percent have immigrated to the United States, Canada, Australia, and New Zealand since 1975. The remaining 35 percent went to Israel. Of the 65 percent opting for resettlement in countries other than Israel, approximately 85 percent chose to come to the United States. Since 1975 about 90,000 Jews have immigrated to the United States. Over 50,000 arrived between 1979 and 1980.[3]

The Soviet refugees were well educated and technically skilled. In the Soviet Union many of them worked as engineers, computer programmers, architects, draftsmen, and doctors. They lived mainly in large cities in the western part of the country, especially in the Ukraine, White Russia, and the Russian Federal Republic (RSFSF). Many of them had studied English in the Soviet Union. Most of them chose to leave because of anti-Semitism, which they believed hurt their own chances for success and limited their children's opportunities. Most of them came in family units of a father, mother, and one child. About 20 percent also came with a grandparent. Almost all of them waited less than a year for their exit visas; two-thirds waited six months or less.[4]

During this same period, 1975 through 1980, more than 360,000 Vietnamese, Laotian, and Cambodian refugees also arrived in the United States. Many of them fled under quite harrowing circumstances. Most did not come directly to the United States but spent months in refugee camps in Thailand, Malaysia, the Philippines, and other parts of Asia and the Pacific. Those who did come directly to the United States also waited in camps until they could be resettled. Many came because they did not want to live under the new communist regime, or felt threatened by the changes in government.

They arrived in large family units—on average, parents, six children, and one or two other relatives. The Vietnamese refugees had less formal education and fewer marketable skills than the Soviets, especially those who arrived after 1978. Among the 1979 and 1980 arrivals, many had been small shopkeepers or fishermen in Vietnam. The majority had no training in English or French. Those who arrived earlier—in 1975, 1976, and 1977—were better educated and had more marketable skills, more experience living in urban communities, and greater knowledge of English and French.[5] Commenting about those who arrived during this early period, Daniel Montero reported that 24 percent of the heads of households had professional, technical, or managerial skills, and 12 percent had clerical and sales expertise.[6] He also claimed that given the high level of educational attainment of the heads of households, many of the early refugees probably came from urban rather than rural areas.

PROFILES OF SOVIET, VIETNAMESE, AND AMERICAN MOTHERS

Soviet Mothers

Most of the Soviet mothers in our sample came from Kiev, Karkov, and Odessa, and had left their homes because of anti-Semitism, which they felt would hurt their own, their spouse's, and their children's economic, professional, and social future. Their mean age at the time of the survey was forty-three. Sixty percent of the mothers had completed at least four years of college; 10 percent had postgraduate degrees. Only 4 percent had less than an eighth grade education. All but 8 percent (including two who were retired) had worked outside their homes as engineers, draftsmen, doctors, teachers, architects, or computer programmers, or in clerical positions. Half of them reported that they had studied English before they came to the United States, and 76 percent were studying English at the time of the survey.

Seventy-two percent of the mothers arrived in the United States in 1979 and 1980, 12 percent came in 1978, and the other 16 percent arrived between 1975 and 1978. At the time of the survey 77 percent were working outside their homes, most of them in clerical positions, as technicians, or as engineers. Their average income was $1,200 a month. The majority rated their facility in reading and understanding English as good, and their ability to speak and write as fair.

On the whole, the Soviet mothers were optimistic about the future in their new country. When asked what they thought their economic position would be five years from now (i.e., the time of the survey), 18 percent said they expected to hold responsible, important jobs and to feel successful; 58 percent said they expected to have good jobs and steady employment; and 10 percent thought they would work steadily at run-of-the-mill jobs. Only one respondent did not believe she would find steady employment, and 12 percent said they had been in the United States too short a time to be able to project themselves five years into the future.

Asked about their language facility, 14 percent thought that they would speak English fluently and use it at work and at home; 36 percent expected to speak English fluently but would continue to speak Russian at home; and 44 percent thought that their English would be serviceable for work and outside activities but expected to speak Russian at home.

Asked how they would identify themselves five years hence, 74 percent of the mothers said as a Jew, an American Jew, or an American; the others said as a Russian American, a Russian, or a Russian Jew. None of them used the term "Soviet" as part of their future identity.

Vietnamese Mothers

Like the Soviets, the majority of Vietnamese mothers in our sample arrived in the United States between 1978 and 1980. Unlike the Soviet refugees, most of them left their homeland illegally. Starting out in small boats, they were picked up en route and taken to refugee camps in Malaysia, Guam, Hong Kong, the Philippines, and other places in Asia and the Pacific. All of the mothers spent some time in camps, ranging from one to nineteen months.

Sixty-eight percent said their main reason for leaving Vietnam was opposition to the new regime—they disliked communism and wanted to live in a free society. Fourteen percent thought their life was in danger because they had worked for the American forces or the South Vietnamese government; 10 percent wanted to be reunited with relatives who had come earlier; 4 percent wanted to escape the war; and 4 percent did not answer. Twenty percent were heads of households, either because they were widowed before they arrived or because their husbands stayed behind in Vietnam.

The mothers' mean age was forty-seven. Most of them had not had more than ten years of schooling in Vietnam; eight had not gone to school at all. At the time of the survey, only 16 percent of the mothers were working outside their homes, mainly as laborers and in service capacities. Their average monthly earnings were $700. Half of them said that they had worked outside their homes when they were in Vietnam, mostly as small shopkeepers.

Seventy percent knew no English when they arrived in the United States. At the time of the survey almost all of them claimed that their speaking, reading, writing, and understanding of English were poor or not serviceable. Half of them were studying English at home or at school.

The Vietnamese mothers were not as optimistic as the Soviet mothers about their future adjustment. Most of them either did not expect to be working outside their home five years hence or could not project themselves far enough into the future to imagine what their economic circumstances would be like. On the matter of language facility, 26 percent did not expect to use English at all, 54 percent believed their English would be serviceable and that they would use it at work, but would continue to speak Vietnamese at home; 8 percent believed their English would be fluent or good and planned to use it all the time. The other 12 percent either did not know, or planned to use Chinese, Vietnamese, and English in some combination.

Regarding their future social identity, half of the mothers expect to identify themselves by their place of origin (e.g., Vietnamese, Indo-Chinese); most of the others, as hyphenated Americans (Vietnamese-American or Asian-American).

American Mothers

Seventy percent of the American mothers we studied were born in Illinois, and 15 percent more were born in neighboring states. Two-thirds were born and lived all of their lives in Chicago. Their average age at the time of the survey was forty.

Fifty-two percent were employed full-time outside their homes, half as teachers, secretaries, clerks, and salespersons, the others as skilled laborers and in service capacities.

When asked to think ahead five years and imagine what their economic circumstances were likely to be, the American mothers were less optimistic than the Soviets. Twenty percent did not expect to be in the labor force. Among those who did, 10 percent expected to hold important, prestigious jobs; 60 percent thought they would have good jobs; and the other 10 percent expected to work steadily at not very interesting or well-paying jobs. Ten percent thought they would be rich, 78 percent thought they would have an average income, and 12 percent expected to earn less than the average worker in Chicago. As has been typical of Americans for decades, when asked to identify themselves with some larger social unit, 72 percent identified themselves as middle class (46 percent added white-collar and 26 percent added blue-collar); the others named such categories as white Catholic, white American, or no special group.

PROFILES OF SOVIET, VIETNAMESE, AND AMERICAN DAUGHTERS

Soviet Daughters

The Soviet daughters' average age was sixteen. Ninety-six percent were attending school at the time of the survey; 64 percent were in high school (twelve were going to a private Jewish high school) and 32 percent were in college. All of them expected to continue their schooling at least through the bachelor's degree, and about half planned to do graduate work. Computer science, medicine, engineering, and the natural sciences were the favorite areas of study and of future careers.

Seventy-four percent had studied English in the Soviet Union, mostly in the schools they attended, a few privately at home. At the time of the survey, most of them evaluated their ability to speak, read, write, and understand English as fluent or good. But practically all of them said that everyone in their family spoke only Russian at home. Seventy percent claimed that they spoke English better than anyone in their family.

When asked to project themselves ten years into the future and consider what their socioeconomic situation was likely to be, most of the daughters painted bright and optimistic portraits. At worst, some expected to hold "good" jobs; most of the others thought they would have prestigious, important jobs. Thirty-six percent expected to be rich; the rest expected to earn comfortable, above average incomes. Half of them expected that they would be fluent in English and would use it all the time at work and at home. The others also thought they would be fluent in their new language but thought they would continue to speak Russian at home.

On the matter of how they would identify themselves ten years hence, half of them said as a Russian-American, 18 percent as an American; 24 percent as an American or Russian Jew or just as a Jew; and 8 percent as a Russian. Unlike their mothers, a hyphenated Russian identity was more popular for the daughters than a hyphenated Jewish one. The daughters, like the mothers, did not refer to themselves as Soviets.

Vietnamese Daughters

The Vietnamese daughters were about two years older than the Soviet daughters. Their average age was eighteen. At the time of the survey 86 percent were attending school; the others were working. Among those in school, 52 percent were still in high school and 34 percent were in college. Like their mothers, the girls did not come to the United States directly from Vietnam. All of them spent months in a refugee camp, where they did not attend school and where there was little opportunity for any formal schooling. Even when they were in Vietnam, it had been difficult for them to continue many of their normal activities, including school.

Fifty-eight percent of those in school said that they expected to attain at least a bachelor's degree, and 16 percent planned to pursue advanced degrees in computer science, business, or medicine.

Far fewer of the Vietnamese, as opposed to the Soviet, daughters had studied English before they arrived in the United States. At the time of the survey one out of three evaluated their ability to speak, read, and understand English as good. Only one out of five rated their English writing ability as good. Almost all of the others rated their English as fair or serviceable.

Ten years hence, 24 percent of the Vietnamese daughters expected to have important, prestigious jobs, 48 percent expected to have good jobs, 16 percent believed they would have steady employment in run-of-the-mill jobs, and 12 percent said they did not know or would not answer. Twenty-six percent expected to be rich, 68 percent comfortable or above average, and 6 percent thought they would be poor. Half expected to speak English fluently at work and planned to speak it at home. The others believed that their English would be good but that they would continue to speak Vietnamese at home.

On the matter of how they will identify themselves ten years hence, 44 percent said as Vietnamese-Americans, 30 percent as Americans, 16 percent as Asians, 4 percent as Asian-Americans, and 6 percent as Vietnamese. The daughters are more likely than their mothers to perceive themselves as hyphenated Americans or as Americans.

American Daughters

The American daughters' mean age was 16.5 years, about the same as that of the Soviet daughters. Seventy-four percent of them were attending school at the time of the survey; three-quarters were in high school, one-quarter in college. Among those in high school, two out of seven were attending a Catholic school.

Eighty-one percent of those who were still in school planned to complete at least a bachelor's degree; half of them were planning to obtain an advanced degree as well. Their most popular career choices were as secretaries, bookkeepers, or other white-collar jobs. Teaching, business, and commercial art were the next most favored job categories.

Among the 26 percent who were not attending school at the time of the survey, three-quarters had finished high school, were working in clerical and sales positions, and did not want to go on to college. The others dropped out of high school in their junior or senior year.

Ten years hence, 20 percent of the American girls did not expect to be in the labor force. Among those who did, one-third expected to have important, prestigious positions, one-half expected to have good jobs that would provide them with a comfortable income, and the others expected to work steadily in run-of-the-mill jobs. Sixty percent expected to be in the average income bracket. When asked to imagine how they would identify themselves in terms of a particular group in society, 40 percent were unable or unwilling to label themselves as being part of any larger social category. Some explained that they did not see people as belonging to any special group, that there are "no classes" in American society. Among the 60 percent who were willing to designate themselves, the modal category and the one selected by two-thirds of the respondents was middle-class American; two said black American, six said Catholic American, and two said working-class American.

SOURCES OF CONFLICT WITHIN FAMILIES

One of the major purposes of this study was to understand how the refugee parents and their adolescent children were relating to each other under the special circumstances of their migration. How much consensus was there about the adolescents' schooling and occupational plans, and about the adolescents' friends and activities? To what extent did the adolescents share the same hopes and aspirations as their parents about the type of person they would marry, the number of children they would have, and the strength of identity with their ethnic community? Their responses would then be compared against those provided by American mothers and daughters who were not experiencing the special problems of cultural and economic resettlement.

The data in Table 10.1 compare the conflicts or lack of them between the mothers and daughters on the issues listed. The figures show that on four of the six topics, more American mothers and daughters report conflicts than do mothers and daughters in the refugee communities. On the issue of daughters' style of dress and schooling, the Americans responded no differently than the refugee women. As for the Soviets and the Vietnamese, the former report more conflict than the latter on four of the six issues. The two exceptions are the daughters' willingness to listen to parental advice and the use of liquor and/or drugs, where, in both cases, there were no differences between the Vietnamese and Soviet

Table 10.1

Conflict Between Mothers and Daughters, by Ethnic Community

Source of conflict	Soviet (% in conflict) Moth.	Soviet (% in conflict) Daught.	Vietnamese (% in conflict) Moth.	Vietnamese (% in conflict) Daught.	American (% in conflict) Moth.	American (% in conflict) Daught.
How a daughter spends time when not in school or at work	18	20	4	12	40	46
Choice of friends	12	18	10	8	20	28
Schooling	20	18	8	6	14	12
Use of liquor and/or drugs	0	0	0	2	6	6
Willingness to listen to advice	10	16	14	16	30	24
Dress style	6	20	6	6	16	12

Table 10.2

Mothers' and Daughters' Expectations About the Highest Degree Daughters Will Attain, by Ethnic Community

Community	Less than B.A.[a]	B.A[b]	More than B.A.[c]	Total
		(percent)		
Soviet	20/18	44/38	36/44	100/100
Vietnamese	52/42	36/34	12/24	100/100
American	40/42	30/34	30/24	100/100

Note: The first figure is the mothers' expectations; the second is the daughters'.
[a] Soviet and Vietnamese mothers: Chi-square = 7.10/$p < .01$. Soviet and Vietnamese daughters: Chi-square = .80/n.s.
[b] Soviet and Vietnamese mothers: Chi-square = .40/n.s. Soviet and Vietnamese daughters: Chi-square = 0.11/n.s.
[c] Soviet and Vietnamese mothers: Chi-square = 6.0/$p < .01$. Soviet and Vietnamese daughters: Chi-square = 2.94/n.s.

women. The age of the Vietnamese daughters may be a factor; on the average, they were two years older than the Soviet and American daughters. Cultural differences may also play an important role. American respondents, speaking to American interviewers in their home country, may have been more open about discussing family problems with strangers than were Soviet or Vietnamese families.

EDUCATIONAL AND OCCUPATIONAL GOALS

Tables 10.2 and 10.3 compare the mothers' and daughters' expectations about the years of schooling and type of work the daughters in each community are likely to pursue. On the educational goals (Table 10.2), we see that the Soviet

Table 10.3
Mothers' and Daughters' Expectations About Daughters' Future Work, by Ethnic Community

Community	Professional[a]	White Collar	Skilled	Unskilled Service	No Answer/ Don't Know	Total
			(percent)			
Soviet	58/56	10/14	6/10	-/-	26/20	100/100
Vietnamese	24/36	14/18	8/12	-/-	34/32	100/100
American	20/34	28/26	n/6	-/-	42/34	100/100

Note: The first figure is the mothers' response; the second is the daughters'.
[a] Soviet and Vietnamese mothers: Chi-square = 7.04/p < .01. Soviet and Vietnamese daughters: Chi-square = 2.17/n.s.

mothers and daughters are more ambitious than either the Vietnamese or the Americans. Four out of five of the mothers and daughters expect the daughters to finish at least four years of college. (Remember that 70 percent of the Soviet mothers had completed at least four years of college in the Soviet Union.) For postgraduate study, the Soviet and Vietnamese daughters have higher goals than their mothers; but the American mothers have higher expectations for their daughters than the daughters have for themselves.

The differences between the responses of the Vietnamese daughters and their mothers reflect the greater expectations that the daughters have about their own upward social mobility. We see this expressed again in Table 10.3, which describes the expectations that mothers and daughters have about the daughters' future occupations.

With one exception, none of the respondents want their daughters to work at unskilled jobs. The Soviet mothers and daughters have the highest expectations that the daughters will hold prestigious positions, mostly as professionals. They also demonstrate the greatest consensus and the smallest percentages of "don't knows" and "no answers." It is rather strange that the Vietnamese and American mothers' and daughters' expectations should be so similar. Almost as many Americans as Vietnamese mothers did not know what type of work their daughters were likely to do. For the Vietnamese mothers, undergoing, as they were, cultural and perhaps psychological stress, this does not seem unusual. For the American mothers it may suggest lack of communication with their daughters or not taking seriously the likelihood that their daughters will have careers. More of the Vietnamese and American daughters than their mothers expect to work in professional positions rather than in clerical or skilled positions.

CHOICE OF SPOUSE AND NUMBER OF CHILDREN

Marriage within the same community is one important way that religious and ethnic groups maintain their uniqueness and their collective identities. For refugee

Table 10.4

Preferences for Daughter's Future Husband, by Ethnic Community

Preference Characteristics	Percent	
	Mother	Daughter
Soviet		
Soviet Jew	20	18
Jewish	40	28
American-Jewish	8	14
Other	12	10
Ethnicity/Religion not important	--	24
No answer/Don't know	20	6
Total	100	100
Vietnamese		
Vietnamese	58	38
Indo-Chinese	12	8
Asian	2	4
American	2	4
Ethnicity/Religion not important	--	28
No answer/Don't know	26	8
Total	100	100
American		
Same background	24	34
Catholic	20	24
Protestant	8	8
Jew	6	4
Black	6	4
No answer/Don't know	34	26
Total	100	100

parents who may not be prepared to accept or cope with all aspects of the host society, their need or desire to have their children find spouses who are "landsmen," who look the way they do, who speak the same language, and who share the same customs and traditions, can be very strong. In this survey we asked the mothers and daughters about their preferences for the ethnic-religious characteristics of the daughters' future husbands. Their responses are shown in Table 10.4.

Both the Vietnamese mothers and daughters were more likely than the Soviets to select a countryman. For both the Soviet mothers and daughters, the Jewish tie (Soviet, American, or any other country of origin) was more important than the country of origin. In both communities, some of the daughters claimed that religion and ethnicity were not important criteria in their choice of a spouse. None of the mothers felt that way. In those families, the daughters may have made a significant move away from the ascriptive traditional ties.

It is interesting that about as many Vietnamese as Soviet daughters said that religion and ethnicity were not important criteria, because in many of their other responses the Vietnamese daughters appeared to be more tied to their families and their traditions than did the Soviet daughters.

The question did not seem to fit the American respondents, reflected in part by the large number of "don't knows" and "no answers," and in their modal choice of response, which was "someone of the same background."

Table 10.5
Expectations of the Number of Children Daughter Will Have, by Ethnic Community

Number of Children	Soviet			Vietnmese			American		
	Moth.[a]	Moth.[b]	Daught.[c]	M	M	D	M	M	D
0	--	--	--	--	--	--	--	--	--
1	31	5	7	5	1	1	2	3	4
2	15	36	32	3	13	21	19	27	16
3	4	6	3	9	8	9	15	5	16
4	--	1	2	12	21	8	8	5	7
5	--	--	--	5	5	1	4	7	4
6+	--	--	--	16	--	--	2	--	--
No preference	--	2	2	--	1	8	--	--	--
As many as can afford	--	--	1	--	--	1	--	--	--
No answer	--	--	3	--	1	--	--	1	1
Average	1.4	2.0	2.1	4.4	3.3	2.7	3.0	2.9	2.8

[a] Number of children mother has.
[b] Number of children mother would like daughter to have.
[c] Number of children daughter expects to have.

Table 10.5 describes the number of children the mothers have borne, the number they would like their daughters to bear, and the number the daughters expect to bear. First, we note that, on average, the Vietnamese mothers have three more children than the Soviet mothers and 1.4 more than the American mothers. Second, the Soviet mothers would like their daughters to have more children, the Vietnamese mothers would like their daughters to have fewer children, and the American mothers would like their daughters to have the same number of children that they had. Third, the number of children the daughters in the three communities expect to have is very similar. On average, the Soviet daughters expect to have 2.1, the Vietnamese daughters 2.7, and the American daughters 2.8. For the Vietnamese daughters the difference between their own and their mothers' expectations is greater than that between the Soviet mothers and daughters. And on this issue, more American mothers and daughters agree than do mothers and daughters in the two immigrant communities. The Vietnamese daughters' preference for fewer children may be considered as still another measure of their subjective mobility.

Finally, in Table 10.6 we report expectations about the daughters' labor force participation after marriage compared with the mothers' work behavior. Among the Soviet respondents, all but 6 percent of the mothers work, and all but 6 percent of the mothers and 4 percent of the daughters expect the daughters to work after marriage. Among the Vietnamese and Americans, the biggest percentage of responses fall in the category "daughter will work, mother does not." In other words, mothers who are themselves homemakers expect their daughters to work outside their homes after they are married. Just as many Vietnamese

Table 10.6

Expectations About Daughter's Participation in Labor Force after Marriage, by Mother's Participation and by Ethnic Community

Work Plans	Soviet[a]		Vietnamese		American[b]	
	Mother (%)	Daughter (%)	M (%)	D (%)	M (%)	D (%)
Mothers work, Daughters will work	92	90	24	20	22	40
Neither work or will work	2	2	10	4	18	6
Daughters will work, mothers do not work	2	6	54	64	52	46
Daughters will not work, mothers work	2	2	10	4	4	4
No answer	2	--	2	8	4	4
Total	100	100	100	100	100	100

[a] Comparison of refugee and American mothers, "Mothers work, daughters will work": Chi-square = 32.00/p < .001. Comparison of refugee and American daughters, "Mothers work, daughters will work": Chi-square = 16.3/p < .001.
[b] Comparison of Soviet with American and Vietnamese mothers, "Mothers work, daughters will work": Chi-square = 7.60/p < .01. Comparison of Soviet with American and Vietnamese daughters, "Mothers work, daughters will work": Chi-square = 3.00/n.s.

mothers expect this as do Americans. Only 4 percent of the Soviet, 8 percent of the Vietnamese, and 10 percent of the American daughters do not plan to work outside their homes after marriage.

SUMMARY AND CONCLUDING REMARKS

This chapter compared the responses of refugee mothers and adolescent daughters against each other and against a group of native-born American mothers and daughters on sources and extent of conflict between the mothers and daughters as well as mothers' and daughters' expectations and aspirations for the daughters' future along such dimensions as educational and occupational achievements, choice of spouse, and number of children.

Looking first at the Soviet and Vietnamese responses, we found that differences between the refugee mothers were greater than those between the refugee daughters, even though both mothers and daughters have been in the United States for the same length of time. The Vietnamese mothers had lower occupational and educational aspirations for their daughters than did the Soviet mothers. However, the Vietnamese daughters' aspirations were closer to those of the Soviet daughters than to their Vietnamese mothers'. They were also more like the Soviet daughters than like their own mothers in the following areas: their belief that race and ethnicity were not important characteristics in the choice of a spouse, in their expectations about working outside their homes after they were married, and in their desire to have fewer children than their mothers.

Both the American mothers' and daughters' responses were closer to those of the Vietnamese than to the Soviets in their expectations about educational levels, occupational achievements, and number of children, and in their desire for the daughters to work outside the home after marriage. The Americans differed from the Soviets and Vietnamese in their reports of conflict between mothers and daughters. We suggested earlier that the fewer reports by Soviet and Vietnamese respondents may reflect cultural differences more than real differences concerning the degree of conflict in those families.

If the Soviet, Vietnamese, and American daughters pursue the plans they described in this survey, then ten years hence we should find most of them having completed at least four years of college, working in professional or white-collar positions, having between two and three children, and still being part of the labor force after they are married. The American daughters would probably be most like their mothers, and the Vietnamese daughters would be least like their mothers. The Vietnamese daughters would be much more educated and technically skilled and have fewer children than their mothers. The Soviet mothers' and daughters' profiles would not match as closely as the Americans', but neither would they be as different as the Vietnamese.

NOTES

1. R. J. Simon, "Russian, Vietnamese, and Mexican Immigrant Families: A Comparative Analysis of Parents' and Adolescents' Adjustment to Their New Society," report presented to the Select Commission on Immigration and Refugee Policy, Washington, DC, November 1980.

2. J. Edelman, "Soviet Jews in the United States: A Profile," *American Jewish Yearbook* 77 (1977): 157–181.

3. B. Leimsidor, "Refugees Leave Soviet Union," *World Refugee Survey*, 1980, 35–36.

4. R. J. Simon and J. L. Simon, "The Soviet Jews' Adjustment to the United States," final report to the National Council of Jewish Federations, New York, April 1982.

5. R. L. Bach and J. B. Bach, "Employment Patterns of Southeast Asian Refugees," *Monthly Labor Review* 103 (1980): 31–36.

6. D. Montero, *Vietnamese Americans: Patterns of Resettlement and Socioeconomic Adaptations in the United States* (Boulder, CO: Westview, 1979).

PART III

Women and Crime

11

Women and Crime:
A Five-Hundred-Year Sweep

Whether one is studying female crime patterns in the last decade of the twentieth century in the United States, or those in the seventeenth, eighteenth, or nineteenth centuries—indeed, even as far back as the fourteenth century— there are striking similarities between the amount and types of criminal activities in which women have engaged. This chapter looks at these criminal activities and the punishments meted out to women since the 1400s, and analyzes whether, and if so how, the crimes and punishments of women have changed in the last 500 years. It focuses in particular on the question of whether justice has been more lenient toward women than toward men in the determination of guilt and in the punishments handed down to the convicted.

Several facts stand out immediately when one studies female crime patterns in the last 500 years. First, the amounts and types of criminal activities in which women are likely to engage are similar and have remained remarkably stable. Second, of the 10 to 30 percent of all reported crimes that are committed by women, females are more likely than males to commit property crimes rather than violent offenses, and women are most likely to commit larceny. Third, those women who do commit acts of violence often kill persons with whom they have intimate ties, usually husbands, lovers, pimps, and infants. Women also serve as accomplices to men who rob and murder for monetary gain.

The following sections look in closer detail at the kinds of crimes for which women have been tried over the last five centuries.

Table 11.1
Percent Distribution of Women Tried on Felony Charges in Fourteenth-Century England

Offense	Percent female among all those charged with each crime	Women charged with each crime as percent of all female offenders
Larceny	8.9	32.4
Burglary	11.0	25.3
Robbery	5.1	11.6
Homicide	7.0	14.4
Receiving stolen goods	27.5	16.3
Counterfeiting	28.8	1.4
Arson	7.6	0.7
Rape	0.0	0.0
Treason	0.0	0.0

Source: Adapted from Barbara Hanawalt, Crime and Conflict in English Communities, 1300-1348, Cambridge: Harvard University Press (1979): 118.

PATTERNS OF FEMALE CRIMINALITY (FOURTEENTH-NINETEENTH CENTURIES)

Slightly more than 10 percent (11.5) of all persons charged with felonies in fourteenth-century England were women. As shown in Table 11.1, women were most likely to be tried for crimes involving property, and larceny was the single most common crime among women. While this pattern was not dissimilar from that of fourteenth-century males, the types of goods stolen by women differed somewhat from those of their male contemporaries. Barbara Hanawalt reports that the value of items stolen by women was often very low and consisted primarily of foodstuffs, clothing, and household goods, while men were more likely than women to steal industrial products, money, and jewels.[1] But the theft of livestock was of substantial interest to both sexes.

In the fourteenth century, women were indicted for a rather small portion (7 percent) of the total number of homicides, while homicide charges were responsible for approximately 14 percent of all trials involving women. But if one considers infanticide, as suggested by Hanawalt and other historians, these figures may greatly underestimate the prevalence of homicide committed by women. In

Table 11.2
Percentage Distributions of Women Charged with Property Crimes in Eighteenth-Century Surrey

Crime	Percent female among all those charged with each crime	Women charged with each crime as a percent of all female offenders
Robbery	7.9	2.4
Burglary and housebreaking	19.5	10.6
Theft from dwelling/house	41.4	6.4
Picking pockets	46.7	0.8
Livestock-theft	3.7	0.8
Petty larceny	29.1	15.7
Simple grand larceny	27.6	61.5
Total (all property crime)	24.2	

Source: Adopted from J.M. Beattie, "The Criminality of Women in Eighteenth Century England," _Journal of Social History_, 8 (1975): 80-116.

any case, it appears as though homicide was a family affair among fourteenth-century women: family members were often involved either as victims or accomplices.

Men figured prominently in all types of crime committed by women in fourteenth-century England. As victims, they were the objects of well over 75 percent of the homicides for which women were tried. As accomplices, they were implicated in over 50 percent of the homicides, 80 percent of the robberies, and approximately 40 percent of the burglaries for which women were tried.[2]

Moving to seventeenth- and eighteenth-century England, the patterns of female criminality identified by Beattie differ somewhat from those prevalent in the fourteenth century (see Table 11.2).[3]

In total, women comprised 24 percent of those accused of property crimes and 18.5 percent of those accused of violent offenses. Although larceny remained the property crime of choice among female offenders, there is evidence of some changes in the substance of the crimes committed. The proportion of females among those indicted for property crimes ranged from under 10 percent for robbery and theft of livestock to over 40 percent for theft from dwellings and for pickpockets. Although not shown in the tables, the crime of shoplifting was also prevalent in the eighteenth century and was almost exclusively a female enterprise.[4]

Turning to personal crimes of violence, we see greater potential differences between fourteenth- and eighteenth-century patterns of female criminality. In eighteenth-century Surrey, 18.5 percent of those charged with crimes against the person were women, a figure markedly higher than that noted for homicides in the fourteenth century. But because the eighteenth-century figures include offenses other than homicide, such as assaults, a truer comparison can be made by considering the proportion of women charged with murder and manslaughter. Thirteen percent of those so charged were women, which is still significantly higher than the 7 percent noted for those charged with homicide in the fourteenth century.[5]

In sum, eighteenth-century women in Surrey seem to have been somewhat more able or inclined than women in earlier days to commit crimes, although still far less so than men. The representation of women among those charged with violent crimes, while larger than that of the fourteenth century, was still quite small. Moreover, murders by women tended to retain their domestic nature with respect to both victims and weapons. As in earlier days, women constituted a greater proportion of those indicted for stealing objects of little value than of those involved in more lucrative enterprises. In addition, the ways of committing small thefts changed with ways of life, and so with urbanization and attendant anonymity, we find women picking pockets.

The same pattern prevailed in nineteenth-century England. Although the percentage of females involved in crime from 1857 through 1875 was higher than at any time earlier or since, the types of offenses women were most likely to commit followed the earlier pattern: larceny, receiving stolen goods, and fraud and currency offenses were most frequent, while offenses against the person remained approximately one-tenth of those committed by men (see Tables 11.3 and 11.4).

We note general similarities and some differences between English patterns of female criminality and those in other countries. In eighteenth-century Paris, about one-fifth of those accused of crimes were women, a fraction identical with that of eighteenth-century Surrey and considerably larger than that found in earlier periods in England. It seems that criminal violence was almost exclusively a male activity in eighteenth-century Paris, but men and women participated more equally in economic crimes than was the case for eighteenth-century Surrey. Not only was the percentage of females among accused thieves high, but more than nine-tenths of the accused women were indicted for theft-related offenses (see Table 11.5).[6] Nineteenth-century Germany, Italy, and the Netherlands show similar patterns.

Overall, the image of female criminality that emerges from our brief historical review is one of continuity. The patterns of crime committed by women have

Table 11.3
Property Offenses Among Men and Women in Nineteenth-Century England and Wales

Year	Men rate	Women rate	Percent female
1836	225.2	48.3	17.5
1840	270.2	64.2	19.9
1845	218.1	54.4	20.6
1850	229.5	56.2	19.8
1857	429.8	159.8	27.2
1860	356.1	148.5	30.5
1865	430.2	147.9	26.6
1870	404.6	124.6	24.5
1875	320.5	99.6	24.7
1880	385.6	103.7	22.1
1885	336.0	84.3	21.0
1890	306.6	75.6	20.8

Source: V.A.C. Gatrell and T. B. Hadden, "Criminal Statistics and Their Interpretation," in E. A. Wrigley, ed., Nineteenth Century Society: Essays in the Use of Quantitative Methods for the Study of Social Data (Cambridge, 1972), pp. 388-389.

remained relatively stable over time in several European societies. The variations that do exist are slight and seem to reflect changes, such as urbanization, that affected the economic structure and the opportunities of women in society.

CRIMINAL PROCESSING AND PUNISHMENT OF FEMALE OFFENDERS

The historical accounts of female criminality in England thus far reviewed suggest that women received more lenient treatment in the courts than their male contemporaries. But some interesting variations may be found in the literature. For example, Hanawalt asserts that while women were more likely to be acquitted than men, pretrial and postconviction treatment of men and women was exactly the same in the fourteenth century. Suspected and convicted female offenders were confined in the ''King's gaol,'' and men and women were often housed

Table 11.4
Black Country Committals to Trial, 1835–1860

Offense Category	Percent Female Among All Those Committed to Trial
Larceny	29.2
Receiving	31.8
Embezzlement	3.0
Fraud, forgery currency offenses	20.1
Offenses against property with violence	6.2
Offenses against the person	11.1
Riot and public order offenses	9.7
Malicious damage	4.0
Other	21.6
TOTAL	25.7

Source: Adapted from David Philip, Crime and Authority in Victorian England: The Black Country, 1835-1860 (London: Croom Helm, 1977), p. 148.

in the same cell. Furthermore, both men and women were subject to the same type of trial and the same punishment—hanging—if found guilty.

In addition to the differential likelihood of conviction, Hanawalt notes two other points of difference between men and women that existed in the law, both of which extended into the eighteenth century. First, women benefitted from the canon law's prohibition against killing an unborn child. If a convicted woman's plea of pregnancy could be substantiated by the court, she would be granted a reprieve until the child was born. Although in most cases the reprieve provided only a temporary benefit, Hanawalt documented one case of an enterprising young woman who managed to invoke successfully six such reprieves on the basis of pregnancy. J. M. Beattie (1986) documents the existence of this practice in the seventeenth and eighteenth centuries and suggests that during this period the reprieved woman was often pardoned.

The second difference between men and women from the fourteenth to the eighteenth century concerns the prescribed punishment for treason. According to Hanawalt, in fourteenth-century England, a man who killed his lord was guilty

Table 11.5

Percentage Distributions of Women Accused of Crimes in Paris in 1765

Offense	Percent female among all charged with each crime	Women charged with each crime as a percent of all females arrested
Theft	32	91
Forgery, etc.	16	3
Homicide	0	0
Begging	25	2
Morals	25	1
Other	15	3

Source: Adapted from George Rude, Crime and Society in Early Nineteenth-Century England (Oxford: Clarendon Press, 1985).

of treason and was drawn and quartered. Legally, a woman's husband was her lord, and if she killed him, she was burned at the stake. Beattie describes this same differentiation in the seventeenth and eighteenth centuries, which was justified on the grounds that "the law presumes there is a special obedience and subjugation on the part of a wife toward her husband."[7] But he also notes that the prescribed punishment for women convicted of treason avoided publicly exposing and mangling their bodies in the name of decency. And it was generally believed that out of compassion women were strangled prior to burning.

In seventeenth- and eighteenth-century England, the most striking differences in the conviction rates of men and women offenders occurred in capital cases rather than in cases carrying noncapital sanctions. But there were also some differences in the punishments accorded men and women for noncapital offenses in late eighteenth-century Surrey. According to Beattie, women were less likely than men to be transported and to be whipped. Women, however, were much more likely than men to be sentenced to a term of hard labor in the house of correction.[8] Rude found that women were virtually never sentenced to be whipped and, when sentenced to jail, they received much shorter sentences than men.[9] But he also found that men and women were equally likely to be fined and sentenced to the house of correction.

By the end of the nineteenth century, imprisonment was the most popular method of punishing noncapital property offenses for both men and women. Table 11.6 provides a cursory estimation of the percentage of men and women in prison in the late nineteenth and early twentieth centuries. The greatest proportion of women may be found in the prisons of the United Kingdom. Women comprised approximately one-third of the prison populations in Ireland, Scotland,

Table 11.6
Distribution of the Prison Population in the Late Nineteenth and Early Twentieth Centuries, by Percent

	England and Wales (1894-1900)	Scotland (1910)	Ireland (1905)	Germany (1870)	France (1896-1900)	Switzer-land (1892-1896)
Men	71.5	71	65.7	91.5	87	85
Women	28.5	29	34.3	8.5	13	15

Source: Adapted from William Bonger, Criminality and Economic Conditions (Boston: Little Brown & Co., 1916).

England, and Wales. This figure contrasts sharply with the proportion of women found in the prisons of France, Germany, and Switzerland, where women made up less than one-sixth of these countries' prison populations.

CONCLUSION

To return to our original thesis: there are striking similarities in female crime patterns and treatment by the law that extend over long time periods and across national boundaries. Much more work needs to be done to fill in the time gaps and to examine data for specific countries in more detail.

NOTES

1. Barbara Hanawalt, "The Female Felon in Fourteenth Century England," *Viator*, vol. J (1974): 253–268.
2. Barbara Hanawalt, *Crime and Conflict in English Communities, 1300–1348* (Cambridge, MA: Harvard University Press, 1979).
3. J. M. Beattie, "The Criminality of Women in Eighteenth Century England," *Journal of Social History* 8 (1975): 80–116.
4. J. M. Beattie, *Crime and the Courts in England, 1660–1800* (Princeton, NJ: Princeton University Press, 1986).
5. David Phillip, *Crime and Authority in Victorian England: The Black Country, 1835–1860* (London: Croom Helm, 1977).
6. George Rude, *Crime and Society in Early Nineteenth Century England* (Oxford: Clarendon Press, 1985).
7. Beattie, *Crime and the Courts*, p. 79.
8. Ibid., p. 613.
9. Rude, *Crime and Society*, p. 63.

12

What Kinds of Crimes Do Women Commit, and What Happens to Them in the Criminal Justice System?

A review of the types of crimes for which women in the United States have been arrested over the past thirty years reveals that property and white-collar offenses, especially larceny, embezzlement, and fraud, are the most frequent offenses, and that the percentage of women has been increasing over time. On the other hand, there has been little change in the percentage of women who have been arrested for violent personal offenses such as homicide and manslaughter. Conviction rates for women in federal and state courts have also gone up, as has the likelihood of their being sent to prison. An important change has occurred in women's prisons, where conditions have improved over the past decade, most notably in the educational and vocational opportunities afforded to inmates.

Almost twenty years have gone by since I wrote *Women and Crime* (1975), which argued that women's greater opportunities and skills, as a function of their increased participation in the labor force and years of schooling, have increased their propensity to commit criminal acts, especially property and white-collar offenses.[1] This chapter analyzes trends in women's involvement in criminal activities, reviewing recent arrest, judicial, and prison statistics and examining the changes, if any, that have occurred vis-à-vis women's socioeconomic status.

Turning first to various indices of women's socioeconomic status, we note that between 1940 and 1987 the percentage of women in the U.S. labor force increased from 27 to 55 percent, and the percentage of married women in the labor force increased from 17 to 56 percent. Indeed, as shown in Table 12.1, as of 1987 a higher percentage of women than ever before—including those who are married and have preschool children—is working full-time.

Table 12.1

Changes in Labor Force Participation Rates of Married Women with Children: 1948–1987[a]

Year	Total	No Children Under 18	Children 6-17 (None < 6)	Children Under 6
1948	22.0	28.4	26.0	10.3
1949	22.5	29.7	27.3	11.0
1950	23.8	30.3	28.3	11.9
1951	25.2	31.0	30.3	14.0
1952	25.3	30.9	31.1	13.9
1953	26.3	31.2	32.2	15.5
1954	26.6	31.6	33.2	14.9
1955	27.7	32.7	34.7	16.2
1956	29.0	35.3	36.4	15.9
1957	29.6	35.6	36.6	17.0
1958	30.2	35.4	37.6	18.2
1959	30.9	35.2	39.8	18.7
1960[b]	30.5	34.7	39.0	18.6
1961	32.7	37.3	41.7	20.0
1962	32.7	36.1	41.8	21.3
1963	33.7	37.3	41.5	22.5
1964	34.4	37.8	43.0	22.7
1965	-34.7	38.3	42.7	23.3
1966	35.4	38.4	43.7	24.2
1967	36.8	38.9	45.0	26.5
1968	38.3	40.1	46.9	27.6
1969	39.6	41.0	48.6	28.5
1970	40.8	42.2	29.2	30.3
1980	50.1	46.0	61.7	45.1
1982	51.2	46.2	63.2	48.7
1983	51.8	46.6	63.8	49.9
1984	52.8	47.2	65.4	51.8
1985	54.2	48.2	67.8	53.4
1986	54.6	48.2	68.4	53.8
1987	55.8	48.4	70.6	56.8

[a] Married women in the labor force as percent of married women in the population.

[b] First year for which figures include Alaska and Hawaii.

Sources: U.S. Bureau of the Census, *Historical Statistics, Colonial Times to 1970*, series D 63-84 (Washington, DC: U.S. Government Printing Office, 1975), Table D 63-74; *Statistical Abstract of the U.S.*, 1988, table 624, p. 374.

In addition to their increased participation in the labor force, women are completing baccalaureate and postgraduate degrees in greater numbers. Between 1950 and 1985, the percentage of women who earned bachelor's degrees increased from 23.9 to 49.4 percent. In 1950 only 29.3 percent of the master's degrees were earned by women; but by the 1980s women were receiving half of the degrees conferred. Although women still lag far behind men at the doctoral level, there has been a major increase here as well, with women being the recipients of one-third of the doctorate degrees in the 1980s, compared to 9 percent in the 1950s.

Not only are more women receiving higher academic degrees and working outside their homes than at any other time since the end of World War II, but higher proportions of them also occupy positions that involve more training, responsibility, and authority.

But in addition to women's greater educational achievements, participation in the labor force, and promotion to positions of higher status, there is also a greater percentage of single-headed female households in which women are the caretakers of young children. In 1970, 10.8 percent of all families in the United States were headed by females. In 1975 the rate increased to 13 percent, in 1980 to 14.6 percent, and in 1988 to 16.3 percent.

ARREST DATA

Table 12.2 traces the percentage of arrests of females for all serious offenses (Type I, *Uniform Crime Reports*) and for all serious violent and property offenses from 1963 to 1987. Women's participation in property and white-collar crime has continued and increased—a pattern that began to form in the late sixties and has continued to the present day. In 1963 women accounted for 12 percent of Type I property offenses; by 1987 that figure jumped to 24 percent. In 1987, 31 percent of all larceny, 44 percent of all fraud, 34 percent of all forgery, and 38 percent of all embezzlement arrests were women. The percentages of women arrested for robbery (8 percent) and burglary (8 percent) have also increased, but at nowhere near the levels for the other property offenses. Women's involvement in violent offenses has not deviated from the pattern established in the 1960s. In 1963 women accounted for 10.3 percent of Type I violent offense arrests; in 1987 women accounted for 11.1 percent of those arrests (see Tables 12.3 and 12.4).

Thus, the overall pattern of women's participation in criminal activities has not changed dramatically in the past decade. The increases observed in the 1980s have been for the same types of offenses reported earlier: property and white-collar offenses, which women have greater opportunities to commit, due to the skills they have acquired through greater participation in the labor force in positions that involve more training and responsibility.

Table 12.5 ranks the proportion of men and women who were arrested in 1972, 1980, and 1987 for the ten most frequently cited Type I and Type II offenses. These ten offenses account for 64.4 percent of all men and 66.4 percent of all women arrested in 1987. Larceny has remained the number one offense for which women are arrested. In 1987 women were less likely than in earlier years to be arrested for drunkenness and disorderly conduct, but more likely to be arrested for drunken driving. Given all of the media coverage that drug-related crimes receive, it is somewhat surprising that drugs account for only 6.3 percent

Table 12.2

Percentages of Females Arrested Among Total Arrests for All Serious (Type I) Crimes and for All Violent and Property (Type I) Crimes: 1963–1987

Year	Total Arrested for Serious Crimes	Percent Female	Total Arrested for Violent Crimes[a]	Percent Female	Total Arrested for Property Crimes[b]	Percent Female
1963	695,222	11.7	124.821	10.3	570,401	12.0
1964	780,501	12.6	137,576	10.4	642,925	13.0
1965	834,296	13.4	151,180	10.2	683,116	14.1
1966	871,962	13.9	167,780	10.1	704,182	14.8
1967	996,800	14.1	191,807	9.8	804,993	15.1
1968	1,047,220	14.2	201,813	9.5	845,407	15.4
1969	1,111,674	15.7	216,194	9.6	892,283	17.1
1970	1,273,783	16.9	241,905	9.6	1,028,858	18.7
1971	1,397,304	17.2	273,209	10.0	1,121,327	19.0
1972	1,417,115	18.0	299,221	10.0	1,114,908	20.2
1973	1,372,220	18.7	290,382	10.2	1,078,842	21.1
1974	1,474,427	19.0	294,617	10.2	1,177,584	21.2
1975	1,901,811	19.5	370,453	10.3	1,528,317	21.7
1976	1,787,106	19.8	338,849	10.5	1,445,607	22.1
1977	1,986,043	20.1	386,806	10.4	1,596,304	22.4
1978	2,169,262	19.9	446,122	10.2	1,723,140	22.4
1979	2,163,302	19.5	434,778	10.2	1,728,524	21.8
1980	2,198,077	18.8	446,373	10.0	1,751,704	21.0
1981	2,293,754	19.1	464,826	10.1	1,828,928	21.4
1982	2,152,480	19.7	443,860	10.4	1,708,620	22.1
1983	2,151,120	20.1	443,686	10.8	1,707,434	22.5
1984	1,834,348	20.8	382,246	10.7	1,452,102	23.4
1985	2,124,671	21.4	431,332	10.9	1,693,339	24.0
1986	2,167,071	21.1	465,391	10.9	1,701,680	23.9
1987	2,266,467	21.6	473,030	11.1	1,793,437	24.4

Overall Rates of Change

1963-87		0.85		0.08		1.03
1973-87		0.16		0.09		0.16
1980-87		0.15		0.11		0.16

[a] Includes male and female arrests for criminal homicide, forcible rape, robbery, and aggravated assault.

[b] Includes males and females arrested for burglary, larceny-theft, and auto theft. As of 1979, arson also is included.

Source: Uniform Crime Reports (Washington, DC: F.B.I., U.S. Department of Justice), 1963-1987, Total Arrests, Distribution by Sex.

of all female arrests. On the other hand, crimes that specifically involve alcohol, if combined, comprised 16.7 of all offenders in 1987, which was similar to the amount they comprised in 1972 (16.7 percent) and 1980 (18.4 percent). Also, in 1980 and 1987 women were much more likely to be arrested for fraud than

Table 12.3
Females Arrested as Percentage of All Arrests for Type I Offenses: 1963–1987

Year	Total Arrested for Criminal Homicide	% Female	Total Arrested for Robbery	% Female	Total Arrested for Aggr. Assault	% Female	Total Arrested for Burglary	% Female	Total Arrested for Larceny	% Female	Total Arrested for Auto Theft	% Female
1963	8,805	15.5	37,836	4.9	68,719	14.0	170,160	3.3	314,402	19.0	85,839	3.7
1964	9,097	15.5	39,134	5.3	79,895	13.6	187,000	3.7	358,569	20.3	97,356	4.2
1965	10,163	15.4	45,872	5.2	84,411	13.5	197,627	3.7	383,726	22.1	101,763	4.2
1966	10,734	15.3	47,031	5.0	98,406	13.2	199,781	3.9	398,623	23.1	105,778	4.1
1967	12,167	14.8	59,789	5.2	107,192	12.9	239,461	4.1	447,299	23.9	118,233	4.2
1968	13,538	14.7	69,115	5.6	106,475	12.4	256,216	4.2	463,928	24.4	125,263	4.9
1969	14,706	14.1	76,533	6.2	113,724	12.6	255,937	4.4	510,660	26.5	125,686	5.3
1970	15,856	14.5	87,687	6.1	125,971	12.6	285,418	4.7	616,099	27.9	127,341	5.1
1971	17,317	15.7	101,728	6.3	140,350	13.3	215,276	4.9	674,997	28.1	130.954	6.0
1972	18,035	14.8	109,217	6.5	155,581	13.2	314,393	5.2	678,673	29.7	121,842	5.7
1973	17,395	14.5	101,894	6.8	154,891	13.2	316,272	5.4	644,190	31.5	107,226	6.5
1974	16,044	14.3	108,481	6.8	154,514	13.4	340,697	5.4	729,661	30.7	120,224	7.0
1975	19,526	14.9	129,217	7.0	202,217	13.1	449,155	5.4	958,938	31.2	110,708	7.0
1976	16,763	14.1	110,296	7.1	192,753	13.1	406,821	5.2	928,078	31.2	135,196	7.0
1977	20,096	14.0	122,514	7.4	221,329	12.8	454,193	6.0	1,006,915	31.8	153,270	8.3
1978	18,755	14.1	141,481	7.0	257,629	12.7	485,782	6.1	1,084,088	31.7	153,270	8.3
1979	18,264	13.7	130,753	7.4	256,597	12.4	468,085	6.3	1,098,398	30.3	143,654	8.9
1980	18,745	12.8	139,476	7.2	258,721	12.4	479,639	6.2	1,123,823	28.9	129,783	8.6
1981	20,432	12.7	147,396	7.2	266,948	12.6	489,533	6.3	1,197,845	29.1	122,188	8.9
1982	18,511	13.3	138,118	7.3	258,899	12.9	436,271	6.6	1,146,705	29.4	108,736	9.0
1983	18,064	13.3	134,018	7.4	261,421	13.5	415,651	6.8	1,169,066	29.5	105,514	8.9
1984	13,676	13.3	108,614	7.2	231,620	13.4	334,399	7.4	1,009,743	30.2	93,285	9.2
1985	15,777	12.4	120,501	7.6	263,120	13.5	381,875	7.4	1,179,066	31.0	115,621	9.3
1986	16,066	12.3	124,245	7.8	293,952	13.2	375,544	7.9	1,182,099	30.7	128,514	9.5
1987	16,714	12.5	123,306	8.1	301,734	13.3	374,963	7.9	1,256,552	31.1	146,753	9.7

Overall Rates of Change

1963-87		-0.19		0.66		-0.05		1.42		0.64		1.60
1973-87		-0.14		0.19		0.01		0.46		-0.01		0.49
1980-87		-0.02		0.12		0.07		0.27		0.08		0.13

Source: Uniform Crime Reports (Washington, DC: F.B.I., U.S. Department of Justice), 1963-1987. Total Arrests, Distribution by Sex.

they were in 1972. For all the other offenses, the pattern has remained fairly stable from 1972 onward.

Among men, the ordering has been even more stable. Except for a decline in the proportion arrested for drunkenness and disorderly conduct and an increase in arrests for drunken driving and narcotics, there have been no marked changes. If we combine all alcohol-related offenses, as we did for women, we find an interesting negative trend: alcohol-related offenses comprised 34.1 percent of male arrests in 1972, 30.8 percent in 1980, and only 25.9 percent in 1987. The sharp decrease in arrests of both men and women for drunkenness and disorderly conduct and the increase in arrests for drunken driving may be as indicative of a shift in police behavior as of the behavior of men and women arrested.

In sum, the data tell us that the proportion of females arrested in 1987 was

Table 12.4

Other Crimes: Females Arrested as Percentage of All People Arrested for Various Crimes: 1963–1987

Year	Total Arrested for Embezzle.	% Female	Total Arrested for Fraud	% Female	Total Arrested for Forgery/ Counterfeiting	% Female	Total Arrested for Offenses Against Family	% Female	Total Arrested for Narcotic Drug Law Violations	% Female	Total Arrested for Prostitu. and Vice	% Female
1963*					30,610	17.6	58,228	9.1	29,604	14.2	26,124	76.9
1964	8,610	17.3	45,998	19.0	30,637	18.2	57,454	9.3	37,802	14.0	28,190	78.0
1965	7,674	17.2	52,007	20.3	30,617	18.4	60,981	8.8	46,069	13.4	33,987	77.5
1966	6,439	19.2	52,041	21.6	29,277	19.8	55,820	9.9	60,358	13.8	34,376	79.5
1967	6,073	19.2	58,192	23.2	33,462	20.8	56,137	8.9	101,079	13.7	39,744	77.7
1968	5,894	19.6	56,710	24.0	34,497	21.8	51,319	8.8	162,177	15.0	42,338	78.3
1969	6,309	20.8	63,445	26.2	36,727	22.7	50,312	9.2	232,690	15.5	46,410	79.6
1970	8,174	24.6	76,861	27.1	43,833	23.7	56,620	8.9	346,412	15.7	49,344	79.3
1971	7,114	24.9	95,610	28.6	45,340	24.5	56,456	8.6	400,606	16.3	52,916	77.7
1972	6,744	26.3	96,713	29.6	44,313	24.8	52,935	9.3	431,608	15.7	44,744	74.1
1973	5,612	23.7	85,467	31.2	41,975	26.7	42,784	9.2	484,242	14.5	45,308	75.5
1974	5,981	26.3	91,176	32.6	39,741	28.6	34,902	11.9	454,948	14.2	53,309	75.6
1975	9,302	31.1	146,253	34.2	57,803	28.9	53,332	11.7	508,189	13.8	50,229	74.3
1976	8,218	31.0	161,429	36.6	55,791	29.6	58,249	10.7	500,540	13.6	58,648	70.7
1977	6,607	22.7	216,672	35.6	67,984	29.1	53,385	10.3	569,293	13.9	77,115	70.7
1978	7,670	25.1	249,207	36.8	73,269	29.7	54,014	10.2	596,940	13.7	89,365	67.7
1979	7,882	25.3	243,461	40.4	70,977	30.9	53,321	9.9	519,377	13.5	83,088	67.5
1980	7,885	28.5	261,787	41.4	72,643	31.1	49,991	10.6	533,010	13.4	85,815	69.5
1981	8,170	28.5	272,900	41.2	81,429	32.1	51,908	10.5	586,646	13.2	103,134	73.4
1982	7,358	30.3	265,663	40.3	79,951	32.6	45,432	11.6	565,182	13.6	111,029	71.0
1983	7,604	32.4	261,844	40.2	74,508	33.4	46,11	11.1	616,936	14.0	119,626	70.2
1984	6,290	36.9	203,175	40.4	63,359	33.7	32,877	13.9	562,255	13.9	88,337	69.9
1985	9,799	35.6	286,941	42.6	75,281	33.2	48,699	12.7	702,882	13.8	101,167	69.5
1986	10,500	36.4	284,790	43.3	76,546	33.9	47,327	15.0	691,882	14.5	96,882	65.4
1987	10,639	38.1	280,809	43.5	78,817	34.4	48,002	17.4	811,078	14.9	100,950	64.8

Overall Rates of change												
1963-87**		1.21		1.28		0.96		0.90		0.05		-0.16
1973-87		0.61		0.39		0.29		0.89		0.03		-0.14
1980-87		0.34		0.05		0.11		0.64		0.11		-0.07

* In 1963, Embezzlement and Fraud were combined.

** For Embezzlement and Fraud, the rates are for the change from 1964 to 1987.

Source: Uniform Crime Reports (Washington, DC: F.B.I., U.S. Department of Justice), 1963-1987. Total Arrests, Distribution by Sex.

greater than the proportion arrested one or two decades earlier; and the increase in female arrest rates among the serious offenses was due almost entirely to greater participation in property offenses, especially larceny. In 1963 roughly one out of five arrests for larceny involved a woman; since 1973 the proportion has been approximately one out of three. And contrary to impressions conveyed by the mass media, the proportion of female arrests for violent crimes has hardly

Table 12.5
Rank Order of Offenses for Which Females and Males Are Most Likely to Be Arrested—1972, 1980, 1987

	1972				1980				1987		
Offense	Female*	Offense	Male**	Offense	Female*	Offense	Male**	Offense	Female*	Offense	Male**
Larceny-Theft	19.1	Drunkenness	21.6	Larceny-Theft	21.2	Drunken Driving	14.5	Larceny-Theft	20.4	Drunken Driving	14.0
Drunkenness	9.5	Drunken Driving	9.5	Drunken Driving	8.0	Drunkenness	11.9	Drunken Driving	8.6	Larceny-Theft	9.7
Disorderly Conduct	8.0	Disorderly Conduct	8.4	Disorderly Conduct	7.3	Larceny-Theft	9.8	Fraud	6.4	Drug Abuse Violations	7.8
Narcotic Drug Laws	6.3	Larceny-Theft	8.0	Fraud	7.1	Disorderly Conduct	7.5	Drug Abuse Violations	6.3	Drunkenness	7.2
Other Assaults	4.0	Narcotic Drug Laws	6.1	Drunkenness	5.2	Drug Abuse Violations	5.6	Disorderly Conduct	5.8	Other Assaults	6.4
Drunken Driving	3.9	Burglary	5.0	Drug Abuse Violations	4.7	Aggravated Assault	5.5	Other Assaults	5.3	Disorderly Conduct	5.5
Prostitution	3.1	Other Assaults	4.5	Liquor Laws	4.2	Other Assaults	4.8	Liquor Laws	4.7	Liquor Laws	4.7
Embezzlement and Fraud	2.9	Liquor Laws	3.0	Other Assaults	4.1	Liquor Laws	4.4	Drunkenness	3.4	Burglary	3.9
Liquor Laws	2.8	Aggravated Assault	2.3	Prostitution and Vice	3.9	Aggravated Assault	2.8	Prostitution and Vice	3.4	Aggravated Assault	2.9
Aggravated Assault	2.0	Vandalism	2.0	Aggravated Assault	2.1	Vandalism	2.6	Aggravated Assault	2.1	Vandalism	2.3

* Percent arrested out of all female arrests.

** Percent arrested out of all male arrests.

Source: Uniform Crime Reports (Washington, DC: F.B.I., U.S. Department of Justice), 1963-1987. Total Arrests, Distribution by Sex.

changed over the past two and a half decades, as evidenced by stable female arrest rates for homicide and aggravated assault.

A more detailed examination of the female homicide rates reveals that between 1976 and 1987, 65.5 percent of all victims of female homicides were persons with whom the women had intimate ties (e.g., current or former spouses, lovers, children, or other family members), compared to 22.1 percent for the male offenders. And among those "intimate" victims, spouses, lovers, and so on accounted for 48.9 percent, compared to 11.8 percent of the male victims. Only 6.2 percent of all felony murders and 4 percent of all robbery murders were committed by women during that same time span.[2] These data suggest that while women's motivations for committing property offenses are comparable to those of men, women commit acts of violence for different reasons. Women are much less likely to kill in the act of committing another offense; rather, they kill for personal and private reasons. In many instances, their victims are their former abusers. This statistic may change, however, as women gain greater economic independence and autonomy—they will be victims less frequently and will be more able to walk away from abusive relationships before they reach the desperation stage that eventually results in the death of the abuser.

Further probing of female arrest rates in Type II offenses reveals that the offenses showing the greatest increases are embezzlement, fraud, and forgery; there are no other offenses, except prostitution, in which women are so highly represented. Should the rate of change continue, female arrest rates for fraud, embezzlement, and forgery will be commensurate with women's representation in society—in other words, roughly equal to male arrest rates for the same offenses—in the next one or two decades.

JUDICIAL DATA

In 1975 having reported the reactions of twenty-three criminal court judges interviewed in the Midwest, I commented: "Most of the judges treat women more leniently than they do men. They are more inclined to recommend probation rather than imprisonment, and if they sentence a woman, it is usually for a shorter time than if the crime had been committed by a man."[3]

Based on additional interviews conducted in 1989, I am still inclined to believe that judges treat women more gently than they do men, mostly at the sentencing stage.[4] There is some evidence to suggest that they are also more inclined to be lenient at the determination of guilt stage. Many trial court judges believe today, as they did twenty years ago, that incarceration is far more degrading for a woman than for a man.

The federal judicial statistics and those available from the states of California, Pennsylvania, and New York reveal a pattern consistent with the recent arrest data, namely, that there has been a 6 percent increase in the number of women who have been charged with and convicted in federal courts, from 10.8 in 1979 to 17.2 in 1987. Twenty percent of the fraud, 49 percent of the embezzlement, 24 percent of the larceny, and 29 percent of the forgery convictions were women in 1987. In the state courts, women accounted for 23 percent of the larceny convictions in California, 26 percent in New York, and 24 percent in Pennsylvania. In each of those states, women were convicted for less than 10 percent of all Type I offenses in 1987.

The data in Tables 12.6 and 12.7 compare the percentages of prosecutions of men and women in New York and Pennsylvania between 1982 and 1987 and 1981 and 1986 that resulted in convictions for specific offenses. They show that for every type of offense in every year, a slightly but consistently higher percentage of men than women who faced prosecution were eventually convicted.

These data support the impressions gained from interviews with judges who maintain that "justice" is not quite blind even at the determination of guilt stage. But in the absence of additional pertinent information, such as prior criminal

Table 12.6
New York: Percent of Prosecutions in Upper and Lower Courts Resulting in
Conviction by Type of Offense and Sex: 1982–1987

Offense		1982	1983	1984	1985	1986	1987
Homicide	Female	61.7	67.0	59.9	69.2	60.0	50.0
	Male	67.8	69.5	70.4	70.7	65.7	55.0
Robbery	Female	58.2	60.0	58.2	53.8	53.7	51.1
	Male	63.6	67.3	65.8	63.2	62.3	57.2
Burglary	Female	61.9	61.8	62.0	57.5	59.4	60.3
	Male	72.4	73.5	72.7	71.7	71.3	69.6
Assault	Female	44.8	44.1	44.7	41.8	37.5	35.4
	Male	50.3	51.0	50.4	50.3	46.1	43.9
Larceny	Female	65.7	65.0	62.8	62.8	62.6	61.5
	Male	69.9	70.1	69.6	69.9	68.1	67.6
Drug Law Violation	Female	63.1	65.4	67.6	69.7	69.3	73.3
	Male	70.1	71.2	72.1	73.4	72.8	74.5

Source: New York State Division of Criminal Justice Services, unpublished data.

record, circumstances surrounding the crime, or type of attorney, we cannot conclude that the higher conviction rates for men are solely a function of the judges' bias in favor of women.

PRISON DATA

In 1987 about 22 out of 100 persons arrested for a serious crime were women. In the same year, approximately 10 out of 100 persons convicted of a serious crime were women, but only about 5 out of every 100 persons sentenced to a federal or state prison were women. The big difference in conviction rates between men and women is, as we have indicated, probably a function of prior criminal record, circumstances surrounding the crime, and judges' bias in favor of women. Many women arrive in the courtroom on their day of sentencing with young children (presumably theirs), whose presence may well influence the judge.

Table 12.8 shows what percentage of those sentenced to federal and state institutions for selected years from 1971 to 1987 were women. As of December 1987, of the approximately 580,000 inmates in state and federal prisons, 29,000 were women. For the sixteen-year period shown, the percentage of women in federal prisons has ranged from 3.7 to 6.4; in state prisons, where the bulk of inmates have been housed, the percentage has ranged from 3.1 to 4.8. But *Uniform Crime Reports* shows that, in 1970, 16.9 percent of all arrests for Type I offenses were women, and in 1987, 21.6 percent of all arrests for serious offenses were women. These data indicate that the rate of commitment to prison

Table 12.7
Pennsylvania: Percentage of Prosecutions Resulting in Convictions by Type of Offense and Sex: 1981–1986

	1981	1982	1983	1984	1985	1986
	(in percent)					
Murder						
Female	59.2	71.1	70.3	75.5	72.6	67.2
Male	65.9	76.5	78.3	78.4	77.9	72.5
Robbery						
Female	37.7	48.8	58.5	47.3	30.4	36.5
Male	57.4	63.6	65.5	66.3	48.7	49.1
Burglary						
Female	37.2	54.6	61.8	55.6	45.7	43.3
Male	56.4	69.4	72.6	73.3	67.7	65.8
Aggravated assault						
Female	26.4	35.2	38.1	33.6	26.4	25.2
Male	30.4	43.2	45.4	46.3	36.4	34.4
Other assault						
Female	21.1	40.8	39.4	44.8	45.7	42.5
Male	28.1	53.9	56.2	57.0	57.8	55.9
Theft						
Female	38.0	71.8	68.4	66.2	63.5	62.1
Male	43.3	59.5	61.5	60.9	63.1	61.5
Forgery						
Female	45.0	63.4	60.2	58.0	58.0	61.4
Male	52.3	65.9	76.0	70.0	65.2	68.0
Fraud						
Female	32.0	43.8	52.7	49.9	60.4	56.9
Male	31.3	47.3	57.9	60.0	57.2	60.7
Drug law violations						
Female	40.7	49.6	57.1	60.5	58.7	59.1
Male	44.3	46.8	57.1	59.9	59.2	57.6

Source: Pennsylvania Commission on Crime and Delinquency, unpublished data.

has not kept pace with the rate of female arrests: the percentage of women arrested for serious offenses has increased, but the rate at which they have been sentenced to state prisons has remained relatively stable.

Table 12.9 shows the types of institutions to which men and women have been committed at the federal and state levels. Three times as many men as women have been committed to maximum and closed institutions at the federal level, and twice as many at the state level. In 1988, 15 percent of the women assigned to maximum security prisons were on death row. Women on death row ranged from 8 percent in 1981 to a high of 17 percent in 1987.

By and large, however, the types of prisons to which men and women are sent reflect the types of offenses for which they were committed. As the data in Tables 12.10 through 12.12 show, the absolute number of women sentenced to prison for homicide has usually been less than 100 per year in three of the most

Table 12.8
Females as a Percentage of All Sentenced Prisoners by Type of Institution: 1971–1987

Date	Number of Sentenced Prisoners in All Institutions	Percent Female	Percent Female in Federal Institutions	Percent Female in State Institutions
1971	198,061	3.2	3.7	4.7
1972	196,183	3.2	3.7	3.1
1973	204,349	3.3	4.1	3.1
1974	229,721	3.5	4.4	3.2
1975	253,816	3.8	4.6	3.4
1976	262,833	3.8	5.4	3.8
1977	300,024	4.1	5.9	3.7
1978	306,602	4.2	6.2	3.9
1979	314,006	4.2	5.9	3.9
1980	328,695	4.1	5.8	4.0
1981	368,772	4.2	5.6	3.9
1982	414,362	4.3	5.5	4.2
1983	437,238	4.4	5.5	4.3
1984	462,442	4.5	5.8	4.4
1985	503,601	4.6	6.0	4.5
1986	546,659	4.9	6.4	4.7
1987	581,609	5.0	6.3	4.8

Note: Figures include all inmates sentenced for more than one year.

Source: U.S. Department of Justice, Prisoners in State and Federal Institutions (Washington, DC: Bureau of Justice Statistics), annual.

populous states—California, New York, and Pennsylvania. For every year, the data across all three states show that for each type of offense for which they have been found guilty, men have been more likely than women to be sentenced to prison.

Note also that within each state, the ordering of the types of crime for which defendants are most likely to receive a prison sentence does not differ noticeably between men and women, with homicide and robbery as the two most likely offenses. In Pennsylvania and California, they are followed by burglary; in New York, drug violation is the third most frequent offense for which men and women are likely to be sentenced to prison. In California, there is no difference in the rank ordering for all six types of offenses between men and women. The differences in Pennsylvania and New York are slight and cover offenses involving assault, burglary, theft, fraud, and drugs.

Table 12.13 compares the offenses for which men and women were sentenced to all state prisons in 1979 and 1986. In 1986 women represented a smaller percentage of the violent offenders than they did in 1979, 40.7 percent as opposed to 49 percent. For the violent offenses, murder and robbery are most frequently cited for both men and women. Among the property offenses, women are more likely to be committed for fraud and theft than for burglary, whereas men are most likely to be committed for burglary.

Table 12.9
Adult Inmate Population by Security Level and Sex: June 30, 1988

	Federal Prisons		State Prisons	
	Men	Women	Men	Women
Maximum security				
Number	600	10	98,364	2,173
Percent	1.5	0.4	19.4	9.3
Close security				
Number	9,712	233	48,213	1,565
Percent	24.0	8.4	9.5	6.7
Medium security				
Number	11,012	698	195,178	11,117
Percent	27.2	25.1	38.5	47.4
Minimum security				
Number	14,213	1,613	131,741	7,013
Percent	35.1	58.0	26.0	29.9
Trusty				
Number	0	0	10,263	524
Percent	0.0	0.0	2.0	2.2
Other				
Number	4,994	228	22,906	1,049
Percent	12.3	8.2	4.5	4.5
Total				
Number	40,531	2,782	506,665	23,441
Percent	100.0	100.0	100.0	100.0

Note: Numbers exclude inmates incarcerated in Washington, DC (men = 8,292; women = 461), and in Cook County, Illinois (men = 5,696; women = 308).

Source: American Correctional Association, 1989 Directory (Laurel, MD), p. xxv.

Table 12.14 shows the age and education of inmates of federal and state correctional institutions from 1960 to 1980 as recorded in the decennial U.S. Census report. Most notable are the increased educational levels of all inmates under custody. By 1980 approximately 27 percent of federal male inmates and 22 percent of federal female inmates had attended college. State inmates show a similar pattern. In 1960, 4 percent of the state male inmates and 5 percent of state female inmates had some college education. These percentages jumped to 18 percent for the men and 19 percent for the women in 1980. About one-third of all federal and state inmates had a high school education by 1980. In 1960 over 50 percent of the men and women had an elementary school education. In

Table 12.10
New York: Persons Convicted in Upper Courts and Sentenced to Prison by Type of Offense and Sex: 1982–1987

	1982		1983		1984		1985		1986		1987	
	Number Convicted	Percent Sentenced to Prison	Number Convicted	Percent Sentenced to Prison	Number Convicted	Percent Sentenced to Prison	Number Convicted	Percent Sentenced to Prison	Number Convicted	Percent Sentenced to Prison	Number Convicted	Percent Sentenced to Prison
Homicide												
Female	121	52.9	122	63.9	96	59.4	124	66.1	126	62.7	54	48.1
Male	1,716	78.7	1,650	80.6	1,544	79.5	1,430	78.7	1,387	81.5	778	76.9
Robbery												
Female	279	31.5	349	35.8	340	29.7	311	30.9	415	41.7	417	36.5
Male	6,392	60.5	8,149	60.2	7,378	58.9	6,768	58.8	7,497	59.7	6,900	62.3
Burglary												
Female	208	12.0	212	15.6	217	24.4	174	17.2	205	17.1	203	27.6
Male	6,124	34.7	6,928	39.4	6,009	40.0	5,961	39.7	6,220	42.7	5,854	43.7

Table 12.10 (continued)

	1982		1983		1984		1985		1986		1987	
	Number Convicted	Percent Sentenced to Prison	Number Convicted	Percent Sentenced to Prison	Number Convicted	Percent Sentenced to Prison	Number Convicted	Percent Sentenced to Prison	Number Convicted	Percent Sentenced to Prison	Number Convicted	Percent Sentenced to Prison
Assault												
Female	155	16.8	139	20.1	158	17.7	192	19.3	176	18.2	127	18.1
Male	1,522	30.4	1,522	30.1	1,795	29.8	1,833	31.9	1,740	34.1	1,265	31.6
Larceny												
Female	437	11.4	600	9.5	545	14.7	567	16.6	619	13.1	453	12.1
Male	2,060	23.3	2,310	23.6	2,500	26.8	2,995	27.1	3,147	30.2	2,314	30.8
Drug Law Violations												
Female	503	16.9	624	19.6	686	19.7	966	21.3	1,440	24.1	1,787	20.6
Male	4,651	37.6	4,823	38.0	5,655	42.7	6,760	41.7	11,219	43.0	12,026	38.1
Total												
Female	1,703	19.8	2,046	21.7	2,042	22.2	2,334	23.4	2,981	25.1	3,041	22.4
Male	22,465	44.7	25,382	46.5	24,881	46.6	25,747	45.4	31,210	46.9	29,137	45.2

Source: New York State Division of Criminal Justice Services, Bureau of Statistical Services, unpublished data.

Table 12.11
California: Persons Convicted in Superior Courts and Sentenced to Prison by Type of Offense and Sex: 1982–1987

	1982		1983		1984		1985		1986		1987	
	Number Convicted	Percent Sentenced to Prison	Number Convicted	Percent Sentenced to Prison	Number Convicted	Percent Sentenced to Prison	Number Convicted	Percent Sentenced to Prison	Number Convicted	Percent Sentenced to Prison	Number Convicted	Percent Sentenced to Prison
Homicide												
Female	97	71.1	87	64.4	86	67.4	101	75.2	100	75.0	100	73.0
Male	1,035	83.2	858	86.7	854	88.8	833	89.9	966	92.3	927	92.3
Robbery												
Female	241	41.1	254	44.5	216	45.8	231	51.9	272	52.2	262	55.7
Male	4,447	64.4	4,135	70.7	3,820	69.9	4,589	70.4	4,451	69.8	4,150	71.3
Burglary												
Female	397	29.5	428	32.2	543	35.7	613	37.8	651	37.5	658	39.7
Male	9,641	41.2	9,181	46.0	9,213	475	9,900	49.4	9,963	50.2	9,350	50.7
Assault												
Female	329	17.6	314	18.8	358	21.2	356	19.7	408	14.0	354	22.6
Male	3,750	29.5	3,475	33.3	3,635	34.6	4,071	36.2	4,342	37.5	4,013	38.9

Table 12.11 (continued)

	1982		1983		1984		1985		1986		1987	
	Number Convicted	Percent Sentenced to Prison	Number Convicted	Percent Sentenced to Prison	Number Convicted	Percent Sentenced to Prison	Number Convicted	Percent Sentenced to Prison	Number Convicted	Percent Sentenced to Prison	Number Convicted	Percent Sentenced to Prison
Theft												
Female	1,635	9.8	1,879	13.6	2,200	12.7	2,622	14.8	2,426	19.8	2,206	18.4
Male	6,313	22.3	6,394	25.7	6,638	27.7	7,418	29.4	7,366	31.1	7,270	32.0
Drug Law Violations												
Female	1,132	7.6	1,417	10.5	1,675	11.2	2,392	10.0	3,115	13.2	3,883	12.5
Male	7,322	14.6	9,074	16.4	11,224	17.2	17,371	17.5	22,995	21.3	26,702	23.3
Total												
Female	3,831	15.4	4,379	17.6	5,078	17.6	6,315	17.8	6,972	20.2	7,463	19.5
Male	32,508	34.7	33,117	36.8	35,384	36.3	44,182	35.2	50,083	35.6	52,412	35.6

Note: For Homicide, "Percent Sentenced to Prison" includes persons sentenced to death.

Source: California Department of Justice, Division of Law Enforcement, Bureau of Criminal Statistics, unpublished data.

Table 12.12
Pennsylvania: Persons Convicted in All Courts and Sentenced to Incarceration by Type of Offense and Sex: 1981–1986

	1981		1982		1983		1984		1985		1986	
	Number Convicted	Percent Incarcerated	Number Convicted	Percent Incarcerated	Number Convicted	Percent Incarcerated	Number Convicted	Percent Incarcerated	Number Convicted	Percent Incarcerated	Number Convicted	Percent Incarcerated
Murder												
Female	56	53.6	54	48.1	64	71.9	74	85.1	45	82.2	45	86.7
Male	428	75.9	469	81.9	499	87.6	522	85.1	398	89.7	371	90.0
Robbery												
Female	60	43.3	105	52.4	120	56.7	98	65.3	66	68.2	85	68.2
Male	1,941	74.4	2,456	73.7	2,173	80.1	2,460	83.6	1,608	84.6	1,648	87.0
Burglary												
Female	89	34.8	172	42.4	131	46.6	129	47.3	110	40.0	84	52.4
Male	3,058	62.2	4,486	60.3	4,394	68.9	4,207	73.5	3,212	77.0	2,945	78.1
Aggravated Assault												
Female	184	23.4	209	22.0	196	33.7	181	39.2	155	38.1	149	37.6
Male	1,609	40.5	1,725	43.4	1,494	56.0	1,552	60.4	1,231	61.3	1,224	67.3
Other Assault												
Female	260	15.4	304	21.1	329	21.0	358	24.9	335	26.3	314	23.2
Male	2,682	29.0	3,077	32.1	3,593	36.7	3,576	38.7	3,227	39.8	3,377	39.7

Table 12.12 (continued)

	1981		1982		1983		1984		1985		1986	
	Number Convicted	Percent Incarcerated	Number Convicted	Percent Incarcerated	Number Convicted	Percent Incarcerated	Number Convicted	Percent Incarcerated	Number Convicted	Percent Incarcerated	Number Convicted	Percent Incarcerated
Theft												
Female	539	18.7	2,947	11.7	2,195	20.0	2,048	21.5	1,822	25.9	1,673	27.2
Male	4,832	35.4	7,243	32.5	6,813	42.5	6,441	44.2	5,599	45.4	5,269	44.5
Forgery												
Female	238	27.7	229	32.8	206	35.4	246	41.1	233	44.6	281	38.1
Male	652	50.9	587	49.9	691	59.8	694	65.4	617	66.1	690	64.5
Fraud												
Female	388	19.8	225	20.0	289	28.4	295	33.6	411	31.1	393	26.2
Male	935	31.3	676	35.5	1,018	38.1	1,123	42.9	1,013	41.9	1,164	41.9
Drug Law Violations												
Female	455	17.4	517	22.2	649	24.8	669	24.8	619	31.2	634	33.1
Male	3,108	28.3	3,121	31.3	3,606	37.5	3,791	38.6	3,686	40.7	4,133	46.6
Total												
Female	2,269	21.7	4,762	17.7	4,179	25.5	4,098	28.2	3,796	35.7	3,658	31.1
Male	19,245	43.2	23,840	44.0	20,675	44.5	24,366	54.0	20,591	53.9	20,821	53.6

SOURCE: Pennsylvania Commission on Crime and Delinquency, unpublished data.

Table 12.13
Offense Distribution of State Prison Inmates by Sex: 1979 and 1986

	Percent of Prison Inmates*			
	1979		1986	
	Male	Female	Male	Female
Violent offenses				
Murder	12.2	15.5	11.2	13.0
Negligent manslaughter	3.8	9.8	3.0	6.8
Kidnapping	2.2	1.4	1.7	0.9
Rape	4.5	0.4	4.4	0.2
Other sexual assault	2.0	0.3	4.7	0.9
Robbery	25.6	13.6	21.3	10.6
Assault	7.7	7.6	8.1	7.1
Other violent offenses	0.3	0.4	0.8	1.2
Total	53.3	49.0	55.2	40.7
Property offenses				
Burglary	18.6	5.3	17.0	5.9
Larceny/theft	4.5	11.2	5.6	14.7
Motor vehicle theft	1.5	0.5	1.4	0.5
Arson	0.6	1.2	0.7	1.2
Fraud	3.8	17.3	3.2	17.0
Stolen property	1.3	0.9	2.0	1.6
Other property offenses	0.8	0.4	0.5	0.4
Total	31.2	36.8	30.4	41.3
Drug offenses				
Possession	1.5	2.7	2.9	4.0
Trafficking	4.3	7.1	5.3	7.3
Other drug offenses	0.4	0.7	0.2.	0.7
Total	6.2	10.5	8.4	12.0

* Figures do not add up to 100 percent because two offense categories ("Public order offenses" and "Other offenses") were excluded from the table.

Source: Adapted from Bureau of Justice Statistics, Profile of State Prison Inmates (Washington, D.C.: U.S. Department of Justice, 1986).

1980 that percentage dropped to 22 percent for the men and 20 percent for the women.

The age distribution of inmates has not changed much over the years, except for a shift from a smaller percentage of male and female inmates in the thirty to thirty-nine age range and a larger percentage in the twenty to twenty-four age range.

Table 12.15 examines the occupational backgrounds of men and women under

Table 12.14
Age and Education of Inmates in Federal and State Correctional Institutions: 1960, 1970, and 1980

	1960				1970				1980			
	Federal		State		Federal		State		Federal		State	
	Male	Female	Male	Female	Male	Female	Male	Female	Male	Female	Male	Female
					(percent)							
Age (years)												
< 15	0.0	0.6	0.1	0.1	0.0	0.6	0.3	0.5	0.3	0.3	0.3	0.4
15-19	8.0	7.8	8.6	10.1	3.7	3.8	8.4	11.6	7.6	5.1	7.9	6.1
20-24	20.7	16.0	19.6	17.0	25.4	27.7	26.2	22.8	22.8	21.4	29.9	23.6
25-29	18.5	20.5	18.2	17.7	19.8	23.5	20.3	18.5	22.4	17.4	24.9	25.9
30-39	31.7	31.6	28.5	32.4	27.2	24.0	24.1	24.8	28.3	25.0	24.7	25.8
40-49	13.5	17.1	15.0	14.2	15.3	17.2	13.4	15.4	11.3	9.0	7.9	9.2
50-64	6.9	6.3	8.7	7.5	7.6	3.3	6.2	4.5	6.3	4.6	3.9	5.7
65 +	0.7	0.0	1.4	0.9	1.0	0.0	1.0	1.9	1.0	17.2	0.5	3.3
Education (years)												
Elementary												
0-4	10.4	10.1	16.6	14.2	6.3	6.4	7.9	5.8	3.7	4.6	3.9	4.8
5-8	39.4	46.7	41.8	39.8	30.9	24.9	33.8	29.6	14.5	18.7	17.7	15.1
High school												
1-3	26.8	25.0	27.2	28.9	33.9	38.6	34.3	37.4	22.2	25.6	30.1	29.1
4	14.8	13.8	10.6	12.3	20.3	21.8	18.6	20.1	32.6	29.1	29.9	31.8
College												
1-3	7.0	3.3	3.1	3.8	6.1	6.0	4.6	5.6	18.3	14.6	15.1	15.5
4 +	1.7	1.2	0.8	1.0	2.4	2.3	0.8	1.5	8.7	7.3	3.3	3.7

Sources: U.S. Bureau of the Census, 1960 Decennial Census, Characteristics of Persons Under Custody in Correctional Institutions, tables 4 and 25; 1970 Decennial Census, Persons in Institutions and Other Group Quarters, tables 3 and 24; 1980 Decennial Census, Persons in Institutional and Other Group Quarters, table 14.

Table 12.15
Occupational Status of Inmates in Federal and State Correctional Institutions: 1960, 1970, and 1980[a]

	1960				1970				1980			
	Federal		State		Federal		State		Federal		State	
	Male	Female	Male	Female	Male	Female	Male	Female	Male	Female	Male	Female
				(percent)								
Total with occupation[a,b,c]	75.0	56.5	61.4	44.8	72.1	57.3	67.6	65.8	72.5	54.8	66.2	61.1
Never worked	4.5	11.5	3.9	12.9	7.1	9.0	7.3	18.6	8.5	21.9	11.8	20.1
No occupational information[d]	20.6	31.9	34.7	42.3	20.8	33.6	25.0	15.6	19.0	23.3	22.0	18.8
Occupation Type												
White collar												
Professional, technical, or administrative	9.1	6.0	3.8	4.4	12.8	17.9	5.8	5.3	9.2	13.2	6.2	11.4
Clerical	4.8	14.8	2.7	10.0	4.7	21.9	5.2	18.5	4.9	7.1	3.8	8.8
Sales	4.8	8.1	2.3	2.9	6.4	5.4	2.5	4.1	5.6	24.1	4.4	18.0
Total	18.7	28.9	8.8	17.3	24.0	45.2	13.4	27.9	19.7	44.4	14.4	38.2
Blue Collar												
Craft	18.7	3.8	12.9	0.4	18.9	0.0	21.3	2.9	20.6	6.5	22.8	3.7

161

Table 12.15 (continued)

	1960				1970				1980			
	Federal		State		Federal		State		Federal		State	
	Male	Female	Male	Female	Male	Female	Male	Female	Male	Female	Male	Female
					(percent)							
Operatives/laborers[e]	35.1	20.0	39.3	18.6	41.5	14.0	48.5	24.2	37.6	15.3	40.5	21.6
Service[f]	9.5	36.0	8.3	49.7	10.4	39.6	12.7	41.7	14.7	28.2	15.1	32.9
Farming, forestry, or fishing[g]	6.2	2.5	6.5	2.6	5.2	1.2	4.1	3.3	7.3	5.5	7.3	3.6
Total	69.5	62.3	67.0	71.3	76.0	54.8	86.6	72.1	80.2	55.5	85.7	61.8
No occupation reported	11.9	8.8	24.2	11.4	--	--	--	--	--	--	--	--

[a] Figures are not strictly comparable across years due to changes in occupational categorizations.
[b] For 1960 and 1970, totals include inmates fourteen years and older, but for 1980, totals include inmates sixteen years and older.
[c] For 1960, figures indicate the number of inmates who reported last working in 1950 or later; for 1970, 1960 or later; and for 1980, 1975 or later.
[d] Included in this category are inmates who last worked in 1959 or earlier and those who did not report the last year that they worked.
[e] Includes all nonfarm laborers and operatives. For 1980, figures include inmates who had been employed in the armed services.
[f] Includes private household workers.
[g] Includes all farm-related occupations, including farm owners and managers as well as laborers.

Sources: U.S. Bureau of the Census, 1960 Decennial Census, Characteristics of Persons Under Custody in Correctional Institutions, table 25; 1970 Decennial Census, Persons in Institutions and Other Group Quarters, table 24; 1980 Decennial Census, Persons in Institutional and Other Group Quarters, table 14.

federal and state custody. We see that the number of incarcerated women who reported never having worked increased over the years. But with the high percentage of "absence of information" about work histories, it is difficult to make too much of that trend. We also see that among women for whom there are occupational data, the number reporting a white-collar occupation, especially in the professional, technical, and administration areas, increased, while the percentage reporting a blue-collar occupation declined. Although this trend seems reversed for the men, again we cannot draw final conclusions based on these percentages because of the number not reporting their occupational category.

INSIDE WOMEN'S PRISONS

The American prison system has been a target of the equal rights movement because, by and large, it continues to provide separate facilities for men and women. Separate prisons were established for women in the 1880s to give them the same benefit of rehabilitation that was being sought for young men and boys in new reformatories.

Advocates of the Equal Rights Amendment who directed their interests at the female offender claimed that the same reasoning that was persuasive to the Supreme Court in *Brown vs. The Board of Education* (i.e., segregation denies to blacks equal opportunities and equality in their educational experiences) should apply to women because of the maintenance of a separate prison system. By definition, schools that segregate by race and prisons that segregate by sex are basically discriminatory.[5]

The fact that women prisoners constitute only 5 percent of all inmates continues to influence the conditions of their incarceration in many important ways. Indeed, the effect begins from the moment a women is sentenced. Because there are fewer female institutions, she is likely to be sent much farther from her community than is her male counterpart. Few states operate more than one female penal institution. All but five states have more than one institution for male offenders, on the other hand, and the decision about which type of institution to commit an offender to is based on age and type of offense.

Thus, women's prisons contain a more heterogeneous population than do prisons for men. They include a wider range of ages, and there is less differentiation by types of offenders.

But not all of the differences between men's and women's institutions result in more negative treatment for women. The stereotypes of women in general give female inmates some advantages. As Burkhart pointed out:

Women just weren't considered as dangerous or as violent as men. So—rather than the mass penitentiary housing used for men—women's prisons were designed on a domestic model with each woman having a "room" of her own. Often no more than stretches [of] open fields or wire fences separate women prisoners and the "free world"—armed guards are rarely visible. Just like women outside, a woman prisoner would be confined to "the home."

"The home" planned for women was a cottage that was built to house 20 to 30 women—who would cook their own food in a "cottage kitchen." The cottages in most states were built to contain a living room, a dining room, and 1 or 2 small reading rooms.[6]

Physically, then, female institutions are usually more attractive and more pleasant than the security oriented institutions for men. They tend to be located in more pastoral settings, and they are not as likely to have the gun towers, concrete walls, and barbed wire so often found at male institutions. Women inmates usually have more privacy than men and tend to have single rooms. They may wear street clothes rather than prison uniforms, and can decorate their rooms with bedspreads and curtains provided by the prison. Toilet and shower facilities also reflect a greater concern for women's privacy. Because women prisoners are perceived as less dangerous and less prone to escape than men, most states allow them more trips outside the prison than they do their male counterparts.

Considering the statistics which estimate that between 56 and 75 percent of incarcerated women have young children, however, the number of institutions accommodating the special needs of mothers with children is disproportionately low.[7] Based on a 1989 survey of women's prisons conducted by Simon and Landis, only 35 percent (thirteen) of the institutions have either "rooms with cribs, high chairs, or other 'baby equipment' " or "rooms in which to talk privately, read, [or] listen to music with older children," and only 50 percent (nineteen) of the responding institutions report having "rooms with toys and other facilities for children up to 6 years of age." Even fewer, 30 percent (eleven), report having "places to prepare food for children."[8]

We also found a great disparity among the institutions in the amount of time allowed for mother-child visitations. Seven of the thirty-seven responding institutions allowed visitations seven days a week. Eleven of the facilities permitted visitations twice a month, and another two allowed visitations only once a month.

At least half (nineteen) of the institutions reported that they had a furlough program whereby mothers could visit their children at home or in halfway houses. Most often, however, these programs had stringent eligibility requirements and were available only to offenders on work release, those convicted of relatively minor crimes, or those within sight of their release dates.

Child visitation is somewhat more problematic in the federal system than in the state system because only a small number of facilities serve the population of federal female offenders. While there may be only one facility within a state that houses female offenders, women adjudicated under the federal system may be housed in any federal facility throughout the country, and are more likely to be incarcerated outside their home states. Indeed, a large majority of all the women incarcerated in the federal system reside in just two institutions, Alderson and Lexington. This situation has obvious negative implications for the continuity of family life, for both men and women.

All of the federal facilities have furlough programs for eligible mothers, and the surveys suggest that they are somewhat more liberal than those offered at the state level. In at least two of the facilities, an inmate may become eligible within two years of release, and at least one other allows eligibility within one year of release.

CONCLUDING REMARKS

Looking back over data compiled during the past twenty-five years, we see a higher percentage of women than ever before—including those who are married and have preschool children—working full-time. Not only are more women working outside their homes, but they are occupying positions in the labor force that involve more training, responsibility, and authority than in the past. Along with women's greater participation in the labor force, promotion to positions of higher status, and increased representation in the professions, there is also a higher percentage of female-headed households in which women are the caretakers of young children.

The crime rates for women, while not dramatic, also indicate increases over time for property and white-collar offenses. The judicial statistics from the states of California, Pennsylvania, and New York confirm this pattern of an increase in the percentage of women charged with and convicted of property crimes.

Women account for about 5 percent of the prison population, and they are more likely than men to be assigned to medium and minimum security institutions at both the federal and state level. A major improvement has occurred over the past fifteen years in the facilities available for contacts and visits with female inmates' children.

In addition, the vast discrepancies between women's and men's opportunities for vocational training and jobs for pay have diminished. Not only do all women's prisons now offer academic classes, but they also offer a broad range of job training that helps female inmates find work once they are released from prison. Some prisons also have industries that offer women an opportunity to earn money while doing time.

Looking ahead to the next twenty years, I do not see an abatement in the number of property offenses women are likely to commit. As women continue to participate in the labor force and continue to move up into more responsible positions, they are likely to continue to commit property offenses which their jobs give them the opportunity to carry out.

Violent crimes, I believe, will show a different pattern. To the extent that women are less likely to perceive themselves as victims generally or as the victims of men, the likelihood of their committing violent acts will decline. Women who find themselves the victims of male aggression and cruelty will recognize that they have options other than bearing such abuse and hoping it will not get worse, or killing or disabling the perpetrator. Violent offenses by women are also likely to decline as they become better able to support themselves physically and emotionally. The higher levels of education attained by women and their greater participation in the labor force underlie this contention, just as these same demographic trends support the likelihood that women's involvement in property offenses will continue to increase.

NOTES

1. Rita J. Simon, *Women and Crime* (Lexington, MA: Lexington Books, 1975).

2. Elizabeth Rapaport, "The Death Penalty and Gender Discrimination," *Law and Society Review* 25, 2 (1991): 366–383.

3. Simon, *Women and Crime*, p. 108.

4. Based on interviews conducted by Angela Musolino and reported in "Judges Attitudes Toward Female Offenders," unpublished manuscript, 1989.

5. R. R. Arditi, F. Goldberg, Jr., M. M. Hartle, J. H. Peters, and W. R. Phelps, "The Sexual Segregation of American Prisons: Notes," *Yale Law Journal* 82 (1973): 1229–1273.

6. Kathryn W. Burkhart, *Women in Prison* (New York: Doubleday, 1973), p. 367.

7. See Clarice Feinman, *Women in the Criminal Justice System* (New York: Praeger, 1986), wherein she cites Glick and Neto (1977) as finding 56.2 percent with one or more children; Phyllis Jo Baunach, "Mothering from Behind Prison Walls," paper presented at the 1979 annual meeting of the American Society of Criminology, as finding 70.4 percent having one or more children; and Brenda McGowen and Karen Blumenthal, *Why Punish the Children? A Study of Children of Women Prisoners* (Hackensack, NJ: NCCD, 1978), who wrote that on any given day, 70 percent of the women in prisons and jails are mothers.

8. Rita J. Simon and Jean Landis, *The Crimes Women Commit, the Punishments They Receive* (Lexington, MA: Lexington Books, 1991).

13

Gender and Violent Crime: A Cross-Cultural Assessment

A comparison of female arrest rates in thirty-one countries over an eighteen-year time span reveals high correlations between female arrests and overall crime rates in any given society. On the average, women account for 1 out of every 10 homicide arrests and for 4 out of every 100 major larceny (including robbery) arrests. In the countries studied, strong positive correlations are found between levels of economic opportunity and industrialization and female arrest rates for homicide and major and minor larceny.

In 1963 Lady Barbara Wooton commented:

It is perhaps rather curious that no serious attempt has yet been made to explain the remarkable facts of the sex ratio in detected criminality, for the scale of the sex differential far outranks all the other traits (except that of age in the case of indictable offenses) which have been supposed to distinguish the delinquent from the non-delinquent populations. It seems to be one of those facts which escape notice by virtue of its very conspicuousness. It is surely, to say the least, very odd that half of the population should be so significantly immune to the criminogenic factors which lead to the downfall of so significant a proportion of the other half. Equally odd is it, too, that although the criminological experience of different countries varies considerably, nevertheless the sex differential remains.[1]

From the time Lady Wooton made those observations, the topic of women and their propensity to commit criminal acts has spawned a considerable intellectual industry. Writing about the percentage of women who have been arrested for criminal acts in the United States, I noted:

What the statistics show about the proportion of women in crime in 1972 are that there are more women involved today than there have been at any time since the end of World War II, and probably before that. But the increase has been in certain types of offenses: theft, forgery, fraud, and embezzlement, not in crimes of violence or in the traditional female crimes, such as prostitution and child abuse. . . . The fact that female arrests have increased for these offenses and not for all offenses is consistent both with opportunity theory and with the presence of a sizable women's movement.[2]

In an appendix to *Women and Crime*, I compared female arrest rates in twenty-five countries over three time periods (1963, 1968, and 1970), and noted that high crime rates and high arrest rates were apparent in the more economically developed and technologically advanced societies. I concluded:

Having reached the era in which women are expected to be "into crime" as they are expected to be "into" many activities that were previously closed or deemed inappropriate or of no interest to them, the topic of female participation in crime is one that should, and probably will, be explored in more depth in the next decade than it has been in the previous half century. Comparative studies of the type only suggested by the comments in this appendix should provide interesting and useful insights into women's propensities, capabilities, and behavior in criminal activities.[3]

The purposes of this chapter are to assess some of the propensities noted earlier, to explore whether the expected changes in women's participation in crime have in fact occurred, and to examine several theoretical frameworks relevant to understanding the pattern of women's criminal involvement. We focus on violent crime and examine the arrest rates of women for homicide and major larceny.[4] For comparison purposes, the analysis also includes minor larceny as a category of nonviolent crime.

Four major questions are addressed: (1) whether there have been significant increases in women's participation in criminal activities generally; (2) whether increases have occurred in specific crime categories, and if so, whether the crimes are more likely to be of a personal, violent nature or more likely to be in the realm of property offenses; (3) if there have been increases, whether they have occurred across all societies or have been apparent only in certain types of societies; and (4) whether any changes appear to be correlated with women's educational and occupational status.

REVIEW OF THE LITERATURE

A major difficulty in integrating studies on women and violent crime stems from the absence of gender as a major analytic variable in contemporary theoretical approaches. As Harris notes, "This failure is more than merely methodological, precisely because it means that purportedly general theories of criminal deviance are now no more than special theories of male deviance."[5] Criminological theories offer scant explanation for the long-observed disparity in the proportions of men and women who are arrested for violent and nonviolent crimes.[6] Consequently, theory has not guided research on women's criminal behavior, and the set of theoretically derived rival hypotheses is small.

The women's liberation movement of the mid-1960s generated a number of theoretical perspectives to fill the void. Building on the arguments of Caesar Lombroso and Sigmund Freud that women's criminal behavior reflected role reversal, a number of scholars proposed what Weis labels the "liberation theory" of female crime.[7] One of the chief proponents of this perspective is Adler:

> The social revolution of the sixties has virilized its previously or presumably docile female segment. . . . The emancipation of women appears to be having a twofold influence on female juvenile crimes. Girls are involved in more drinking, stealing, gang activity, and fighting-behavior in keeping with their adoption of male roles.[8]

A variant of this approach is the "human liberation" or "role convergence theory" of criminal behavior, which argues that criminal behavior is least frequent in settings in which boys are taught traditionally feminine values (e.g., violence is never appropriate) and girls traditionally masculine values (e.g., self-sufficiency).[9] This theory was developed to account for the similarity and relative pettiness of deviant acts of middle-class boys and girls, and the dissimilarity and violence apparent in the deviance of working-class boys and girls. Both of these approaches focused on the magnitude of differences in the socialization of women and men.

In contrast, the "role validation" perspective proposes that criminal behavior is an illegitimate expression of femininity rather than a sign of masculinity. Davis argues as a structural functionalist that prostitution is an extension of the female sex role.[10] Pollak,[11] Hoffman-Bustamante,[12] and Simon[13] argue that opportunities for criminality are sex-role determined. Women primarily commit petty property crimes (e.g., shoplifting) because these are the only opportunities available to house-bound women whose major social role is that of consumer. This perspective suggests that as women expand their roles, enter the labor force, and increase their education, they will experience the same opportunities and motivation as men to commit crimes. Increases in the status of women per se should be associated with increases in their criminal conduct, which should in turn be reflected in an increase in the numbers of women arrested.

Hill and Harris label these explanations as "objectivist" as opposed to "subjectivist" explanations, which stress attitudes and interpret increases in women's criminality as changes in their self-perceptions that lead them to commit more crime.[14] This dismissal of structural approaches is in line with Harris's earlier contention that such models cannot readily account for the crime rate of women being much lower than that of men, or for the greater propensity of women to commit nonviolent property crimes rather than violent personal and property crimes.[15] The structural strain theory of Emile Durkheim and Robert Merton would predict higher crime rates among women than men because their traditional roles deny access to legitimate means of achievement, forcing them to become criminal "innovators." Similarly, Harris contends, differential opportunity theory would interpret traditional sex roles as blocking access to both legitimate and illegitimate means. In their frustration, women would be expected to commit relatively more violent crimes than men. Neither of these expectations is borne out in official police data or in the profile of offenders sketched by victimization surveys.

Nevertheless, the liberation and opportunity hypotheses continue to direct the bulk of research on women and crime today. The typically employed research design correlates changes in women's status in the United States with the Uniform Crime Reports statistics over a period of time. The problem with this design is that the study is couched within one society, which offers little variance in crime statistics and the social, economic, or psychological factors thought to influence them. A richer design maximizes social structural variation by comparing national crime data derived from a larger number of countries. Several researchers have followed this design (e.g., Widom and Stewart[16] and Hartnagel[17]) but have drawn comparisons across a number of countries for only one year, which is a cross-sectional design. As is discussed more fully below, this strategy is problematical. An even better, more rigorous approach is both comparative and longitudinal: crime rates are analyzed by country and across time, and conclusions are based on the empirical evidence from a widely varying set of countries for a lengthy time period. This is the approach employed here.

METHOD

The data are drawn from the Correlates of Crime Archive, which contains crime data printed in *International and Crime Statistics*, a biannual publication of the International Police Organization (INTERPOL).[18] Member countries voluntarily report the number of crimes recorded in total and by type (homicide, major larceny, minor larceny, fraud, etc.), the number cleared, and the number of offenders arrested (by gender and adult/juvenile status).

The validity and reliability of INTERPOL data have been severely criticized by numerous researchers. Most recently, Archer and Gartner depict INTERPOL data as "by far the least satisfactory."[19] They are especially critical of the organization's arbitrary definitions of offense categories. This constitutes a more serious threat to validity than the well-known tendency of member countries to use different operational definitions of types of crimes[20] or to underreport crimes systematically.[21] Archer and Gartner's contention is refuted, however, by Bennett and Lynch's comparison of INTERPOL data (used in the Correlates of Crime Archive) with the figures Archer and Gartner collected directly from nations. A test of the comparability between the two data sources found them virtually identical (r = .95).

Whatever biases and inconsistencies exist in INTERPOL figures, they are minimized when crime figures are analyzed for one nation over a considerable period of time. The data set analyzed in this chapter contains information on each of thirty-one countries over the 1962–1980 period.

Six crime variables were defined using INTERPOL data. The first three were total crime (the total number of crimes reported to police), overall arrests (the number of women and men arrested in all of the crime categories reported to the police), and female arrests (the number of women arrested in all of the crime categories). Each of the three variables was converted to an annual rate through division by the nation's population for each year. The three remaining crime variables separately measured women's arrests for homicide, major larceny, and minor larceny. For each variable, the denominator was the number of women and men arrested for that category of offense, and the resulting figure was the percentage of women among those arrested for the offense.

There are known inconsistencies in what nations report as arrests. Some countries count only the people apprehended, while others report only those formally arrested. The within nation design of this study makes this cross-nation variation acceptable, if we assume that member nations do not change their definition of an arrested offender over time.

Four social and demographic variables were used. Women's enrollment in secondary education institutions was measured as the percentage of all secondary education students who were women in a given country. Women's labor force participation was calculated as the percentage of the total national labor force comprised by women. Two other variables measured social structural characteristics of the countries: level of economic opportunity was measured by the per capita private consumption of gross national product (GNP), and level of industrialization was indicated by the percentage of the labor force in industry. Other variables useful for testing the liberation and opportunity hypotheses described in the preceding section (such as the percentage of women employed in managerial and professional positions; the percentage of women who have completed the equivalent of four years of college or more; and statutes pertaining to women's rights to hold and inherit property, to divorce, to vote, and to obtain an abortion) were not available over a period of years and for a large enough group of countries to be analytically useful.

World Bank and United Nations publications were the sources for the annual data on the number of women enrolled in secondary educational institutions, the level of economic opportunity, and the level of industrialization in a nation. The International Labor Organization published the data on women's labor force participation.

ANALYSIS AND FINDINGS

The first step in the analysis was to collapse the nineteen years' worth of data into three time periods. Period A, 1962–1965, Period B, 1969–1972, and Period C, 1977–1980. This was done to stabilize the rates and smooth their minor year-to-year fluctuations. Grouping the data in this fashion also reduced the auto-

Table 13.1
Total Crime Rate over Three Time Periods

Country	Period A (1962-65)	Period B (1969-72)	Period C (1977-80)	Group Means: Periods A,B,C	Rate Change Period A-B (percent)	Rate Change Period B-C (percent)
Sweden	4885.58	7853.51	10235.68	7658.26	60.75	30.33
New Zealand	4696.58	6291.36	9634.57	6874.17	33.96	53.14
Korea	3580.52	1404.41	1486.84	2157.26	-60.78	5.87
Austria	3297.63	3634.55	4285.04	3739.07	10.22	17.90
West Germany	3157.27	3982.67	5707.56	4282.50	26.14	43.31
Israel	3147.78	4469.45	5977.00	4531.41	41.99	33.73
Denmark	3059.91	5704.32	6958.66	5240.96	86.42	21.99
Canada	3052.67	5365.08	7149.32	5189.02	75.75	33.26
Finland	2899.60	6137.32	10132.46	6389.79	111.66	65.10
Fiji	2456.23	4275.79	6059.49	4263.84	74.08	41.72
Libya	2372.21	1693.84	1154.28	1740.11	-28.60	-31.85
Japan	2035.25	1311.92	1267.68	1538.28	-35.54	-3.37
England/Wales	1892.15	2617.75	4631.06	3046.99	38.35	76.91
Australia	1807.76	2887.35	8190.29	4295.13	59.72	183.66
France	1772.48	2805.01	4308.39	2961.96	58.25	53.60
Kuwait	1772.39	1067.66	647.30	1162.45	-39.76	-39.37
Luxembourg	1619.12	1990.07	2649.29	2086.16	22.91	33.13
Jamaica	1592.44	1756.17	2461.58	1936.73	10.28	40.17
Zambia	1283.16	2243.99	2580.39	2035.85	74.88	14.99
United States	1269.96	3058.11	5309.87	3212.65	140.80	73.63
Netherlands	1269.35	2390.63	4339.49	2666.49	88.33	81.52
Norway	1241.43	1919.28	2636.73	1932.48	54.60	37.38
Hong Kong	992.75	1223.52	1474.13	1230.13	23.25	20.48
Cyprus	783.58	461.98	387.73	544.43	-41.04	-16.07
Burma	744.26	752.91	171.46	556.21	1.16	-77.23
Philippines	690.05	66.07	121.92	292.68	-90.43	84.53
Malawi	635.17	745.98	998.47	793.21	17.45	33.85
Ivory Coast	300.15	251.29	184.38	245.27	-16.28	-26.62
Malaysia	292.89	349.45	568.27	403.54	19.31	62.62
Sri Lanka	266.88	483.85	704.67	485.13	81.30	45.64
Nigeria	146.33	173.28	247.38	189.00	18.42	42.76
Median for Time Period	1721.33	2253.34	4381.99	2785.55	30.91	94.47
Mean for Time Period	1903.66	2560.28	3634.24	2699.39	34.49	41.95

correlation effect present in time series data and enabled unbiased correlation coefficients to be calculated between two data trends grouped in identical time period categories.

Crime Rates

Table 13.1 presents the total crime rates for the thirty-one nations over the three time periods, in descending order, based on the crime rate in Period A. The data show that crime rates have gone up in twenty-three of the thirty-one nations and that there has been a steeper increase in crimes reported between Periods B and C than between Periods A and B. Australia, the United States, Finland, and the Netherlands showed the largest increases across the three periods. The eight countries in which crime rates fell were developing nations (e.g., Burma, Cyprus, the Ivory Coast, and Kuwait).

Arrest Rates

Table 13.2 shows the overall arrest rates in those same countries during the three time periods. Similar to the trend in crime rates, arrest rates increased in twenty of the thirty-one nations, but the increase was steeper in the earlier period (between A and B) than in the later (between B and C). The nations showing the largest increase continued to be largely industrialized—Sweden, Canada, and the United States. Similarly, four of the nations with decreasing total crime rates showed the biggest declines in arrest rates as well—Kuwait, Cyprus, Burma, and the Philippines.

Pearson product moment correlation coefficients were calculated between the crime rates and the overall arrest rates for the three time periods. The coefficients were quite strong: $r = .73$ for Period A, $r = .73$ for Period B, and $r = .75$ for Period C.

Female Arrest Rates

The total crime rate and overall arrest rate figures provide some measure of the magnitude of offenses by men and women and the ability of police organizations to apprehend offenders. Within the national context presented by these data, it is interesting to examine the female arrest rates.

As the data in Table 13.3 show, there has been a steady increase in thirteen of the thirty-one countries. Only three nations showed a consistent decline in female arrests—Kuwait, Israel, and the Ivory Coast.

While cross-national comparisons are somewhat inappropriate for reasons mentioned above, it is striking that the nations with the greatest increases in arrests of women also have relatively high female arrest rates, namely, New Zealand, the United States, Canada, England, Sweden, and Australia. On the whole, women's arrests account for about one-eighth of the total arrests in each time period.

The repeated appearance of several countries on the three lists of nations showing the greatest increases across the three periods in Tables 13.1, 13.2, and 13.3 led us to examine the extent to which female arrest rates rise or fall in accordance with total crime and overall arrest rates. The Pearson's r's between total crime and female arrest rates were similar to those reported for the overall arrest rates: $r = .63$ in Period A, $r = .68$ in Period B, and $r = .73$ in Period C. As expected, the correlations between overall arrest rates and female arrest rates were even higher: $r = .72$ in Period A, $r = .88$ in Period B, and $r = .90$

Rabbis, Lawyers, Immigrants, Thieves

Table 13.2
Total Arrests over Three Time Periods

Country	Period A (1962-65)	Period B (1969-72)	Period C (1977-80)	Group Means: Periods A,B,C	Rate Change Period A-B (percent)	Rate Change Period B-C (percent)
Israel	989.53	1072.24	457.96	839.91	8.36	-57.29
West Germany	769.39	944.93	1287.40	1000.57	22.82	36.24
New Zealand	719.54	1063.83	1740.67	1174.68	47.85	63.62
Burma	585.79	459.38	313.72	452.96	-21.58	-31.71
Luxembourg	545.05	504.49	438.20	495.91	-7.44	-13.14
Austria	526.72	577.66	598.02	567.47	9.67	3.52
Finland	465.09	680.79	834.39	660.09	46.38	22.56
Kuwait	460.43	190.00	109.39	253.27	-58.73	-42.43
Korea	417.15	291.62	319.34	342.70	-30.09	9.51
Australia	397.73	544.57	572.71	505.00	36.92	5.17
England/Wales	342.75	496.49	676.07	505.10	44.85	36.17
Netherlands	334.11	463.27	526.87	441.42	38.66	13.73
France	326.25	788.21	721.60	612.02	141.60	-8.45
United States	325.39	539.43	896.40	587.07	65.78	66.18
Cyprus	290.58	188.33	125.19	201.37	-35.19	-33.53
Canada	278.56	379.17	791.55	483.09	36.12	108.76
Jamaica	276.03	725.11	918.12	639.75	162.69	26.62
Libya	269.77	224.38	176.89	223.68	-16.83	-21.16
Sweden	264.78	437.68	1002.08	568.18	65.30	128.95
Zambia	263.68	208.38	206.49	226.18	-20.97	-0.91
Japan	259.45	189.13	198.10	215.56	-27.10	4.74
Fiji	212.74	355.35	453.12	340.40	67.03	27.51
Norway	154.96	198.22	194.72	182.63	27.92	-1.77
Hong Kong	147.10	185.47	239.84	190.80	26.08	29.31
Ivory Coast	130.02	161.96	115.91	135.96	24.57	-28.43
Sri Lanka	121.08	239.20	153.11	171.13	97.56	-35.99
Denmark	104.26	150.41	251.09	168.59	44.26	66.94
Philippines	102.82	55.09	43.83	67.25	-46.42	-20.44
Malawi	100.97	110.42	158.54	123.31	9.36	43.58
Malaysia	50.84	45.52	63.36	53.91	-10.46	43.59
Nigeria	30.43	45.93	51.01	42.46	50.94	11.06
Median for Time Period	281.72	430.87	611.62	441.40	52.94	41.95
Mean for Time Period	331.06	403.76	472.18	402.34	21.96	16.95

in Period C. The strength of the association suggests that the factors influencing changes in a nation's crime and arrest rates also affect the nation's female arrest rates.

We turn next to an analysis of female arrests for homicide and major larceny (Tables 13.4 and 13.5). For purposes of comparison, we also report the percentage of female arrests for a nonviolent offense, minor larceny, which includes theft and receiving stolen goods (Table 13.6).

Commenting first on the homicide data, we note that the percentages decreased across the three time periods, and that the decline was slightly steeper between

Table 13.3
Total Female Arrest Rates over Three Time Periods

Country	Period A (1962-65)	Period B (1969-72)	Period C (1977-80)	Group Means: Periods A,B,C	Rate Change Period A-B (percent)	Rate Change Period B-C (percent)
West Germany	134.27	197.26	290.91	207.48	46.91	47.48
Austria	84.91	94.37	107.89	95.72	11.14	14.33
New Zealand	75.65	202.88	390.83	233.12	168.18	92.64
Luxembourg	66.92	77.35	69.65	71.31	15.59	-9.95
Israel	63.32	53.32	51.84	56.16	-15.79	-2.78
England	52.42	72.90	151.37	92.23	39.07	107.64
Netherlands	48.63	67.01	67.92	61.19	37.80	1.36
Finland	48.02	77.81	97.34	74.39	62.04	25.10
United States	47.19	97.29	215.79	120.09	106.17	121.80
France	46.37	148.18	143.58	112.71	219.56	-3.10
Australia	43.37	88.34	142.92	91.54	103.69	61.78
Japan	40.15	37.82	60.28	46.-8	-5.80	59.39
Sweden	36.11	62.01	138.11	78.74	71.73	122.72
Jamaica	34.38	157.06	62.94	84.64	356.84	-60.21
Korea	32.32	26.69	31.67	30.23	-17.42	18.66
Canada	26.70	60.16	115.60	67.49	125.32	92.15
Cyprus	19.02	8.94	9.11	12.36	-53.00	1.90
Burma	15.92	17.57	26.14	19.88	10.36	48.78
Denmark	13.54	12.66	17.94	14.71	-6.50	41.71
Norway	13.52	20.04	17.73	17.10	48.22	-11.53
Libya	10.75	4.28	4.79	6.61	-60.19	11.92
Fiji	7.21	12.80	19.28	13.10	77.53	50.63
Kuwait	7.16	7.09	4.85	6.37	-0.98	-31.59
Hong Kong	6.55	5.43	24.41	12.13	-17.10	349.54
Zambia	4.46	3.20	5.01	4.22	-28.25	56.56
Ivory Coast	4.28	4.12	3.78	4.06	-3.74	-8.25
Philippines	3.78	1.69	1.96	2.48	-55.29	15.98
Sri Lanka	3.67	8.87	8.39	6.98	141.69	-5.41
Malawi	2.17	2.73	4.80	3.23	25.81	75.82
Nigeria	1.11	3.08	2.67	2.29	177.48	-13.31
Malaysia	0.77	0.69	0.79	0.75	-10.39	14.49
Median for Time Period	34.27	28.18	46.09	36.18	-17.76	63.52
Mean for Time Period	32.09	52.70	73.87	52.88	64.24	40.17

Periods A and B than between Periods B and C. On average, women accounted
for a little more than one out of ten homicide arrests. The percentages for major
larceny increased an average of 10 percent across the three time periods. Nevertheless, women accounted for only 4 out of 100 major larceny arrests.

As expected, examination of the data in Table 13.6 on females arrested for
minor larceny reveals a higher percentage of arrests than for homicide and major
larceny, and a steady increase across the three time periods. On the whole,
women account for about one out of every eight arrests for minor larceny.

We computed Spearman's rank order correlation among the percentage of

Table 13.4
Percentage of Females Arrested for Homicide over Three Time Periods

Country	Period A (1962-65)	Period B (1969-72)	Period C (1977-80)	Group Means: Periods A,B,C	Rate Change Period A-B	Rate Change Period B-C
			(percent)			
Norway	30.1	2.5	11.4	-91.66	354.18	14.67
Denmark	25.0	14.0	12.4	-44.00	-11.43	17.13
England/Wales	23.4	15.8	13.7	-32.48	-13.29	17.63
Austria	23.2	18.8	20.7	-18.97	10.11	20.90
New Zealand	22.9	14.0	10.3	-38.86	-26.43	15.73
Korea	21.7	17.5	17.3	-19.35	-1.14	18.83
West Germany	18.5	12.9	11.0	-30.27	-14.73	14.13
United States	18.2	15.6	13.7	-14.21	-12.07	15.81
Libya	18.0	15.9	9.7	-11.67	-38.99	14.53
Australia	16.6	12.8	14.0	-22.89	9.38	14.47
Fiji	16.0	8.3	6.1	-48.13	-26.51	10.13
Jamaica	14.9	7.8	2.8	-47.65	-64.10	8.50
Japan	14.6	18.0	21.4	23.29	18.89	18.00
France	14.2	14.4	13.4	1.41	-6.94	14.00
Finland	13.2	16.0	8.8	21.21	-45.00	12.67
Netherlands	10.5	6.0	5.7	-42.86	-5.00	7.40
Canada	8.7	11.7	10.5	34.48	-10.26	10.30
Malawi	7.5	4.8	11.9	-36.00	147.92	8.07
Kuwait	7.0	6.4	11.5	-8.57	79.69	8.30
Luxembourg	6.4	14.5	5.7	126.56	-60.69	8.87
Ivory Coast	5.9	9.6	7.4	62.71	-22.92	7.63
Israel	5.2	4.6	3.3	-11.54	-28.26	4.37
Nigeria	4.7	7.3	3.8	55.32	-47.95	5.27
Sri Lanka	4.7	5.5	6.1	17.87	10.11	5.45
Sweden	4.1	12.1	9.7	195.12	-19.83	8.63
Hong Kong	3.8	5.0	9.6	31.58	92.00	6.13
Malaysia	3.3	1.8	3.3	-45.45	83.33	2.80
Zambia	2.8	1.0	0.3	-64.29	-70.00	1.37
Cyprus	2.1	23.3	12.5	1009.52	-46.35	12.63
Philippines	1.6	1.4	2.0	-12.50	42.86	1.67
Burma	0.9	1.1	1.7	27.59	53.15	1.23
Mean Percent	11.92	10.34	9.41	-13.31	-8.97	10.56

female arrests for homicide, major larceny, and minor larceny within each time period and found the following:

	Periods A	B	C
Homicide and major larceny	.44	.45	.39
Homicide and minor larceny	.38	.47	.47
Major and minor larceny	.65	.59	.59

Table 13.5
Percentage of Females Arrested for Major Larceny over Three Time Periods

Country	Period A (1962-65)	Period B (1969-72)	Period C (1977-80)	Group Means: Periods A,B,C	Rate Change Period A-B	Rate Change Period B-C
			(percent)			
Denmark	16.0	7.9	5.1	-50.53	35.19	9.66
Austria	10.3	8.5	5.3	-17.33	-37.34	8.03
Jamaica	9.1	23.9	4.7	162.95	-80.21	12.55
France	9.0	8.7	7.3	-3.67	15.38	8.32
Korea	6.8	2.4	1.4	-65.15	-43.04	3.51
Canada	4.8	6.1	5.7	27.52	-6.92	5.49
Luxembourg	4.3	7.8	12.4	79.03	59.20	8.16
West Germany	4.0	3.6	5.4	-11.03	51.27	4.30
Cyprus	3.9	2.2	4.5	-44.27	104.11	3.53
United States	3.9	5.2	6.4	33.42	24.27	5.14
Netherlands	3.7	4.4	4.8	18.48	9.40	4.27
Finland	3.6	3.5	9.3	-3.31	164.86	5.46
Israel	3.6	2.2	3.6	-39.83	65.28	3.11
Norway	3.2	3.6	5.2	13.25	44.85	3.99
Australia	3.2	3.4	5.8	7.62	71.09	4.11
New Zealand	2.6	5.3	11.8	101.52	123.02	6.58
England/Wales	2.5	2.9	4.4	15.85	53.33	3.23
Sweden	2.1	2.7	4.6	30.62	68.50	3.14
Sri Lanka	2.0	3.4	6.4	67.66	90.50	3.93
Nigeria	2.0	2.1	2.1	5.00	0.95	2.07
Ivory Coast	1.8	3.0	1.9	64.13	-36.42	2.26
Libya	1.6	2.3	2.8	43.75	22.61	2.24
Philippines	1.4	1.6	1.9	15.44	17.83	1.59
Hong Kong	1.2	0.8	0.6	-27.83	-25.30	0.87
Japan	1.1	1.7	6.8	48.67	305.95	3.21
Kuwait	1.1	1.8	2.2	73.58	16.85	1.68
Malawi	0.8	1.6	1.4	92.68	-11.39	1.27
Burma	0.6	0.3	0.5	-50.79	51.61	0.47
Fiji	0.6	0.8	0.9	31.03	21.05	0.75
Zambia	0.3	0.5	1.1	35.29	139.13	0.63
Malaysia	0.2	0.0	0.1	-100.00	0.00	0.07
Mean Percent	3.58	3.99	4.39	11.40	10.90	3.99

Overall, the strongest relationships in each time period were between major and minor larceny. The former category, as noted, involved both violent and property offenses.

The data presented thus far show that crime rates and arrest rates have increased at about the same levels and that the female arrest rates correlate strongly with the overall arrest rates. Examination of the data for women's involvement in the major violent offense category revealed a slight decline in the overall percentage of female homicide arrests across the three time periods. Female arrest for major larceny remained steady at a relatively low percentage. Women's arrest for minor

Table 13.6
Percentage of Females Arrested for Minor Larceny over Three Time Periods

Country	Period A (1962-65)	Period B (1969-72)	Period C (1977-80)	Group Means: Periods A,B,C	Rate Change Period A-B	Rate Change Period B-C
			(percent)			
West Germany	21.6	31.2	29.7	44.08	-4.59	27.50
Netherlands	20.9	25.2	22.0	20.65	-12.63	22.68
Austria	20.8	25.9	25.3	24.40	-2.05	23.98
Sweden	20.4	19.8	21.6	-3.04	9.31	20.58
United States	20.3	22.4	30.6	10.66	36.49	24.43
England/Wales	19.4	19.1	28.4	-1.39	48.46	22.31
Japan	18.8	22.3	34.3	18.60	54.25	25.11
Luxembourg	18.2	24.6	17.6	35.00	-28.61	20.14
Jamaica	14.9	18.6	11.5	25.13	-28.51	14.98
France	14.9	17.7	18.1	19.39	2.09	16.89
Finland	14.4	16.3	11.5	13.12	-29.45	14.07
Norway	13.6	18.5	14.3	35.36	-22.38	15.47
Australia	12.1	19.2	31.9	58.20	66.23	21.07
New Zealand	11.7	25.8	25.3	120.10	-2.09	20.96
Cyprus	10.2	6.0	10.0	-41.64	67.00	8.72
Canada	9.7	16.5	15.0	69.69	-9.71	13.70
Korea	9.5	9.2	8.1	-2.94	-12.34	8.95
Israel	8.1	7.1	13.2	-12.00	85.65	9.46
Burma	6.0	6.9	14.1	15.03	104.21	8.89
Philippines	5.3	5.1	7.6	-3.75	48.54	6.03
Denmark	4.9	4.7	5.9	-3.49	25.96	5.16
Hong Kong	4.5	4.1	18.2	-10.13	345.34	8.93
Fiji	4.3	4.5	5.9	5.59	29.58	4.90
Nigeria	4.1	7.6	6.1	84.88	-19.26	5.93
Sri Lanka	3.9	3.6	4.3	-6.49	19.44	3.92
Ivory Coast	3.2	1.9	3.0	-41.25	56.91	2.68
Libya	3.1	1.6	2.8	-47.57	74.07	2.51
Malawi	2.6	2.8	3.4	5.77	21.82	2.90
Zambia	1.9	2.7	4.5	38.14	67.91	3.04
Kuwait	1.8	4.7	5.0	161.80	6.22	3.80
Malaysia	1.7	1.6	1.5	-8.19	-4.46	1.59
Mean Percent	10.9	13.1	14.8	31.70	31.50	13.00

larceny increased more steeply than for major larceny, but has not attained the levels anticipated by many researchers writing in the 1970s.

SOCIETAL CORRELATES OF CRIME

Another set of questions raised earlier in this chapter concerns the relationship between the percentage of women arrested for violent offenses and the socio-economic and demographic characteristics of their societies. Durkheim and Merton's structural strain theory would predict higher violent female crime rates in those societies in which there is greater suppression of women's rights. As women feel more downtrodden and oppressed in their aspirations for social and economic independence, they are more likely to "innovate" by committing violent acts against those whom they regard as the source of their suppression. Thus, women in societies that do not allow divorce, forbid them to inherit or hold property, and bar them from participation in institutions of higher education and in various labor markets are more likely to commit homicide than women who live in societies where they enjoy the full rights of citizenship granted to men.

Continuing this line of argument, societies in which there are high rates of female property offenders are likely to support women's participation in higher education and the labor force, and are more likely to extend political rights (e.g., the right to vote), social rights (e.g., divorce), and other economic rights (inheritance and the right to hold property in one's own name) to women.

Two questions drove this phase of the analysis: Are women's propensities to commit violent offenses negatively correlated with women's labor force participation and higher educational attainment, and are women's propensities to commit property offenses positively correlated with such indicators?

Examining first, in Table 13.7, the correlations between female labor force participation and the percentage of females arrested for the two violent offenses, we found no strong correlation coefficient in any of the three time periods. Only between minor larceny and female labor force participation in Period C (1977–1980) was there a moderately strong relationship ($r = .43$). The table also shows a strong relationship between the percentage of females attending institutions of secondary education and female homicide arrests ($r = .56$) in Period C; and for female minor larceny arrests ($r = .51$ in Period A and $r = .45$ for Period B).

In addition to the two demographic indicators, we also were able to array societies by levels of economic opportunity (e.g., the private consumption of gross domestic product divided by the population), and industrialization (the percentage of the work force engaged in industry). Running correlations between each of those measures and female homicide, major larceny, and minor larceny, we found high correlation relationships between both those indicators and female arrests for violent and property offenses in the three time periods. While the strongest correlations were between female minor larceny and the level of economic opportunity and the level of industrialization, female homicide and major larceny arrests were also strongly and positively correlated with higher levels of industrialization and higher rates of economic opportunity.

CONCLUDING REMARKS

The data show that there have been comparable levels of increase among crime, arrest, and female arrest rates from 1962 through 1980. The fears raised in the late 1960s and early 1970s that women's participation in crime would increase dramatically have not been realized. For homicide and major larceny, women's participation has, if anything, decreased slightly. Thus, at least in the thirty-one countries for which longitudinal data are available, women continue to play relatively minor roles in violent criminal activities.

Table 13.7
Pearson Product Moment Correlations Between Crime and Societal Variables over Three Time Periods

Variables	Period A (1962-65) r=	Period B (1969-72) r=	Period C (1977-80) r=
1. Correlations Between Female Labor Participation and:			
Female Homicide Arrests	-0.07	0.12	0.10
Female Major Larceny Arrests	0.23	0.12	0.18
Female Minor Larceny Arrests	0.28	0.26	0.43
2. Correlations Between Female Enrollment in Secondary Education and:			
Female Homicide Arrests	0.20	0.14	0.56
Female Major Larceny Arrests	0.22	-0.01	0.19
Female Minor Larceny Arrests	0.51	0.45	0.36
3. Correlations Between Level of Industrialization and:			
Female Homicide Arrests	0.37	0.40	0.51
Female Major Larceny Arrests	0.50	0.40	0.46
Female Minor Larceny Arrests	0.68	0.66	0.70
4. Correlations Between Level of Economic Opportunity and:			
Female Homicide Arrests	0.31	0.35	0.54
Female Major Larceny Arrests	0.57	0.42	0.65
Female Minor Larceny Arrests	0.56	0.53	0.65

The data do show a consistent relationship between levels of industrialization and economic opportunities and female crime. Over the nineteen-year time span, we find that the more industrialized the society and the greater the economic opportunities, the higher the female participation in both violent and property offenses.

Unfortunately, we did not have sensitive enough measures of women's status in the countries as a whole for the time periods involved to assess the relationship between societies in which women enjoy political and social opportunities and civil rights and their propensity to commit crimes. To measure those relationships we would need data on women's rights to hold and inherit property, to divorce, to obtain abortions, to vote, and to hold public office; and on the percentage of women in professional and managerial positions, and the percentage of women who have completed at least four years of postsecondary education. Such indicators would have allowed us to test more thoroughly the strength of the relationships between women's status and their propensity to commit violent as well as property offenses.

NOTES

1. Quoted in Rita J. Simon, "American Women and Crime," *The Annals: Crime and Justice in America: 1776–1976* 423 (1976): 32.

2. Rita J. Simon, *Women and Crime* (Lexington, MA: D. C. Heath, 1975), p. 107. Unfortunately, data on the number of women in each nation's population were not routinely available, so the women's arrest rate was calculated using total population as the denominator.

3. Ibid., p. 118.

4. Major larceny is considered a violent offense because it includes robbery with dangerous aggravating circumstances.

5. Anthony R. Harris, "Sex and Theories of Deviance: Toward a Functional Theory of Deviant Type-scripts," *American Sociological Review* 42 (1977): 3–16.

6. In addition to homicide, major larceny, and minor larceny, the other offense categories are fraud, counterfeit, drug offenses, and a miscellaneous category of other offenses not including the six cited above.

7. Joseph G. Weis, "Liberation and Crime: The Invention of the New Female Criminal," *Crime and Social Justice* 6 (1976): 18.

8. Freda Adler, *Sisters in Crime* (New York: McGraw-Hill, 1975), p. 87.

9. Nancy B. Wise, "Juvenile Delinquency Among Middle-Class Girls," in Edmund W. Vaz, ed., *Middle-Class Juvenile Delinquency* (New York: Harper and Row, 1976).

10. Kingsley Davis, "Prostitution," in Robert K. Merton and Robert A. Nisbet, eds., *Contemporary Social Problems* (New York: Harcourt Brace Jovanovich, 1961).

11. Otto Pollak, *The Criminality of Women* (Philadelphia: University of Pennsylvania Press, 1950).

12. Dale Hoffman-Bustamante, "The Nature of Female Criminality," *Issues in Criminology* 8 (1973): 122.

13. Simon, *Women and Crime.*

14. Gary D. Hill and Anthony R. Harris, "Changes in the Gender Patterning of Crime, 1953–1977; Opportunity vs. Identity," *Social Science Quarterly* 62 (1981): 660.

15. Harris, "Sex and Theories of Deviance."

16. Cathy S. Widom and Abigail J. Stewart, "Female Criminality and the Status of Women," *International Annals of Criminology* 24 (1986): 137–162.

17. Timothy F. Hartnagel, "Modernization, Female Social Roles, and Female Crime: A Cross-National Investigation," *Sociological Quarterly* 23 (1982): 483.

18. Richard R. Bennett and James P. Lynch, "Does a Difference Make a Difference? Comparing Cross-National Crime Indicators," unpublished manuscript, The American University, Washington, DC, 1986.

19. Dane Archer and Rosemary Gartner, *Violence and Crime in Cross-National Perspective* (New Haven, CT: Yale University Press, 1984), p. 18.

20. Charles R. Wellford, "Crime and the Dimensions of Nations,"*International Journal of Criminology and Penology* 2 (1974): 2.

21. Gideon Vigderhouse, "Methodological Problems Confronting Cross-Cultural Criminological Research Using Official Data," *Human Relations* 31 (1978): 231.

14

Coverage of the Davis, Harris, and Hearst Trials by Leading Magazines

This chapter examines the treatment female defendants Angela Davis, Jean Harris, and Patricia Hearst received in three types of magazines: feminist, general interest, and traditional women's magazines. Jean Harris, the scorned older woman, had no champion among any of these media. Philosophy professor and communist leader Angela Davis was the favorite of the feminist publications. Patricia Hearst, the young heiress, was adopted by the traditional women's magazines but scorned by the left- and right-wing general interest ones.

Daily the media offer explanations of the world around us. Television, newspapers, and magazines provide us with information about newsworthy events. But what events are determined to be "newsworthy" and which people "count"? In the media, these decisions are made by those who choose the stories that appear, the stories that offer us explanations.

Of the thousands of homicide and other violent crimes that occur each year in the United States, the media select certain ones for special attention and publicity. The criteria for selection usually include the social status of those involved in the perpetration of the act, the victim, and/or the heinousness of the act itself.

In examining the attention that the media paid to Angela Davis, Jean Harris, and Patricia Hearst, we note that these are unusual offenders. First of all, they are women, and women usually account for less than 15 percent of all violent acts; second, they are of middle- and upper-middle-class backgrounds (two of them are well educated with successful careers). In addition to the "star" quality of the offenders, each act involved extraordinary dramatic effects. In the Harris case, the victim was a world-famous doctor; in the Davis and Hearst cases, the political ramifications were significant. It is no surprise, then, that all three cases received extensive publicity. The focus of this chapter is on the quality and tone of that publicity.

Before examining the media's treatment, we turn to profiles of each of the women, who differed by age, marital status, lifestyle, and political views. Angela Davis was black, the vice presidential candidate of the American Communist party, and a professor of philosophy. Jean Harris was white, fifty-seven years old, a divorced mother of two grown sons, and headmistress of an elite private boarding school. Patricia Hearst, a twenty-two-year-old heiress to the Hearst fortune, was kidnapped and recruited as a member of a political terrorist group. Each woman was charged with having committed at least one major violent offense: homicide, conspiracy to commit homicide, kidnapping, or bank robbery. All of them elected to present their case before juries, who responded to them differently: Angela Davis was acquitted, Jean Harris was convicted of second-degree murder, and Patty Hearst was found guilty of a lesser charge. Jean Harris was sentenced to a prison term of at least fifteen years, and Patty Hearst was pardoned by President Jimmy Carter after she served two years in prison.[1]

MEDIA COVERAGE

In addition to the extensive publicity they gave these women, the media also expressed strong and different opinions about their behavior and how the law should treat them. This chapter compares the coverage these women received in feminist, general interest, and traditional women's magazines. Among the feminist magazines we examined *Ms, New Woman, Savvy, Essence, Working Woman*, and *Self;* among the traditional women's magazines we looked at *Ladies Home Journal, Good Housekeeping, McCall's, Redbook, Family Circle*, and *Woman's Day*.[2] Under the general interest category we surveyed *Saturday Evening Post*, the *Nation, National Review*, the *New Republic*, the *New York Times Magazine, Ebony, Esquire, New York Magazine*, and *Harper's*.

We had different expectations about what we would find in the three types of magazines. Recognizing that in recent years traditional women's magazines had varied their contents and broadened their scope, we nevertheless still expected that they would respond to each of the three defendants differently and that their reactions to the defendants would be different from the reactions of the feminist and general media magazines.[3] We expected the women's magazines to provide little or no coverage of Angela Davis; if there were stories about her, they would be negative in tone. Patricia Hearst, we thought, would receive the most attention, and by and large the attention would be positive and forgiving. We believed Jean Harris would fall somewhere in between Davis and Hearst—she would not be ignored or treated in as negative a fashion as Angela Davis, but neither would she receive the attention or the positive press that would be accorded Patricia Hearst.

For different reasons, we expected that the general interest magazines would have difficulty condoning or condemning each of the three women. We thought

that they would be more troubled by and less forgiving in the Harris case—
Harris had shown herself to be a successful member of the establishment, but
her recent behavior clearly indicated that she was losing control of her life. We
expected that these magazines would have more respect for Angela Davis than
for Jean Harris or Patricia Hearst. Her position as a professor at a prestigious
university and her political activities would cause them to treat her seriously and
critically.

We anticipated that the general interest magazines would give a more diver-
sified response to Patricia Hearst than to the other women. The more left of
center the magazine, the more disdainful and punitive it would be toward Patricia
Hearst. These magazines would perceive the relatively short prison sentence, as
well as the presidential pardon, as exemplifying unequal justice—because she
was the daughter of a Hearst, she had available to her the kind of extraordinary
legal talent that many defendants could not afford. We believed that those magazines to the right of center, on the other hand, would exhibit sympathy and
understanding toward Patricia and her family, largely because of the suffering
she had endured.

Among feminist magazines, we believed that Angela Davis would be likely
to receive the most extensive coverage and the most respect, admiration, and
sympathy. Her militance, her defiance, and her poise would be admired, and
the meaning of her political views would be accepted without careful scrutiny.

Jean Harris, however, would be more complicated. We expected the feminists
and the traditional women's magazines to have similar reactions to her. On the
one hand, she shared many characteristics with the readership of traditional
magazines, albeit she was more successful. Her age, also, would work in her
favor—a fifty-seven-year-old woman who has been discarded by her lover of
many years in favor of a younger woman arouses empathy and sympathy. On
the other hand, ambivalence would arise from the revelations about her behavior
with her lover and her lack of control over her own desire.

Because the Harris story is more complicated socially and emotionally than
the others and corresponds to no clear political position, we felt that none of the
feminist magazines were likely to pay too much attention to her. We thought
that Patricia Hearst, in contrast, was likely to be viewed as negatively by the
feminists as she was positively by traditional women's magazines. The latter
would focus on who Patricia Hearst was, not who she became; and the feminist
magazines would focus negatively on her emergence as a "rich man's daughter
from her former role as an urban guerrilla." The feminist magazines would
denounce her family connections, and her return to the family fold would be
perceived as a threat to the women's movement.

THE TRADITIONAL WOMEN'S MAGAZINE

Both Jean Harris and Angela Davis were noticeable by their absence from
traditional magazine coverage. With one exception (an interview with Diana

Trilling about Jean Harris in *Vogue*) there were no stories about either Harris or Davis at any time before, during or after their trials.[4] The *Ladies Home Journal*, which annually lists America's seventy-five most influential women, never selected Davis for their list, nor did they consider her newsworthy.

Patricia Hearst, on the other hand, was eminently newsworthy. The traditional magazines printed stories not only about her directly, but also about or by members of her family, her former fiancé, a girlfriend, a friend of her mother, and the Hearts' family cook. For example, a July 1974 *Ladies Home Journal* profile of Patricia's mother, Catherine, was very sympathetic to Mrs. Hearst, characterizing her as "stoic" and as a mother who "loves her daughter even though she does not understand what has happened to her."[5]

Another article, also in *Ladies Home Journal*, is a profile of Patricia Hearst drawn by the Hearst's cook.[6] Patricia is described by the cook as being "a sturdier, more independent girl" than her sisters, and as someone who also had a great "need for love." Patty is described as a girl with spunk who was brutally kidnapped. The cook seems to lean toward the view that Patricia joined her captors because of her need for love anywhere she could find it.

In early 1976, *McCall's* published a piece by Hearst's fiancé, Steven Weed, and his ghostwriter.[7] Weed described Patricia's schoolgirl crush on him when he was her high school math teacher, but insisted that this was no ordinary schoolgirl crush: "She seemed as much a woman as a seventeen-year-old." He described Hearst as "sexually precocious" as well as "stubborn and independent." When they had set up a household together, Patricia was portrayed as trying very hard to be everything that a mate should be. Weed wrote that Hearst was single-minded in pursuit of her goals. He also said that she was "double-natured, at one moment warm and caring and the next moment scathingly sarcastic."

The next piece appeared in *McCall's* and was written by a young woman of Hearst's age and social background—another insider's view.[8] The author believed that Hearst was an active and dedicated member of some leftist group, claiming that as a young girl in school Patty was "defiant and stubborn." The Symbionese Liberation Army (SLA), wrote the author, "gave her danger, real stakes, the sense that everything mattered." The story, designed to be sympathetic, shows Hearst as having little choice in her course of conduct after the kidnapping. Yet it also suggests that Hearst made a conscious choice to be a freedom fighter.

Another group of articles appeared after Hearst was tried and convicted of bank robbery. Hearst's defense attorney, F. Lee Bailey, filed a two-part series in *Ladies Home Journal*.[9] Meeting Hearst for the first time, Bailey found her "physically and emotionally . . . numb . . . incredibly small." She spoke in a "flat . . . monotone, and if she could answer in one word, she never bothered with two." It is in these articles that Hearst is clearly singled out for the first time as a victim. All the previous pieces, whether superficially sympathetic or not, had portrayed Hearst more as a wrongdoer than a victim. Here, for the first time, we read descriptions of Hearst's captivity and subsequent time with the SLA.

Another piece was entitled "Why Patty Hearst's Trial Was Unfair." Bailey writes that the case was lost for one of two reasons: either the judge improperly allowed evidence into the trial about Hearst's behavior after the robbery, or the government, the jurors, and many Americans felt that Patty Hearst had become a symbol of the lax discipline in our permissive society.

Not surprisingly, a two-parter in *Good Housekeeping* by Al Johnson, Bailey's associate, makes much the same argument and evokes the same feelings of injustice.[10] Johnson is far less cynical than Bailey, injecting into the story his feelings for the poor, battered Patricia Hearst, describing her as an emotional cripple. He portrays the defense as a fight for Hearst's very life, convinced that she is dying and that a prison term would kill her. This is by far the most sympathetic published portrayal of Hearst.

The last two stories on Patricia Hearst in the traditional women's magazines were based on interviews with her. The first appeared in *Redbook*, where Hearst was portrayed as happier and more stable than in previous articles.[11] Characterizing Hearst as a "bright, energetic, and thoroughly spontaneous young woman," the author mentions Patricia's "very private, special sisterhood" with her real sisters. The author compares Hearst's captivity to white slavery or forced prostitution, portraying Hearst as a good girl who was turned into a zombie through "male aggression."

In sharp contrast to their lack of coverage of the Harris and Davis trials, the traditional women's magazines gave the Hearst saga extensive and varied coverage. Perhaps Shana Alexander had it right when she wrote that Patty Hearst could be "anyone's daughter" and that all of us are vulnerable.[12] Davis and Harris, on the other hand, were "special types"—the readers of the traditional women's magazines could distance themselves from these women and see their behavior as arising out of unusual circumstances.

THE FEMINIST MEDIA

Of the three defendants, Angela Davis received the most extensive coverage in the feminist media. She was their heroine: a black intellectual, revolutionary activist from the middle class who renounced her background and cast her lot with the oppressed.

Kate Millett, in a two-part series that appeared in *Ms* in August and September 1972, accused the prosecution of trying Davis as a woman,[13] on the evidence of love letters exchanged between her and prisoner George Jackson.[14] Millett, who wrote of Angela Davis in the most adoring of tones ("a rare and great woman"; "she takes my breath away"), claims that the case against Davis was circumstantial, a reprisal for Davis's activities in the Black Liberation Movement and in prison reform.

In addition to Millett's two-part series, *Ms* carried excerpts from Angela

Davis's autobiography and an article, "Black Women," that she had written for the *Black Scholar*.[15] It also carried Karen Durbin's review of her autobiography, which was not as one-sided as Millett's series.[16] Durbin characterized Davis as "a true intellectual, someone who finds the world of pure ideas a vivid and compelling place." But Durbin, unlike Millett, also maintained enough distance from her subject to observe: "I wonder if, had Davis been fat, ugly and inarticulate, we would be reading her story now, selling for $8.95 and dustjacketed with a glossy photographic portrait of Davis' handsome, sensitive face, dramatically silhouetted against a backdrop of dark red."

Ms also ran stories on Jean Harris and Patricia Hearst. Lindsey Van Gelden, in an article on Harris, captured well the ambivalence of the feminist movement and its media toward Jean Harris.[17] In her opening paragraph Van Gelden wrote, "Perhaps the most striking thing about her case is the 'schizy' incongruity of it all, the accomplished, independent, frosty-cool educator versus the sap operatic stereotype of the jilted love-junkie, the woman who couldn't live without her man."

It is the "love-junkie" aspect of Jean Harris about which the feminist media are so intolerant. Much of Van Gelden's uneasiness and ambivalence toward Jean Harris is the result of her feelings about Harris's lawyer, Joel Aurnou.[18] Van Gelden wrote of him:

Aurnou's defense relies on a rather stereotypical image of the long-suffering, faithful female. "She is a lady, refined. . . . [Tarnower] saw her as a companion he could take anywhere and not be embarrassed, whereas his other women had other talents, chiefly sexual." Various writers and legal investigators, I've heard, are currently beating the bushes to find supposed back-street boyfriends of Harris' who would presumably destroy her virtuous image. Aurnou assured me that such searches are in vain: "Harris was true blue. When you have a Magnificent Obsession there isn't room for anyone else." Does this mean that only a Madonna can feel suicidally depressed about her relationship? Isn't this the same criterion that has been applied to rape victims who have had to present proof of chastity before juries find them sympathetic?

New Woman excerpted the last chapter of Diana Trilling's book, *Mrs. Harris: The Death of the Scarsdale Diet Doctor*, and in so doing presented Harris in a most positive light, vividly recounting her poised, articulate, and thoughtful statement to the court after the jury had announced its verdict.[19] But Diana Trilling also wrote: "Mrs. Harris didn't come crawling to him [Dr. Tarnower] for drugs, but the way in which she crawled to him for love was like nothing so much as the behavior of an addict. She was totally shorn of self-respect."

In the end, Diana Trilling prescribed containment, enclosure, restriction as the medicine Jean Harris needed to mend socially and to rebuild her body:

The structure of prison life could turn out to be a better source of freedom for Mrs. Harris than her adorned but limitless world. More important, the gifts of mind may now be put to use as they never were before. There is work to be done in the sphere of prison education, serious work of a kind for which she has the training, energy and intelligence. She may now be splendid in a way that she never knew how to be or dared to be.

If the feminist media were awed by Angela Davis and ambivalent about Jean Harris, they felt a mixture of sadness, disappointment, contempt, and disdain toward Patricia Hearst. They found her an unsophisticated woman or young girl who lacked intellect and insight into many of her experiences. Indeed, the only sympathetic coverage she received in the feminist media occurred while she was still in captivity.

In 1974 *Ms* carried an article in which Lucinda Franks blamed Patricia's parents for not loving her enough, for not having provided her with enough emotional security to withstand the brainwashing she underwent at the hands of the SLA.[20] The most eloquent evaluation of Patricia Hearst by the feminist media is to be found in the Franks piece. Franks took Patricia Hearst seriously and respected her: "She had told us that she is prepared to die for her revolution, and I think we must believe her. She speaks with the voice of a young woman so alienated and disaffected by the malaise of this country that no other option seems open to her."

In contrast, Robin Morgan wrote in the March 1979 issue of *Ms*, which appeared after the trial but before the pardon, when Patricia Hearst was still in prison:

I had the feeling that it was difficult for Patricia to be curious or to feel very deeply about anything; that she was barely listening to her own words as well as anyone else's; that she was utterly preoccupied, yet unacquainted with herself; that she had turned inward but had somehow got no further, as if in terror of finding nothing there. Women of the powerful are trained for precisely such vapidity.[21]

Morgan is critical of Hearst, disappointed that she is not more of an intellectual and a feminist. At her kindest, Morgan is ambivalent and wishes Patricia Hearst a speedy release.

THE GENERAL INTEREST MAGAZINES

One would have expected the Harris trial to have generated the most general media interest. Harris was white, upper middle class, middle aged, divorced, the mother of two, and successful in her own right. More people would have been able to identify with her than with Hearst, who was young, rich, and sheltered, or with Davis, who was black, a revolutionary, and an intellectual. Moreover, Harris's victim was a nationally known celebrity doctor.

But the Harris trial received much less coverage in the general media than did the Davis or Hearst trials.[22] Compared, for example, to twenty-two stories about Davis and eighteen about Hearst, there were only three about Harris in the magazines surveyed. When we extended our list and included *Time, News-*

week, and *U.S. News and World Report*, the amount of coverage of the Davis and Hearst trials was much greater than that of the Harris trial.

In one of the three pieces on the Harris trial, Sue Halpern wrote in the *Nation*: "The case has been made into a public spectacle, a morality play, directed by the social fathers—the Establishment. . . . it is intended to put women in their proper place—that is, a submissive place. They're assuaging anxieties engendered by the women's movement. The lesson is that women won't be able to get away with murder."[23] Halpern also criticized women who were writing books about Harris for adding to the sensationalism without lending any depth, insight, or understanding to the case or the participant.

Anne Bernay's article in the *New Republic* was unsympathetic to both Harris and Tarnower, claiming they got what they deserved.[24] Bernay diagnosed Harris as being "hopefully masochistic." In the end, according to Bernay, Harris "had no ego, no identity, no center, no control over the forces in her life. The Harris-Tarnower affair should be exploited as a cautionary tale of the evils of female submissiveness and then used as a piece of promotional copy for the women's movement."

Unlike Angela Davis and Patricia Hearst, the little coverage that Jean Harris received in the general interest media was negative and punitive. As we shall see, the *Saturday Evening Post* made Patricia Hearst its special property, and *Ebony* adopted Angela Davis. But no author or magazine came forth as Jean Harris's defender, apologist, or benefactor.

Among the general interest magazines, *Ebony* gave Angela Davis the most coverage, publishing three major articles about her over a two and a half year time span.[25] In each, Davis was characterized as a successful, glamorous black woman who had attracted not only national but international attention. About her politics, about the Communist party, about terrorism, they said little. On the other hand, they paid much attention to her childhood, to her education, and to the fact that she was black and beautiful. They also tried to tie Angela Davis to the mainstream civil rights struggle, a theory not supported by the facts.

William Buckley's column in the *National Review* compared Angela Davis to Gloria Steinem.[26] It had a cynical tone and asked rhetorically why Steinem and her organization would wish to be associated with Davis.

The *Nation* and the *New Republic* expressed concern that Angela Davis receive a fair trial. The *New York Times Magazine* put Davis on the front cover and ran an extensive article about her trial.[27] The picture accompanying the article showed her in a miniskirt with the caption "Imperious Beauty." The article provided in-depth coverage of the events of the trial, but its main focus was Davis's codefendant Russell Magee, who was described as a victim, ignored by everyone, while Davis was a political exploiter and manipulator.

The *Saturday Evening Post*'s coverage of Patricia Hearst was comparable to *Ebony*'s coverage of Angela Davis.[28] It described Patricia as an attractive young American girl who had been to hell, survived, and had now returned. Even more than the traditional women's magazines, it championed the cause of Patricia

Hearst as the victim. It welcomed her lovingly back into the fold and urged everyone to let bygones be bygones. The April 1976 issue had several articles emphasizing this theme. One editorial began with these words: "We are glad Patty Hearst is alive. Her greatest sin was to be born and reared rich. In this day and age wealth puts a sensitive young person at a considerable disadvantage, especially during the college years." The same editorial compared Hearst to returned prisoners of war:

Patty Hearst had a number of decided disadvantages compared to the military P.O.W.'s. She had received no training at all on how to cope with the political prisoner status.

Once returned to society, Patricia Hearst had no easy path. Like the returned P.O.W.'s and missionaries, she initially showed signs of confusion. She could not trust her parents who she characteristically thought had turned against her.

We are glad Patty Hearst is alive. Already she has survived great danger. We hope she will be dealt with fairly, even-handedly and gently—with some understanding of the ordeal that she went through. There but for the grace of God could go a child of a thousand other parents in our land.

Another piece in this issue was written by Charles L. Gould, former publisher of a Hearst-owned paper and a long-time Hearst family friend. Gould's description of Hearst was of a "wee-mannered child" who grew and developed into "a lovely, gracious, gentle and outgoing person." He warns the reader, "Your wife or mother or daughter would have broken as did Patricia, had any of them been subjected to the same treatment."

The *Nation* and the *New Republic* charged the media with covering the Patty Hearst story in a "life-like parody of Hearst journalism." They accused others in the press of "bloated journalism" and sensationalism. The *Nation* summed up its reaction to the case and to the coverage it had received as follows:

She was a kidnap victim. She was a gun-moll robber. She was a revolutionary. She was a poor little rich girl. Conventional, eccentric, exploited, she was always a celebrity. She and her case lent themselves best to the crude taste of her family's reactionary press. The question of who she was seemed to matter more than what she was, innocent or guilty.

There is no large lesson in this grubby story. . . . But if all this had happened to a young woman who was not named Hearst, she would still be in prison—doing, instead of making, time. The idea of equal justice for all is once again the principal victim of the Hearst melodrama.[29]

And the *New Republic* wrote:

Revolutionary terrorism may be the most serious and least understood issue closing in on bicentennial America. The press coverage of the Hearst case seems symptomatic of our ignorance, much of it deliberate and defensive. What might have been a remarkable opportunity to use a famous name to educate the public on the new scope and complexity of the problem has been largely lost in the comforting stereotypes and platitudes we use to inure ourselves to political violence.[30]

William Buckley, who does not generally share the *Nation*'s or the *New Republic*'s liberal editorial views, made much the same assessment of Hearst. To the refrain of "Whatever Lola Wants, Lola Gets," Buckley described his perception of Patty Hearst, of what happened to her and why it happened.[31]

When, as a teenager, she had set her cap at a young teacher, Steve Weed, she persuaded her parents to transfer her to the school in which he taught, and she promptly had an affair with him. In due course she moved in with him, in an apartment her parents rented for her, and adopted the lifestyle of the day, a lifestyle that was big on personal gratification, short on responsibility, unmindful of hurt to family and friends. She was doing her thing.

But when Patty Hearst got more than she asked for, at much more than the usual cost of selfish peccadillos, when she was brutally put to the test, seemingly there was nothing there to sustain her: no religion (she had dropped away from the Church years before), no feeling of community with family, with class, with culture, with country—no underpinnings to strengthen her will to resist.

In a reversal of the *Post*'s analogy to the prisoners of war, Buckley wrote:

America's prisoners of war in Vietnam had shown what disciplined men of resolution could endure if the goal—in their case, simply God and Country—was kept in sight, cherished, honored. But Patty Hearst, untrained, undisciplined, pitifully young—totally unmotivated—had nothing, and succumbed.

Buckley concluded his piece on the only note of pity he permitted himself. "She told a story with holes you could drop the Grand Canyon through, but despite it all, Patricia Hearst, in her first presentation in Judge Carter's court, was more convincing than Tania the Bank Robber, Tania the Revolutionary posing with tommy gun in front of the coiled serpent of the SLA. And more pitiable."

CONCLUDING REMARKS

Some of our expectations about how the three kinds of magazines would cover the Davis, Harris, and Hearst trials were fulfilled, and some were not.

The major difference between our expectations and the data was that we anticipated more coverage of the Jean Harris trial than it actually received from each of the three types of magazines. The indifference of traditional women's magazines to her trial and to Harris herself was most surprising. While we expected that they would be ambivalent and troubled by her, we thought her case would be of sufficient appeal (the older loyal woman, discarded by her lover for a younger model after years of faithful service) to merit sympathetic coverage and analysis. Instead, the traditional women's magazines ignored her. The feminist magazines, as expected, scorned her. The general interest media analyzed the strengths and weaknesses of her case and her lawyer's strategy, but avoided value judgments and provided less extensive coverage than for the Davis and Hearst cases.

The Davis coverage fit our expectations quite closely. The traditional women's magazines ignored her, the feminist magazines made her their own, and the general interest media recognized her significance and treated the substantive issues raised in her trial as serious and important.

So, too, was the coverage of Hearst consistent with our expectations. The traditional women's magazines gave her much more attention than they did Davis and Harris, and by and large the coverage was positive and forgiving. The feminists paid less attention to her than to Davis and tended to be disdainful and negative toward her. The general interest magazines varied more in their reactions toward her than they did toward Harris and Davis. The *Saturday Evening Post* adopted her, just as *Ebony* adopted Davis. But both magazines of the left (the *Nation*) and the right (*National Review*) were negative and condescending in their treatment.

There is little in the literature to explain the media's rejection of Harris. While the *Saturday Evening Post*'s supportive response to Hearst must be seen in the context of her position as part of a media empire, media coverage of the Harris case is more difficult to explain. Society, and therefore the media, could not accept the image of an older woman and her lover. Thus, while Angela Davis was a heroine and Patty Hearst was a victim, Jean Harris was neither.

As Sydney Schanberg wrote, "Whether we're white or black, struggling or well-heeled, we're all crammed full of conventional wisdom, stereotypes, easy definitions of groups and communities."[32] It is these easy definitions and stereotypes that unfortunately determine what is newsworthy and who "counts."

NOTES

1. The initial appearance of the media events was as follows: the first stories about Davis appeared in 1969 and ran until 1975; stories about the Hearst kidnapping ran from 1974 to 1979; and the Harris case was in the news from 1980 through 1982. Each of the cases has had stories reappear at significant dates, such as Patty Hearst's wedding.

2. We did not find articles on any of the three defendants in *Savvy, Self, Family Circle,* or *Woman's Day.*

3. We recognize that traditional women's magazines have been affected to some extent by the women's movement and by the socioeconomic, political, and cultural changes that have occurred in American society since the 1960s. We refer specifically to the higher proportion of women in the labor force, to the increased number of female-headed families, to the increased number of mature women who are going back to colleges and universities, and to the movement for passage of the Equal Rights Amendment (ERA). Nevertheless, we believe that the traditional women's magazines still retain their "model" image of the woman as homemaker, wife, and mother—a person interested in good nutrition for her family and in making her home an attractive, comfortable place in which to live, someone who has most of the responsibility for the family entertainment and social activities, and as a parent responsible for the physical and psychological well-

being of her children. But because the traditional media are also responsive to the afore-mentioned changes, the topics and issues considered appropriate for a woman's magazine have broadened. Articles now appear about the stock market, tax shelters, budgetary analysis, the environment, and population control. Even in the most traditional of these magazines, there is an emphasis on appealing to and presenting issues of interest to the "modern woman." Recognizing that the editorial policy of a magazine would influence decisions of coverage, we surveyed a wide range of general interest magazines.

4. Mary Cantwell, "Diana Trilling on Women, Sexual Pride... and Jean Harris," *Vogue*, September 1981, p. 548.

5. Adeline Ross, "The Private Ordeal of Catherine Hearst," *Ladies Home Journal*, July, 1974, p. 65.

6. Judith Stone, "Patty Hearst: The Hearst Family Cook Provides Another View," *Ladies Home Journal*, October 1974, p. 92.

7. Steven Weed with Scott Swauton, "My Life with Patty Hearst," *McCall's*, January 1976, p. 88.

8. Leslie Redlich, "The Puzzle of Patty Hearst," *McCall's*, February 1974, p. 28.

9. F. Lee Bailey with John Greenup, "Patty Hearst: The Untold Story," *Ladies Home Journal*, September 1976, p. 36; continued as "Why Patty Hearst's Trial Was Unfair," ibid., October 1976, p. 50.

10. J. Albert Johnson with Phyllis Batelle, "Patty Hearst—The Way It Really Was and Is," *Good Housekeeping*, February 1977, p. 94; continued, under same title, in ibid., March 1977, p. 104.

11. Kathy Barry, "The Real Patricia Hearst Story: 'What I Couldn't Say Until Now,' " *Redbook*, October 1978, p. 112.

12. Shana Alexander, "Patty Hearst Was Punished for Our Sins,"*Esquire*, February 27, 1979, p. 34.

13. Kate Millett, "Kate Millett on Angela Davis," *Ms*, August 1972, p. 107.

14. Millett writes of the letters: "In fact they are not really love letters, they are essays. Essays on the role of black women on the depravity of the black bourgeoisie, on the need for prison research, and on the importance of a knowledge of history. They are letters of a woman who is in love with ideas and with an ideal of freedom."

15. Angela Davis, "Angela Davis on Black Women," *Ms*, August 1972, p. 55.

16. Karen Durbin, review of *Angela Davis: An Autobiography*, *Ms*, February 1975, p. 38.

17. Lindsey Van Gelden, "The Scarsdale Diet Doctor Murder Case: Jean Harris Won't Be the Only One on Trial," *Ms*, August 1980, p. 69.

18. Kate Millett did not like Archie Moore, Angela Davis's attorney, but that did not affect her feelings about Davis.

19. Diana Trilling, "I Did Not Murder Dr. Tarnower," *New Woman*, March 1982, p. 32.

20. Lucinda Franks, "As American as Apple Pie," *Ms*, October 1974, p. 66.

21. Robin Morgan, "Why Should We Care About Patty Hearst?" *Ms*, March 1979, p. 60.

22. Here we recognize that the length of time each was a "media event" is a factor in the actual number of articles written about the three women. *Readers' Guide to Periodical Literature* was surveyed for relevant articles. Stories were found on the following time scale: Angela Davis, March 1969–February 1976; Patricia Hearst, March 1974–March 1979; Jean Harris, March 1980–March 1982. (As a check, the *Guide* was

surveyed for the appearance of the name two years previous to the first citation on each individual.) Clearly the time span is weighted in favor of Davis. However, accounting for the time factor and the prominence of the Hearst name, it is still apparent that Harris was all but ignored by the feminist, traditional women's, and general interest magazines. Considering an average number of articles per year, the coverage of the women's stories is as follows: Davis, 3.0 articles per year; Hearst, 4.0 articles per year; Harris, 2.0 articles per year.

23. Sue M. Halpern, "Ping! Not Some Chicano Woman," *The Nation*, March 16, 1981, p. 341.

24. Anne Bernay, "Cad and Mouse," *New Republic*, March 7, 1981, p. 9.

25. Charles L. Sanders, "The Radicalization of Angela Davis," *Ebony*, July 1971, p. 114; Robert DeLeon, "A New Look at Angela Davis," ibid., April 1972, p. 53; Louis Robinson, "How Psychology Helped Free Angela Davis," ibid., February 1973, p. 44.

26. William F. Buckley, "Mss. Davis and Steinem," *National Review*, December 31, 1971, p. 1486.

27. Sol Stein, "Campaign to Free Angela Davis and Russell Magee," *New York Times Magazine*, June 27, 1971, p. 8.

28. Charles L. Gould, "Patty Hearst in Perspective," and "An Editorial: The Peril of Patricia," *Saturday Evening Post*, April 1976, p. 4.

29. "Case Closed," *The Nation*, December 11, 1976, p. 612.

30. R. Morris, "Patty Hearst and the New Terror," *New Republic*, November 22, 1975, p. 8.

31. "Truth or Consequences?" *National Review*, March 5, 1976, p. 201.

32. Sydney H. Schanberg, "Deciding Who Counts," *New York Times*, December 11, 1984.

15

Women as Political Terrorists

Little is known about the roles women perform in terrorist organizations, the extent to which women are involved in terrorist activities, and the kinds of women who are drawn to various types of terrorist movements. This chapter offers some speculations and provides some data on these issues. It culls information from different historical periods, societies, and cultures.

Using as much data as we could locate from a variety of countries and historical periods, this chapter examines the roles women perform as terrorists and political criminals. But we acknowledge at the outset that our data describe only a small proportion of the known terrorist organizations.

We tried to collect information from a variety of historical periods, nationalities, and cultures, in the hope that this approach would allow us to throw light on some current misconceptions about the female terrorist. Unfortunately, the available information is unsystematic and largely anecdotal. Consequently, we can draw only a roughly sketched collective profile of the typical female terrorist and discuss only briefly the roles that women have played and continue to play in terrorist groups.

The main question, and the one that serves as the focus for our discussion, is whether, as trumpeted in the popular press, women's terrorist activities are a "side effect" of the women's liberation movement. For example, in September 1974, Daniel Green, a reporter for the *National Observer*, wrote the following analysis of women's liberation, which took up much of the newspaper's front page.

THE DARK SIDE OF WOMEN'S LIBERATION: CRIME TAKES A FEMALE TURN

Before the advent of militant feminism, female radicals were little more than groupies in the amorphous conglomeration of revolutionary and antiwar groups that came to be known collectively in the 60's as The Movement. Like camp followers of old, they functioned principally as cooks, flunkies, and sex objects.

Sexual equality came to the Movement in the gas-polluted streets of Chicago during the '68 Democratic Convention. Enraged by the tactics of Mayor Daley's police, Middle American daughters raised for gentler things shrieked obscenities and hurled rocks as ferociously as veteran street fighters. From then on, guerrilla women were dominant figures in the splintered Movement, particularly the defiantly militant Weatherman faction, which they purged of "macho sexism" and renamed the Weather Underground.[1]

The proponents of such a view are not limited to alarmists in the media, but include sociologists as well. Hofmann, for example, reports that among Italian and West German sociologists the "significant female membership in radical and terrorist groups is being viewed as an unwelcome consequence of the women's liberation movement."[2] Is such a view plausible?

If the women's liberation movement has brought about an increase in the participation of women in radical and terrorist groups, then one would expect that prior to the women's liberation movement the role of women in radical political protests would be much less noticeable. Historical evidence, however, does not support this conjecture. Not only is the active participation of women in revolutionary movements commonplace, but women in revolutionary movements have not limited their participation to supportive, housekeeping roles.[3]

For example, Broido's 1977 history of the revolutionary movement in Russia during the reign of Alexander II shows that women were founders and leaders of many revolutionary groups and were regarded by some men as the driving force of the revolution.[4] In this vein, Serge Krauchinsky, a Russian revolutionary of the 1870s, wrote of the profound sense of duty which "women possess in much greater measure—let us admit it—than men." He continued, "That is why the Russian revolutionary movement owes its almost religious fire above all to them, and why, so long as there are women in it, it will remain invincible."[5] Moreover, the revolutionary activity of women in Russia is not a period anomaly; it has substantial continuity. Consider, for example, the leadership role played by Alexandra Kollontai in the Bolshevik Revolution.[6]

Historically, women have also been active in revolutionary movements in Latin America. Jaquette claims that female revolutionaries can be traced back at least as far as Cecilia Tupac Amaro, who led an Indian revolt in 1780 against the Spanish.[7] In the early nineteenth century, Juana Azuduy, Juana Robles, and Loreto Sanchez de Peon were famous female revolutionaries. Azuduy held the rank of lieutenant colonel in the revolutionary army of Alto Peru (now Bolivia). Both Robles and Sanchez de Peon were renowned for their exploits as spies and messengers. In the mid-twentieth century, women also held important positions in the Cuban Revolution. There is further evidence of female participation in the five rural guerrilla movements (Peru, Colombia, Bolivia, Guatemala, Venezuela) that followed in the wake of the Cuban success. However, the extent of their participation and its nature are not known.

In the last decade, with the proliferation of revolutionary and terrorist groups in Latin America, the female terrorist has become a familiar face in the news, playing an active leadership role. As Tupac Amaro is reported to have said, "First, let me tell you that a woman is never more equal to a man than behind a forty-five pistol."[8]

A study of insurgent movements in the Far East conducted by the U.S. Department of the Army reported that about one-third of all guerrillas captured in Korea in 1951–1952 were women.[9] In Malaya between 5 and 15 percent of the Min Yuen (the underground army of the insurgent movement) were women, and several women were said to have played leadership roles in the Huk uprising in the Philippines.

One cannot, of course, make sweeping generalizations from such limited findings, but the range suggested by the U.S. Army study is consistent with estimates by other researchers. According to McClure, women constitute one-fifth to one-third of the participants in terrorist groups in Germany and Japan.[10]

What kinds of women become terrorists? Biographies, diaries, and police reports reveal that they are usually well educated and are drawn from the middle or upper classes, even though the revolution for which they struggle is intended to better the lot of the lower classes.[11] For example, the women in the Baader-Meinhof gang, Ulrike Meinhof and Gudrun Ensslin, came from middle- to upper-middle-class backgrounds, as did the four women of the Symbionese Liberation Army (SLA).[12] Fusaka Shigenobu, founder of the Japanese Red Army (JRA), is the daughter of a Tokyo insurance executive.[13] And the early female Russian terrorists of the 1800s came largely from the nobility.[14]

We can gain some insight into the terrorist and revolutionary careers of women by investigating the age patterns of the participants. The women's ages extend from adolescence through the late thirties. The average age of German and American female terrorists is the mid-thirties. For the Japanese it is just under thirty.[15] The Department of the Army reported the following age distributions for captured male and female Korean insurgents:[16]

Age	Male	Female
Under 17	5%	26%
18–30	49	30
31–40	32	20
Over 40	14	24
Total	100%	100%
	(2000)	(700)

We see that the age distribution of women is much more uniform than that of men, which is highly concentrated in the eighteen to forty age bracket.

In examining these distributions, two questions come to mind. Why are there proportionally more girls (26 percent) than boys (5 percent) under age seventeen? And why are there proportionally more women (24 percent) than men (14 percent) over forty? In answer to the first question, one might make a plausible argument that young girls are often socially invisible and hence make choice recruits for insurgent movements. Only future research and accumulation of more data will show whether this is the case. The greater proportion of women than men over age forty suggests that once a woman joins a revolutionary group, she stays. The age pattern might also reflect women's reluctance to undertake revolutionary activity while they have young children at home. Alternatively, it may be that male guerrillas are more likely than their female counterparts to experience combat. If so, their chances of death are greater, explaining the lower proportion of men in the highest age group. To evaluate these explanations we need to know what roles women play in terrorist groups.

There is a good deal of disagreement about whether the division of labor by gender is traditional or egalitarian in terrorist groups. Some argue that women join terrorist groups because their men do. Jaquette, for example, notes that female revolutionaries are often wives or lovers of male revolutionaries. This may well be true, but it is not clear whether the women simply follow their men, or whether love blossoms between comrades. In general, those who hold that women follow their men into insurgency (''whither thou goest'') also claim that women's roles in revolutionary groups mirror female roles in society. They provide supportive companionship, nurse the sick, and run errands. They are fetchers and carriers.[17] By contrast, other writers hold that women terrorists are vicious and fanatical, adopting supermacho roles.

For those familiar with American criminological theory, the argument that women terrorists adopt a supermacho identity must remind them of Cohen's theory of reaction formation in male juvenile delinquents.[18] Cohen's theory, now regarded as inadequate, is that lower-class males, because they are unable to succeed according to the middle-class standards by which they are judged, adopt an identity and behavior pattern the direct opposite of middle-class norms. A similar argument seems to be used to explain women's terrorist activity. We feel that such psychological romanticizing of women terrorists befuddles the question of their real motives, and is neither verifiable nor falsifiable.

Of course, some women terrorists may fall into one pigeonhole or another—the housekeeper versus Amazon dichotomy—but arguments on this score seem to generate more heat than light. Moreover, one cannot help but hear an echo of the Victorian debate over the female criminal: Is she a poor, misled creature or is she a messenger of the devil? To go beyond this superficial analysis requires finer distinctions in our terminology.

Contemporary terrorist groups can be divided into two categories: idealists and nationalists.[19] Inspired by vague notions of world liberation and emphasizing the dramaturgy of violence, the idealist terrorists are the most eccentric and bizarre of all terrorist groups. Included in this category are the Japanese Red Army, the Baader-Meinhof gang, and the SLA. By contrast, nationalist groups stress the political rights and liberation of the people in a specific geographic area. Included in this category are the Irish Republican Army (IRA), the Palestine Liberation Organization (PLO), and perhaps the Tupamaros and the Algerian

National Liberation Front (FLN). This dichotomy is not entirely satisfactory because it leaves no place for groups like the British suffragists in the second decade of this century (Hachey, 1976), but it does accommodate the groups currently of paramount interest to researchers and the public.[20]

In idealist groups, there seems to be little, if any, division of labor by sex. Thus, for example, both Ulrike Meinhof and Gudrun Ensslin planned and carried out many of the violent acts of the Baader-Meinhof group. Similarly, women in related terrorist groups such as the Revolutionary Cell and Red Army Faction— whose founder, Fusaka Shigenobu, was a woman—"are often involved in kidnapping, murder, arson and bombings."[21] The presence of women in activist-leadership roles in these groups may be a function of their anarchical political ideologies, compounded by an extreme scarcity of members. Since the groups are very small, they may have found that a division of labor results in nothing being accomplished. For them, the actual shootings and bombings in the name of their cause are far more important than who is doing the shooting and bombing (unless, of course, the social identity of a member can be transformed into ideological ammunition, e.g., Patty Hearst). It is in these groups that the members are most likely to come from the middle and upper classes.

By contrast, nationalist terrorist and revolutionary groups, such as the IRA and the FLN, are more stable and have attracted more people to their causes. Nationalist groups also draw members from a greater variety of social classes. Since the 1960s, for example, peasants and the urban poor have become increasingly important as terrorists and revolutionaries in Latin America.[22]

Fanon's study of the Algerian Revolution demonstrates how women's roles in revolutionary groups may change as the group's relationship to its enemies changes.[23] It also illustrates our contention that revolutionary theory and practice can lead to a breakdown in traditional female roles, rather than a breakdown in roles targeted by terrorist activity.

In the beginning, Algerian women were not involved in the movement except in the mountains, where they cared for and helped the guerrillas. Thus, until 1955 the revolution was fought almost entirely by men. As the French gradually adapted themselves to Algeria's male-dominated FLN guerrilla tactics, new forms of combat were needed by the revolutionaries. The wives of some militants became involved, and gradually the movement began to accept all types of women: widows, divorcées, old, and lastly, young women.

The involvement of women in the movement changed the traditional roles of women. But the existence of the traditional roles also created a setting in which female guerrillas could be outstandingly effective. For example, the French attempted to destroy the Algerian culture by breaking down customs about women wearing veils and restricting women's movements outside of the home. The Algerians responded by Europeanizing some women (i.e., unveiling them) so that they could pass as European and mix with the enemy more freely. Their duties included acting as liaison agents, message bearers, and lookouts; carrying weapons, bombs, and money; infiltrating and spying; and maintaining safe houses. Often women would carry the bombs or weapons for a terrorist attack into the target areas. The men would retrieve them at the last moment and carry out the attack. When the French learned of the tactics using unveiled women, the Algerians had veiled women carry contraband. This worked until the French began to search everybody on the streets systematically.[24]

In the Algerian case, women performed certain tasks because their special status as women gave them freedom of movement. Initially, women had certain advantages over men in terrorist activities. Not only could they do what men did in terms of shooting and bombing, but they could also get away with certain things because they were women—they could move and operate in areas where men would arouse suspicion. The frequent use of this advantage, however, incurred diminishing returns. As more and more women were apprehended, women became "visible" to the French, and thus were unable to operate more openly than men.

The important point is that revolutionary tactics demanded abandoning the traditional roles assigned to women in Algeria. In this case, revolutionary activities led to the liberation (used here in both the national and the sexual sense of the term) of women, rather than vice versa.

Accounts of men's and women's activities in the FLN and the IRA suggest that nationalist movements tend to have a more rigid division of labor between men and women than do idealist revolutionary movements. In nationalist movements women are more likely to act as couriers, spies, and occasionally saboteurs, in contrast to the more sex-neutral patterns found in the idealist groups. These differences may be due to the ideology of the movement or to its size, which reflects the availability of men to perform all of the "front-line" activities.

The story of Maria McGuire's involvement in the Provisional IRA (Provos) casts light on the division of labor by sex in another nationalist guerrilla movement. According to her account, McGuire was middle class, educated, and in her twenties when she joined the IRA for patriotic reasons. Her family was apolitical, and she had had little contact with the IRA before joining the group. She left the Provos after one year, so her experience probably differs somewhat from that of people with more enduring involvement.

McGuire's first tasks centered around policy discussions and preparation of scripts and tapes for broadcast. McGuire claims that although she was not involved in making decisions about policy, the leaders wanted to discuss policy matters with her because of her middle-class, non-Republican background, a type of background rare among IRA members. But her role in those policy discussions, focused as it was on the relationship between the Provos and the British, seemed to have become more important as her time in service lengthened. While her involvement was at first confined to the political aspects of the movement, she subsequently became involved in the Provos' military operations when she accompanied David O'Connell, a Provisional leader, to the Continent to buy arms. Her role on this trip was to provide cover for O'Connell, making it easier for him to blend in. She also carried the money for the arms deal because it was less suspicious for her, as a woman, to do so. The arms deal was botched, but she became something of a Provisional hero because of her escape from the police. She eventually left the Provisional movement when she could no longer accept or justify its policies concerning the bombing and killing of civilians.

We cannot say whether McGuire's experience in the IRA generalizes to that of all IRA women. Her experiences and the activities in which she engaged appear to be consistent with what we know about the roles of women as terrorists in nationalist movements: she carried contraband and money and acted as a cover for male leaders.

Some female supporters of revolutionary movements would place women in a lower and more oppressed position than they presently occupy. Women actively involved in the Ayatollah Khomeini movement illustrate such a position.

In sum, the evidence that we have marshaled suggests that women's terrorist activities are not a side effect of the women's liberation movement. Rather, in some cases, such as the Algerian Revolution, it appears that one of the unintended consequences of women's participation is a weakening of traditional customs and sex roles. Female terrorists, like male terrorists, tend to be drawn from the middle or upper classes, although this seems to be true more of idealistic revolutionary movements than of nationalistic ones. There is also some evidence that women, once recruited into insurgency movements, are more likely than men to stay in the movement.

We note that women appear as likely to support the Ayatollah Khomeini as they are to demonstrate against the military-industrial complex of West Germany or the United States. These women dedicate themselves to class, ethnic, and religious movements that not only offer no advantages to women, but which, if victorious, would be detrimental to their own liberation. More substantial evidence suggests that the division of labor by sex tends to be fairly rigid in nationalistic movements but very flexible, or even nonexistent, in idealistic terrorist movements.

Clear thinking about terrorism and the involvement of women in terrorist movements is hard to come by, in part because the enormous diversity of terrorist groups makes it easy to examine the evidence selectively. By surveying as much evidence as possible, we hope to stimulate future research and better conceptualization.

NOTES

1. Daniel A. Green, "The Dark Side of Liberation: Crime Takes a Female Turn," *National Observer*, September 1974, p. 2.

2. Paul Hofmann, "Women Active Among Radicals in West Europe," *New York Times*, August 14, 1977, p. 7.

3. Eric Hobsbawn, *Primitive Rebels: Studies in Archaic Forms of Social Movement in the Nineteenth and Twentieth Centuries* (New York: Praeger, 1963).

4. Vera Broido, *Apostles into Terrorists: Women and the Revolutionary Movement in the Russia of Alexander II* (New York: Viking, 1977).

5. Quoted in ibid., p. 185.

6. Alexandra Kollontai, *The Autobiography of a Sexually Emancipated Communist Woman*, trans. S. Attanasio (New York: Schocken, 1975).

7. Jane S. Jaquette, "Women in Revolutionary Movements in Latin America," *Journal of Marriage and the Family* 6 (1973): 344–354.

8. Ibid., p. 352.

9. U.S. Department of the Army, "Human Factors: Considerations of Underground Insurgents," Pamphlet 505-104 (Washington, DC: Department of the Army, 1966).

10. Brooks McClure, Testimony Before Senate Subcommittee to Investigate the Administration of the Internal Security Act and Other Internal Security Laws, "Report: Terrorist Activity: Hostage Defense Measures, Part 5" (Washington, DC: U.S. Government Printing Office, 1975).

11. Maria McGuire, *To Take Arms: A Year in the Provisional IRA* (London: Macmillan, 1973); Thomas Powers, *Diana: The Making of a Terrorist* (Boston: Houghton Mifflin, 1971).

12. Bernard K. Johnpoll, "Perspectives on Political Terrorism in the United States," in *International Terrorism*, edited by Yonah Alexander (New York: Praeger, 1976).

13. McClure, "Terrorist Activity," p. 311.

14. Broido, *Apostles*, pp. 730–776.

15. McClure, "Terrorist Activity," p. 282.

16. U.S. Department of the Army, "Human Factors," p. 75.

17. H. A. Cooper, "Women as Terrorists," in *The Criminology of Deviant Women*, edited by Freda Adler and Rita J. Simon (Boston: Houghton Mifflin, 1979), pp. 150–158.

18. Albert Cohen, *Delinquent Boys: The Culture of the Gang* (New York: Free Press, 1955).

19. McClure, "Terrorist Activity," p. 275.

20. Thomas E. Hachey, "Political Terrorism: The British Experience," in Alexander, *International Terrorism*. Hachey discusses briefly the British suffragist movement (1910–1919). The Women's Social and Political Union (WSPU) was led by Emmeline Pankhurst. They broke windows at the Home Office, the Foreign Office, and homes of selected political leaders. Once arrested they went on hunger strikes in jail. Other terrorist acts included burning post boxes, cutting telegraph lines, fire-bombing, and using bogus telegraph messages to send the army all over the place. Perhaps the most interesting part of Hachey's discussion is the way in which the British public responded to these acts. A goodly portion of Parliament and the populace were inclined to treat the women as ordinary criminals, not as political rebels.

21. "Terrorists: Closing in on an Elusive Enemy," *Time*, October 9, 1978, p. 64.

22. James Petras, "Revolution and Guerrilla Movements in Latin America: Venezuela, Guatemala, Colombia, and Peru," in *Latin America: Reform or Revolution?* edited by James Petras and Maurice Zeitlin (Greenwich, CT: Fawcett, 1968), pp. 329–369.

23. Franz Fanon, *A Dying Colonialism* (New York: Grove Press, 1965).

24. Ibid., pp. 48–57.

PART IV

Friendships and Public Opinion on Gender Issues

16

Married Women and Their Friends

This chapter examines the role that married women play in the initiation and maintenance of friendships by comparing friendship patterns of middle- and working-class women based on interviews with over 200 married women. It describes the number and duration of friendships, the likelihood that friendships established prior to marriage will be maintained, and the criteria used in the selection of friends. Working-class women are more likely to perceive their neighbors as close friends, and middle-class women are more likely to have friends whom they share with their husbands. Middle-class women are more active in initiating "couple" friendships, and they spend more time with their friends as couples.

Friendship has not been an area of enormous interest to sociologists. Although there are brief references to friendship patterns in community studies of Middletown, Plainville, Yankee City, Deep South, and Elmtown (Lynd and Lynd, 1929; West, 1945; Warner et al., 1949; Davis et al., 1941; Hollingshead, 1948) and in analytic descriptions of the society as a whole, such as Robin Williams (1960) provides in *American Society*, the topic is not considered important enough to merit elaboration in any of these studies.[1] Empirical studies of friendship have also been few and far between.

In two articles published in the 1960s, Babchuk and Bates described friendship patterns among a group of middle-class couples.[2] The major purpose of their research was to examine how many close friends married couples have and the relative influence of husbands and wives in forming and maintaining close friendships.

Our study has much in common with the Babchuk-Bates research. We are interested in examining the role of married women in the initiation and maintenance of friendships, the number and duration of friendships, the likelihood

Table 16.1
Proportion of Neighbors Who Are Close Friends by Social Class (in percent)

Social Class	Half or More	Few	None	Total
Middle	14	38	48	100(86)
Working	20	51	29	100(102)

that friendships established prior to marriage would be maintained, and the criteria used in the selection of friends. Our study differs from theirs primarily in that we compare friendship patterns among middle- and working-class women, and interview only wives.[3]

The sample frame for the study was obtained from the voter registration list of a community of about 50,000 people located near the Illinois-Indiana border. Five hundred names were selected at random; of those, 50 percent participated either by filling out a mail questionnaire or in an interview conducted in their home by one of the authors. A comparison of husbands' occupations and respondents' education revealed no significant differences. While it was not possible to make as meaningful a comparison between the nonrespondents and the participants, we made some assessments as to the relative status of persons in the two categories by using addresses and then locating residences in different sections of the city. No significant differences between respondents and nonparticipants were found.

We expected that middle-class women would report that they had more friends as a couple than would working-class women. But, we thought, middle-class women would be more dependent upon their husbands for the friends they have as a couple, would perceive the friends their husbands had prior to marriage as "their" friends, and would be less likely to maintain the friendships they had formed prior to marriage. Working-class women, on the other hand, would be more likely to substitute relatives for friends, and the friends they did have would be women in the neighborhood with whom they could visit across fences or driveways, or while taking care of their children.

We examined the last points first, and found that there was a greater propensity for working-class women to perceive their neighbors as their friends. This propensity (described in Table 16.1) is unrelated either to the length of time respondents have lived in the neighborhood or to their employment outside their homes.

The average number of friends middle-class women claimed they and their husbands have as a couple is 19.4; among working-class women, the average number is 14.5. There is no difference in the number of friends women in both

Table 16.2

Frequency of Social Contacts with Relatives by Social Status (in percent)

	Once a Day	Twice a Week	Once a Week	Once or Twice a Month	Less than Once a Month	Total
Middle Class	20	25	35	10	10	100(87)
Working Class	20	25	29	15	11	100(104)

categories claim they have but do not share with their husbands. It is interesting that about 20 percent of the women in both categories report having no friends that they do not share with their husbands.

We had expected that the fewer "friendships as couples" reported by the working-class women would be related to the number of relatives that live in the community and the frequency of their social contacts with those relatives. We found, however, that 62 percent of both middle- and working-class women reported having parents and/or in-laws who live in the community, and over 70 percent reported other close relatives in the community. As the figures in Table 16.2 show, there were no differences in the frequency of social contacts with relatives between the two classes.[4]

Inquiries about initiation, sources, and patterns of friendships revealed that 60 percent of both middle- and working-class women initiated the friendships about half the time. Among the remaining 40 percent, there was a slightly greater tendency for middle-class women to initiate the friendships than there was for working-class women.

About two-thirds of the women in both categories said that hardly any of the friends they and their husbands share as a couple are business associates or men with whom their husbands work; and two-thirds of the women in both categories claimed that friends of their husbands prior to marriage became their friends as well. About the same percentage also claimed that persons who were friends of theirs before marriage became friends of their spouses after marriage.

In both categories 40 percent of the women said they do not spend any evenings in the company of friends away from their husbands. Among the remaining 60 percent, the mean number of evenings was 2.2 per month for working-class women and 1.5 per month for middle-class women. When asked about how many evenings per month they and their husbands spend with friends, 11 and 15 percent of the women in both categories said "none." Among the others, the average number was 3.8 for middle-class and 3.4 for working-class women.

In their study of friendship patterns among middle-class couples, Babchuk

and Bates (1963; Babchuk, 1965) reported that husbands initiate mutual friendships about two-thirds of the time. They also found that among the friendships
established before marriage by either the man or woman, those of the husband
were more likely to survive marriage and become friends of the married pair.

The male dominance theme that runs all through the Babchuk-Bates findings
does not appear in the responses of our middle-class housewives. It is possible
that had we interviewed the husbands (Babchuk and Bates interviewed husbands
and wives), they would have provided a different impression and one more in
accord with the "male dominance" image. But that is not the way their wives
see it. Instead, our data indicate, there are only slight variations in the friendship
patterns of middle- and working-class housewives. Middle-class women claim
that they and their husbands have more friends as a couple than do working-
class women. The middle-class women are slightly more active in initiating those
"couple friendships," and they spend more time with their friends as couples.
Working-class women, on the other hand, are a little more likely to spend time
with friends without their husbands. They are also more likely to perceive their
neighbors as close friends.

We also asked participants about friends that they maintain apart from those
they share with their husbands. Again, there were no significant differences
between the middle- and working-class respondents. Middle-class women are
more likely than working-class women (56 compared to 30 percent) to see these
friends during the day, even though the same proportions in both categories are
housewives. There is no difference between the two categories of women concerning how they spend their time with their friends.

About one-third of the women in both categories claimed to maintain friendships formed prior to marriage; about three-quarters of these friendships were
formed during grade and high school. Three-quarters of all the women claimed
they maintain friendships via correspondence, writing to an average of four
persons. Babchuk and Bates found that their subjects stressed the importance of
"nonlocal" friendships; but on further probing they also found that friends who
were described in the warmest of terms had been neither seen nor corresponded
with for many years.

Both middle- and working-class women reported having made an average of
about four (4.4 and 4.1) friends in the past year, and most report that they did
not lose a friend during that time. The average numbers lost were 1.8 (middle-
class) and 1.1 (working-class), thus leaving a net gain of about three new friends
per year. When we add the number of friends women report they have as couples
to those friends they do not share with their husbands, the total comes to about
twenty-seven for middle-class and about twenty-two for working-class women.
With about two-thirds of the respondents having reported that they have been
married at least fifteen years, the figure of a net gain of three friends indicates
that the past year must have been unusually fruitful. It is more likely, though,
that they underestimated or misperceived the number of friends they lost.

Our two final items concerned the criteria respondents used in choosing friends, and the relationship to respondents of the people closest to them. The two criteria named most often by middle- and working-class women were "the personality of the person" and "similar interests." On the last item, more than half the women in both groups named siblings, girlfriends, and parents, in that order.

CONCLUSIONS

We conclude by noting that, on the whole, middle- and working-class women are very much alike in their friendship patterns. The major differences are that working-class women are more likely to perceive neighbors as close friends, while middle-class women report that they and their husbands share more friends than do working-class women and their husbands.

We did not find the male dominance theme that was so prominent in Babchuk and Bates's account of friendship patterns of middle-class couples. The wives in our study have at least taken the initiative in forming about half of the friendships that they and their husbands share. The middle-class women also report that about the same proportion of their friends before marriage as compared to their husbands' friends prior to marriage have become "couple friends."

Spending time with relatives does not seem to interfere with friendships, and maintaining friendships by correspondence is a common experience among both middle- and working-class women. Both groups probably either exaggerated the number of "new" friends they had made during the past year, or "forgot" that they had in fact lost contact with persons who had been friends at one time. Personality characteristics and common interests are the most important criteria in the selection of friends for both middle- and working-class women. And when asked to rank the five persons that are closest to them (leaving out husbands and children), girlfriends ranked below siblings but above parents.

NOTES

1. A. Davis, B. B. Gardner, and M. R. Gardner, *Deep South* (Chicago: University of Chicago Press, 1941); A. B. Hollingshead, *Elmtown's Youth* (New York: Wiley, 1948); R. S. Lynd and H. M. Lynd, *Middletown* (New York: Harcourt, Brace and World, 1929); W. L. Warner, M. Meeker, and K. C. Eells, *Social Class in America* (Chicago: Science Research Associates, 1949); J. West, *Plainville, U.S.A.* (New York: Columbia University Press, 1945); R. M. Williams, Jr., *American Society* (New York: Knopf, 1960).

2. N. Babchuk, "Primary Friends and Kin: A Study of the Associates of Middle Class Couples," *Social Forces* 43 (May 1965): 483–493; N. Babchuk and A. P. Bates, "The Primary Relations of Middle-Class Couples: A Study of Male Dominance," *American Sociological Review* 28 (June 1963): 377–384.

3. Class was determined by husband's occupation. Respondents who said their husbands held professional, managerial, clerical, and sales positions were categorized as

middle class; those who reported that their husbands were skilled craftsmen and laborers were categorized as working class.

4. Babchuk also found that there was no relationship between frequency of interaction with relatives and the number of friends or the frequency of interaction with those friends.

17

Careers and Close Friendships Among Successful Women

How important are intimate friendships to successful, career-oriented women, and how much time are they willing to devote to cultivating and maintaining close friendships? Based on long personal interviews with women doctors, lawyers, professors, and entrepreneurs, this chapter looks at women's views on intimate friendships and their interest in maintaining long-term ties. The opinions expressed range from total indifference, and an absence of close friends, to strong commitments to the ideal of intimate friendship.

Sisterhood—intense, exclusive bonds of friendship among women—became a rallying cry for the women who began to expose and protest the oppression of women in the nineteenth century. In 1848 women's rights activist Elizabeth Cady Stanton expressed the isolation women felt and the need for close relationships with other women:

Woman herself must do this work—for woman alone can understand the height, and the depth, and the length and the breadth of her own degradation and woe. Man cannot speak for us—because he has been educated to believe that we differ from him so materially, that we cannot judge of our thoughts, feelings and opinions by his own.[1]

But times, and the position of women in society, have changed. Women no longer describe themselves in terms of "degradation and woe," especially those women who have achieved success in the professional world. This chapter looks at the ways in which professional women bond today, and addresses the question of how women's friendships have changed and continue to change as their lives take on new roles and dimensions.

As success increasingly becomes a force to be reckoned with, women are changing their priorities in friendship. The successful professional women of today—doctors, academicians, lawyers, entrepreneurs—may not be looking for close, intimate friendships with other women, but rather for friends who can help them on the job, who can provide entry into the highest echelons of the work force, who can give strong emotional support in the workplace. The traditional spheres of home and marriage may be of less importance in these friendships; instead, shoptalk takes prominence, as do competition, success, and economic survival.

In order to compare the place and estimate the importance that close friends have in the lives of successful, career-oriented professional women, we have compiled data based on in-depth interviews two to three hours in length with twenty-seven women and six men, all of whom have achieved professional and market recognition. The interviews were conducted in Washington, D.C., Champaign-Urbana and Chicago, Illinois, New York, and London. We want to emphasize at the outset that we are describing the experiences of women who have "made it" in their given occupation or profession. Some of these women describe themselves as "driven"; all perceive themselves to be as fully dedicated to their work as any of the successful professional males we interviewed for purposes of comparison. The picture that emerges about the place and importance of close friends among these women should not be generalized to friendships among women as a whole. By the amount of money they earn, and by the types of positions they occupy, the women we interviewed are different from the large majority of their gender.

Many of them expressed thoughts similar to the following: "This notion of sisterhood and deep bonds between women was something that might have been true in the late sixties and seventies. But today friendships between women are based more and more on work-related issues and are used primarily to provide emotional support for career ambitions." (The respondent, at forty-one, heads a national coalition of black women.)

As expressed by a number of highly successful women, friendship itself is becoming less important for some, and simply less likely for others. In both cases, time constraints, job demands, and family pressures all take precedence, severely curtailing the time that can be allotted to contact with friends. Indeed, time seems to have replaced money and success as the most precious commodity in these women's lives. "I think that time, more than money and more than sex, more than anything, is the scarcity that women talk about in this room. The two scarcities that women feel [are] time for friendship and time for themselves," said one respondent.

So, how do they cope? At one extreme is a thirty-seven-year-old doctor who is the director of clinical programs at a major New York hospital. She does not have *any* friends to speak of. She maintains contact with three college friends, but they are always the ones to initiate contact. She feels no need to confide in people, including her husband, although she does consider him a friend. "I'm in a profession where I have to befriend in a peculiar way so many people that

I don't feel the need for friends. When I get home, for the most part, I'd just as soon not have to be involved with people. [My husband] is a very good friend. I know that I can confide in him, but I don't really use that relationship for a friendship."

The majority of the women we interviewed told us that friendship is important to them, but that regular contacts with friends lose out in the daily struggle to find the time and place for competing demands. Sixteen of the twenty-seven women interviewed felt that friends were important; eleven felt that they were not. Ten of those who felt that friends were important were married; of those to whom friends were not important, six were married.

There are two ways for those women who consider friendships important to accommodate their needs. The first is to plan well in advance times when they will meet with their friends. But that, too, leads to frustration. The women interviewed would generally talk to their friends once a month, and see them even less frequently. In many cases, these women have close friends who live in different areas of the country, and contact has dropped to phone calls once every few months. A law professor describes her relationship with two close friends who live in distant cities in this way: "I speak to them a few times a year and I see them if I happen to be passing through their respective towns on business. My friends are people who are willing to accept me as not pursuing friendships."

The second and more common method of dealing with a desire for friends is to create friendships on the job. For example, a woman who runs her own political consulting firm explains that "there is always a reason for meeting friends, a framework surrounding it, such as business reasons." Another Washington, D.C., professional woman, a bank president, sees her friends more often than most of those interviewed, because they all tend to show up at the same receptions. And when this bank president sponsors parties for prospective clients of the bank, she always invites her friends, whose charm and social graces, she says, "liven things up and make everyone feel comfortable."

Dr. Alexandria Symonds, president of the Association of Women Psychiatrists, raises the possibility that women are becoming much more like men insofar as "they're taught to repress their feelings, so relationships gradually become less important and their work is more important. Perhaps more women are developing the kind of character structure that men have been encouraged to develop: a more expansive, detached kind of character."

As career-oriented women are finding more and more close friends in the workplace, a fundamental part of those friendships is the exchange of ideas. It is, in fact, crucially important for most of the women we interviewed to be able to talk about work. They feel alienated from those friendships dating back to the time before they entered the work force. Indeed, it is common practice for most of these women to drop or lose interest in high school and college friends.

The same is true in cases where friends lead more "traditional" lives—having jobs but not careers—and are not driven toward professional achievement. One of the respondents, who owns a public relations firm, insists that she looks for ambition and competitiveness in friends now, qualities absent in the close friendships she developed as a homemaker when she formed bonds with six women in similar circumstances. Today, while she regularly sees those same people, none of whom are pursuing a career, she feels that they regard shoptalk as bragging on her part. So she has been caught in what she perceives as a void: she cannot relate to the women she knew before becoming a businesswoman, while most of the women professionals she meets in her current position do not devote the same amount of attention to family that she does. What has happened is that she turns more to her husband for emotional support and advice.

While professional women often coordinate and cooperate with other women in their work, many are also finding a new element in their associations or friendships: competition. The traditional notion of female friendships is that of a nurturing spirit. Men, by contrast, are classically perceived as competitive. Carol Gilligan (*In a Different Voice*) characterizes women's identity within a "context of relationship," that is, women define themselves by their relationships with other people—wife, mother, child, friend, lover. "Similarly," says Gilligan, "the standard of moral judgment that informs their assessment of self is a standard of relationship, an ethic of nurturance, responsibility, and care."[2] In a survey of five career-oriented women, Gilligan found that "these highly successful and achieving women do not mention their academic and professional distinction in the context of describing themselves.[3]

While the portrayal of men may not have changed much over the years, the image we have of professional, career-oriented women is that they feel much less responsible for accommodating as many people and interests as they have in the past. A number of the women we interviewed acknowledged competition in their friendships. They dealt with these feelings—which they consider somehow detrimental to the friendship—by making a conscious effort to suppress them.

Symonds agrees that women are becoming increasingly competitive, and mentions several ways they have integrated those perceptions. "Some women have accepted being openly competitive. Most women are uncomfortable being competitive and don't like to admit that to themselves, so it's disguised more." One of the practicing attorneys in our study says that she talks less about professional aspects of her life when she is with similarly situated women attorney friends. The most extreme example of this type of behavior was found in London, where one partner in a law firm told us: "Over the years we've learned that people become very jealous of you. We're all frightened of making the others jealous or uncomfortable. So we tend to talk about things that we know will please the other people."

Symonds points out that "women were always competitive about getting a man in the old days; now it's switching over to their work." What's new today is that "women are competing with men for the same jobs. They're not comfortable with that open competition, which men have always been trained into since childhood.''

However, the nurturing ''instinct'' has taken another form in some cases: women assume much of the caretaking responsibility in their close friendships, inhibited by the prospect of making demands on their friends. Rather, they will be the ones to whom their friends turn for advice—a role they often enjoy. One respondent puts the blame squarely on her ego: ''I think some of that is a notion of independence, always wanting to be independent of other people. I get selfish gratification out of being known as unselfish.'' The only exception is in their marriages, where most of the women actively seek their husband's support and guidance.

The men in Gilligan's study, on the other hand, focus on their own individual achievement. ''Instead of attachment, individual achievement rivets the male imagination, and great ideas or distinctive activity defines the standard of self-assessment and success.''[4] Among the men we interviewed, as well as those surveyed in a number of other studies, male executives find it difficult to maintain close ties with their colleagues. A Washington, D.C., judge explains the fear he has of developing close friendships on the job:

In the workplace, among the males, there is certainly a reluctance to get too close because you never know when things will boomerang. It's the fear that what you say will be used against you, so you have to watch out what you say and who you say it to. Patterns and attitudes are developed early on. The competitiveness in men is very prevalent. If that predominates, it can kill a lot of stuff. It not only kills it because you're reticent, it kills it because when you have a relationship, you're still trying to show how you're better than the other guy.

The women in our survey do not express such extreme competitive feelings, but occasionally the rivalry between women in the workplace leads to feelings of betrayal. One college professor had to face outright envy: ''There was a woman I was very friendly with when I came to Champaign-Urbana. I found her to be exceedingly envious about what she perceived as my success, and undercut me, always being critical, and not in a constructive way. I finally gave up that friendship because it was so painful and destructive. It's too competitive. It's not nurturing.''

Although women find it easier than men to create friendships on the job, there is little loyalty among them as women per se. The networking so prevalent in the seventies is absent among the women we spoke to. What help is given to other women is provided through informal contacts. The reason for the lack of formal networks: no time. Often they regard ''success in a man's world'' as their contribution toward helping women. It seems that the purpose of networking in the seventies—to provide support for success and ambition—is fulfilled today by one's own individual network of friends. And that, too, is the importance of friendship for most of the women we spoke to. Rather than the constant, daily nurturing provided by frequent and intense contact, friends are important just because they are there, because they can be contacted if necessary, and because they provide a sense of identity for women following similar paths.

Just as there is little formal networking among women, it is rarely the case that women look toward other women as mentors. Most of the women interviewed have had male mentors. Whereas most males in our survey regard mentors as people whom they admired as role models, most of the women consider mentors to be men who have helped them get ahead. Representative of this is a staff director of a Congressional subcommittee: "In every job I've had, I've had a man who was my supervisor who saw what I could do and pushed me along. They have been older men who recognized that I was smart and made sure that I got ahead." Another Chicago professor mentions a law school professor who "took me under his wing and has opened every door that has ever been opened." While men tend to feel close emotionally toward their mentors, often mentioning their father as a role model, women rarely discuss intimate details of their lives with their mentors, relying on them instead for career advice.

A further by-product of women's increased participation in the professional work force is the growth of close friendships with men. Several of those interviewed actively sought out male friendships "for business purposes." One of our respondents explained that "they give you a male perspective that you need, particularly in business. They give me good advice and solutions that I just wouldn't have recognized and neither would my female friends." Inevitably, this closeness leads to sexual tension which must be resolved in order for the relationship to continue, and which is resolved, according to most women. Men, on the other hand, feel such discomfort more intensely. All the men interviewed believe that sexual undertones prevent close friendships with women.

RELATIONSHIPS WITH THEIR MOTHERS

Most of the women in our survey described themselves as "loners," "outsiders," and "different" from their peers in elementary and high school. Not only did these women view themselves as unpopular, nearly all of them had troubled relationships with their mothers. In many cases, a mother was unable to understand her daughter's ambitions, while the daughter had little respect for the way her mother had chosen to lead her life. This inability to understand each other often extends into a daughter's adult life. One respondent told us:

I find it more difficult to communicate with my mother as I have gotten older—that's why these other women have become important—to share experiences that she's never had. She did work, but work was supplemental. Her career was her family. If I'm talking about board room politics, or if I'm talking about the tribulations of setting up an office, my mother has never had to do those kinds of things.

Others said bluntly, "My mother bores me." In other instances, this disparity of experience has led to a sharp role reversal in these women's lives. When her father died, a Washington, D.C., real estate agent was surprised to learn that she, rather than her mother, had been appointed executor of his will. In assuming authority over her mother's life, she has become a role model for her:

My mother is an accountant, who always worked for my father. She did what my father told her to do. I'm trying to get her to understand everything that is going on. Though I'm in charge, I say to her we'll do what you want to do, but you have to figure it out. My mother is coming into the twentieth century with a vengeance. She's beginning to be angry that she never knew what was going on.

Many of the women we spoke to felt the same way: their mothers are a responsibility, not someone with whom they could share confidences or values.

Many of the women we interviewed see their husband as their closest friend, and the only person toward whom they allow themselves to feel dependent. We see a certain irony in the relationship that these successful women have vis-à-vis their husbands compared to women who play more traditional roles. Traditional women are more dependent on their husbands for financial support and economic security than are career women. But the traditional women are not as dependent on their husbands for emotional support, comfort, friendship, and love as are successful professional women. The former turn to their sisters, their mothers, their friends, for those kinds of support. The professional career woman is more likely to have cut herself off from those ties.

Toward the end of the interview, one of the women said: "I am not willing, or able, to put the time into friendships; I want to spend most of it on work and some on family. I'll probably be sorry for that twenty years from now." That attitude characterizes the one train of thought running consistently through all our conversations with these high powered, high achieving women: the fulfillment and delight of career success takes a heavy toll, perhaps the heaviest, when it comes to friendship. The full price to be paid remains to be seen.

NOTES

1. Theodore Stanton and Harriet Stanton, eds., *Elizabeth Cady Stanton, as Revealed in Her Letters, Diary and Reminiscences* (New York: Harper and Brothers, 1922), p. 144.

2. Carol Gilligan, *In a Different Voice* (Cambridge, MA: Harvard University Press, 1982), p. 160.

3. Ibid., p. 159.

4. Ibid., p. 163.

18

Confrontation or Consensus? The Differences Between Women and Men on Political and Social Issues

Using national poll data and going back on some issues to the early 1940s, this chapter (portions of which appeared in Women's Movements in America) *compares women's and men's responses to political and social issues that are important in women's lives. Abortion, the Equal Rights Amendment, family size, domestic division of labor, work opportunities, and equal pay are some of the issues considered. The major finding is that men and women are much more likely to agree than to disagree on all of these issues, and consensus rather than confrontation characterizes their relationships.*

The demand for suffrage was a major rallying cry of the earliest women's movement in the United States. Leaders of the National American Women's Suffrage Association (NAWSA) and its offshoot, the National Women's Party, argued that with the vote, women would demonstrate their greater (as compared to men) social consciousness and humanitarianism. Armed with the right to vote, women would declare their independence from male influence and elect persons to office who were more competent, more honest, and more caring than those nominated and elected by their husbands, fathers, and brothers.

Not only would women manifest their independence and greater social consciousness by voting for more qualified candidates, but they would also demonstrate their political power by nominating and supporting other women for public office. Once in office, women governors, representatives, senators, indeed, even presidents, would change the character of the nation. Under women's leadership, new, effective, and peaceful ways of resolving domestic and foreign disagreements would be found. There would be better care for children. The aged and the sick would have greater security. Workers would labor under better conditions and for fewer hours. These were but some of the bounties that suffrage would provide.

The momentous time finally arrived with the passage of the Nineteenth Amendment to the Constitution in 1920. What has been the impact of that change on American society? How many women presidents, governors, and senators have been elected since that time? The answer is appallingly few. We have had no woman president, nor has one ever been nominated by a major political party. One woman was nominated for the office of vice president, in 1984. At no time have there been more than two women in the U.S. Senate in any one session. Hattie Caraway was the first woman elected, after having been appointed to the Arkansas seat in 1931 at the death of her husband; in 1932, with the help of Huey Long, she was elected to the Senate. In 1953, twelve women served in the House of Representatives and one served in the Senate. In 1978 the House had eighteen women members; the Senate had no woman member until Muriel Humphrey was appointed to fill her late husband's seat. Through 1980 only four women had been elected to full terms. In 1988 there were twenty-three women serving in the House and two, Nancy Landon Kassebaum (R-Kan) and Barbara Mikulski (D-Md), serving in the Senate.

Women candidates do not fare any better in gubernatorial races. The first woman governor was Nellie Ross Taylor, elected in 1924 to fill the seat of her husband, who died in office. From 1924 to 1980, only five women were elected to governorships. In 1990 there were four women governors, in the states of Arizona (appointed following the impeachment of Governor Edward Meachem), Kentucky, Nebraska, and Vermont, and five serving as lieutenant governors. During the 1980s there was an increase in the number of women serving in state legislatures. But the expectations of the suffragists regarding women and political office have not been fulfilled. As of April 1988, women held only 15.8 percent of state legislative seats, 228 in the state senates, and 949 in state houses.

At the local level, the percentage of women occupying elective offices is even lower. As of 1985 women comprised only 14.5 percent of mayors and members of municipal township governing boards; and as of 1987 women comprised only 8.6 percent of county governing boards. As cited in *Ms* magazine (April 1988), the Center for the American Woman and Politics at Rutgers University has estimated that although there has been a 300 percent increase in the number of local women office holders since 1974, at no level of office do women hold more than 15.8 percent of available positions.

The persistent underrepresentation of women in elected positions contrasts with increased public support for qualified women officeholders as voiced over the years in public opinion polls. In 1987 Gallup found that 82 percent of respondents answered yes when asked, "If your party nominated a woman for president, would you vote for her if she were qualified for the job?" Broken down by sex, the shift in attitudes by men and women over a fifty-year period has been dramatic.

We note two things about the data in Table 18.1. First, the gap between male and female preferences has closed: where once (in 1937) one-third more of the women than the men polled were likely to favor a woman, by the 1970s there

Table 18.1
Percent Who Would Vote for a Woman President

Year	National	Women	Men
1937	34	40	27
1945	33	37	29
1949	48	51	45
1955	52	57	47
1958	52	55	51
1963	55	51	58
1967	57	53	61
1969	54	49	58
1971	66	67	65
1975	73	71	75
1976	76	74	78
1978	80	81	80
1983	80	80	80
1984	78	78	78
1987	82	83	81

Source: The Gallup Organization, Princeton, NJ, 1952-1988.

was no difference between male and female voters. Second, those who said they would vote for a woman increased to 82 percent, from a low of 34 percent fifty years earlier. But those attitudes have yet to be tested, since no woman candidate has gained the nomination.

VOTER TURNOUT AND VOTING PREFERENCES AMONG WOMEN

Did suffrage in fact lead to a high turnout of women at the polls? Only 26 percent of eligible women voters actually voted in the first presidential election after suffrage was granted [1] However, by 1952, voting participation of women approached that of men; and by the 1984 presidential election women registered and voted in higher numbers than men.[2]

Table 18.2
Voter Turnout in Presidential Elections, by Percentage

Year	National	Women	Men
1952	62	60	64
1956	59	57	61
1960	63	61	66
1964	69	67	72
1968	68	66	70
1972	63	62	64
1976	59	59	60
1980	59	59	59
1984	60	61	59

Sources: 1952-1960:   The Gallup Report, March 1976, no. 128:14;
1964-1984:   U.S. Bureau of the Census.

And how did the women vote? Was there a difference in the candidates women supported as opposed to men? How important is gender in presidential elections? For these data we go back thirty-five years and compare male and female voting patterns from the 1952 presidential election through the 1988 election. Table 18.3 describes the percentage who voted for the elected candidate.

The most significant observation about the percentages in Table 18.3 is the similarity between male and female preferences. The biggest difference is 9 percent, which occurred in 1984. There is no consistent pattern of voting preferences for women. Compared to other demographic characteristics such as race, education, religion, and occupation, gender introduces much less variance in voting behavior. For example, in 1964 (Johnson versus Goldwater), there was a 2 percent difference by gender but a 35 percent difference by race, a 14 percent difference by education, a 17 percent difference by occupation, and a 21 percent difference by religion.[3]

Although women's choices for political office do not seem to differ significantly from those of men, gender could influence attitudes toward public issues. One way of testing whether women's voting preferences conform to those of men is to examine male and female opinions on important national issues during the same period for which we compared the presidential voting preferences. For

Table 18.3
How Men and Women Voted in Presidential Elections, by Percentage

Year	National	Women	Men
1952 Eisenhower	55	58	53
1956 Eisenhower	58	61	55
1960 Kennedy	50	49	52
1964 Johnson	61	62	60
1968 Nixon	43	43	43
1972 Nixon	62	62	63
1976 Carter	50	48	53
1980 Reagan	51	49	53
1984 Reagan	59	55	64
1988 Bush	54	52	56

Source: The Gallup Organization.

these data we go back to 1948 and report male and female opinions over the next three and a half decades.

In the period from 1948 to 1952, national issues included support for revision of the Taft-Hartley Labor Act, understanding how government works, sex education in the high schools, U.S. military involvement in Korea, a draft law, interest in political affairs, a welfare state, government spending, a permanent military alliance between the United States and Western Europe, and the first use of atomic bombs. Men and women agreed on all of the issues except for U.S. potential involvement in Korea, on which 45 percent of the men as opposed to 33 percent of the women advocated "do what is necessary even at the risk of starting World War III." Women also differed from men on items that asked about understanding of and interest in government and political affairs. A higher percentage of women consistently indicated that they could not understand what was going on (78 percent versus 63 percent of men) and that they were not particularly interested in political affairs (69 percent women versus 55 percent of men), and a higher percentage of women than men consistently indicated that they had no opinion about the substantive issues.

A similar pattern prevailed in the early 1960s, when the issues were welfare and relief programs, involvement in Vietnam, government funded job programs, Social Security, the death penalty, the stance to be taken vis-à-vis the Soviets, money spent on national defense, the costs of sending a man to the moon, attitudes toward having a colored family live next door, preference for living under communism or fighting an all-out nuclear war, and fear about U.S. involvement in another war. The substantive issues on which men and women differed were Vietnam (55 percent of the men as opposed to 42 percent of the women favored greater U.S. involvement); the Soviet Union (60 percent of the men as opposed to 46 percent of the women advocated adopting a tougher stance); willingness to fight an all-out nuclear war rather than live under communism (87 percent of the men compared to 75 percent of the women); fear about the United States getting into another war (42 percent of the men as opposed to 24 percent of the women answered that they were not worried); and the death penalty (64 percent of the men favored it as opposed to 55 percent of the women). On other substantive issues (money spent on a welfare state; the responsibility of the government to find jobs; increasing the Social Security tax; costs of sending a man to the moon; having a "colored" family move in next door), there were no differences between men and women. Women were more likely to agree that "politics seem so complicated, we cannot understand what is going on" (63 percent as opposed to 52 percent for men), and women were more likely than men to have no opinion or to say they were undecided on every issue.

In the early 1960s, the responses indicated that women were demonstrating a greater concern about U.S. involvement in actions that might lead to war and were less likely to favor the death penalty. A decade later the issues posed were busing school children in order to integrate schools, allowing amnesty for young men who fled the United States to avoid the draft, beliefs about the poor, permits for handguns, the death penalty for convicted murderers, and lessening involvement in world affairs. Women were more likely to favor amnesty for men who left the United States to avoid the draft (42 percent for women, 32 percent for men). They were also more likely to favor a law requiring a police permit before anyone could purchase a gun (82 to 62 percent), and they were less likely to favor the death penalty for convicted murderers (51 versus 64 percent).

Do we find more evidence of women's greater compassion and desire for peace in the early seventies? The answer is a weak and equivocal yes, based on the above-mentioned responses. Not until 1976, however, did larger and more consistent differences between men's and women's attitudes on public issues emerge. While there were no differences by gender on how much money should be spent on improving the nation's education system, on busing, and on whether more money should be spent to fight crime, women did differ from men on a range of domestic and foreign policy issues. Women were more likely than men to favor greater protection for the environment (58 to 48, and 51 to 35 percent), to oppose the death penalty (77 to 67 percent), to favor police permits for use of handguns (80 to 65 percent), and to support programs that would reduce the income gap between rich and poor (73 to 61 percent). On foreign policy, women were more isolationist than men (43 to 31 percent), more favorable toward having the United States stay out of world affairs (39 to 28 percent), less likely to support increased spending for the military (67 to 80 percent), and less likely to favor a return to the draft (39 to 52 percent). In addition to these specific issues, women expressed less confidence in their government and more concern that their country was in "deep and serious trouble" (27 to 39 percent, and 48 to 37 percent).

The trends that emerge in the contemporary period are that women have greater compassion for the poor, more concern about protecting the environment, and greater antipathy toward violence, and are more inclined to advocate that the United States insulate itself from active involvement in world events, especially from those actions that might lead to military intervention. Women are also less optimistic that "all would be well" with their country, and less confident about the future than men.

DIFFERENCES BETWEEN MEN AND WOMEN ON ISSUES INVOLVING WORKING WOMEN

What about issues that more directly affect the day-to-day lives of women? How similar are their views to those of men on matters such as married women working outside their homes, equal pay for equal work, and the number of children they would like to have?

The first set of polls compares male and female attitudes about married women working outside their homes (see Table 18.4). Over the fifty-year time span, there was never more than an 8 percent difference between men and women on the issue of married women working outside their homes. In the postwar era and in the early period of the women's liberation movement, the gap between men and women grew smaller, until it all but disappeared by the mid seventies, as a higher percentage of both men and women indicated their approval of married women holding jobs outside their homes.

Beginning in 1942, the item described in Table 18.5 (with slight variations) appeared on national surveys. Going as far back as 1942, there was widespread support for equal pay among men and women, and since 1962 the differences between men's and women's views have almost disappeared.

When asked in general about perceptions of employment discrimination, we see in Table 18.6 that in 1987 a higher percentage of women perceived discrimination than in 1975. The trend was weaker and reversed among men: 50 percent felt that women were discriminated against in 1975; in 1987, only 46 percent believed women did not have equal job opportunities.

The data in Table 18.7 show that in 1970 men and women agreed that a woman with the same ability as a man has as good a chance to become the executive of a company. Over the next seventeen years, men were slightly more likely than women to believe that a woman's chance of becoming an executive was as good as a man's. But polls also show that working women are more likely than men to believe that they have equal opportunities on matters such as salaries, responsibilities, and promotions (Table 18.8).

Table 18.4
Percent Approving of Married Women Working

Year	Women	Men
1936	18	12
1938	25	19
1946	42	34
1967	47	40
1975	71	69
1977	64	67
1978	74	71
1982	75	73
1983	75	75
1985	84	85
1986	76	78

Sources: The Roper Organization for <u>Fortune</u>, as cited
in Hazel Erksine, "The Polls: Women's Role," <u>Public Opinion</u>
<u>Quarterly</u>, 1977, p. 35 (for 1936 and 1946); The Gallup
Organization (for 1938, and 1972-1986; The Roper Organization for
<u>Saturday Evening Post</u>, 1977 (for 1967).

Given the publicity and support that the women's movement has received over the years, the results of a poll that asked, "For whom would you rather work?" (Table 18.9), are surprising. While the percentage of women who chose another woman increased by more than 100 percent between 1953 and 1987, twice as many women still prefer working for a man. For men, on the other hand, the shift has been more dramatic; in 1987 over half of the male respondents said it made no difference to them.

WOMEN AND MARRIAGE

Most women want the whole package: marriage, children, and a career (see Table 18.10). Clearly women do not want careers instead of marriage or in place of childless marriages.

What sort of marriage do men and women contemplate in the era of "the working woman?" Do both sexes envisage major changes in the traditional division of labor between husbands and wives, or are men more likely to favor

Table 18.5
Do you approve or disapprove of paying women the same salary as men, if they are doing the same work?

Year	Women	Men and Women	Men
		(Percent "same salary")	
1942	92		78
1945		76	
1954		87	
1962	92		88
1973	96		94
1977		94	

Sources: Surveys by American Institute of Public Opinion (Gallup), 1942 and 1962; Daniel Starch and Staff, Inc., 1973; and NBC News, November 29-30, 1977, as cited in Public Opinion January/February 1979, p. 36; 1945 and 1954, Gallup, as cited in Erskine, 1977, p.287.

Table 18.6
Do you feel that women in this country have equal job opportunities with men or not?

Year	Women		Men	
	Yes	No	Yes	No
	(in percent)			
1975	49	46	46	50
1982	41	54	46	50
1987	35	56	48	46

Source: The Gallup Organization.

Table 18.7
If a woman has the same ability as a man, does she have as good a chance to become the executive of a company or not?

Year	Women			Men		
	Yes	No	No Opinion	Yes	No	No Opinion
	(in percent)					
1970	39	54	7	39	56	5
1975	37	59	4	43	54	3
1982	40	56	4	45	49	6
1987	46	50	4	50	42	8

Source: The Gallup Organization.

maintaining the status quo whereby women assume responsibility for house-keeping and child care? Table 18.11 describes responses of men and women to this question over an eleven-year period.

Although the traditional division of labor between wives and husbands has lost some support, marriage has not gone out of style. In 1985 a higher percentage of both women and men preferred a more egalitarian marriage to a traditional marriage in which women carry a greater share of the housekeeping and child-rearing responsibilities. The differences between men and women are not great, and clearly, for both sexes, marriage is almost unanimously preferred over other living arrangements.

In 1970 and in 1985, men and women were asked to assess whether the "institution of marriage" was stronger, weaker, or about the same as it was "ten years ago" (see Table 18.12). For each time period, a majority of the men and women believed that the institution was weaker than it was ten years ago. But the percentages were lower in 1985 than in 1970, when 72 percent of the men and 75 percent of the women believed marriage as an institution was weaker than it had been ten years earlier. Perhaps that is because in 1970 respondents were looking back on a decade of social turmoil in which marriage and the family were targets of attack and derision. By 1985 that upheaval had run its course.

There has been a dramatic shift in both attitudes and behavior concerning the "ideal" number of children a family should have. This shift may be attributed not only to changes in women's roles and perceptions of their status in society, but also to beliefs about the danger of "overpopulation" and the success of a social movement espousing zero population growth.

Although the question regarding ideal family size has been phrased slightly

Table 18.8

Do you feel you stand an equal chance with the men you work with on salary, responsibility, promotions, and becoming an executive?

Year	Working Women			Men		
	Equal Chance	Not Equal	Don't Know	Equal Chance	Not Equal	Don't Know
	(in percent)					
Salary:						
1970	54	33	13	45	49	6
1979	55	32	13	54	40	6
1985	57	33	10	48	46	6
Responsibility:						
1970	67	21	12	56	39	5
1979	68	20	12	62	32	6
1985	73	18	9	61	33	6
Promotion:						
1970	51	32	17	43	50	7
1979	52	33	15	49	42	9
1985	53	35	12	45	49	7

Sources: 1970, Lou Harris; 1979 and 1985, The Roper Organization for Virginia Slims, 1979 as cited in Public Opinion, August/September 1981, p. 32; 1985, as cited in Shirley Wilkins and Thomas A.W. Miller, "Working Women: How It's Working Out," Public Opinion, October/November 1985, p. 46.

differently in the forty-five years in which it has appeared on national polls, its essence has been: "What do you consider is the ideal size of a family: a husband and wife and how many children?" Between 1941 and 1959, as shown in Table 18.13, the modal response for women was "at least four children." Men's responses varied more than women's from year to year, but on none of the five polls up to and including 1959 did the level of their responses match those of the women in the "four plus" category. The year 1966 marked the beginning of the smaller family trend, which was reflected in the opinions of the men and women polled. In 1973 and up through 1986, the choices between men and women moved closer together and shifted from a preference on the part of women for at least four children to two children. Women's preferences changed much more than men's. From 1978 to 1986 a higher percentage of women than men wanted two or fewer children.

Table 18.9
For whom would you rather work?

Year	Women			Men		
	For a Man	For a Woman	No Difference	For a Man	For a Woman	No Difference
1953	57	8	29	75	2	21
1970*	40	5	53	47	3	43
1975	60	10	27	63	4	32
1982	52	15	30	40	9	46
1987	37	19	39	29	9	57

* Based on views of men and working women only.

1970: From your experience, would you rather work under a man or a woman, or doesn't it make any difference to you?

1953, 1975, and 1987: If you were taking a new job and had your choice of a boss, would you prefer to work for a man or for a woman?

Sources: 1970, Lou Harris; 1953, 1975, 1982, and 1987, The Gallup Organization.

HOW WOMEN PERCEIVE THEMSELVES

Women who work outside the home perceive themselves differently than do homemakers. As shown in Table 18.14, in 1984 about twice as many of the former believed they should have an equal role with men. But over a twelve-year period more than half of the women employed outside their home and at least 70 percent of the women who were housewives did not support full equality with men in the running of business, industry, and governmental affairs.

Education played an important role in influencing women's responses. In 1984, 63 percent of the women who were employed outside their homes and who graduated from college placed themselves in the fully egalitarian position, as opposed to 33 percent of the working women who were high school graduates. Among the housewives, 33 percent of the college graduates favored equality compared to 19 percent of the high school graduates.[4]

Consistent with those data are the responses in Table 18.15, which show that both men and women, and women more than men, believe that it is a husband's position that determines the family's overall status.

In 1983, when the question was phrased in nonsexist language, women were

Table 18.10
Considering the possibilities for combining or not combining marriage, children, and a career, and assuming you had a choice, which one of those possibilities do you think would offer you the most satisfying and interesting life?

Choices	1974	1985
Combining marriage, career, children	52	63
Marriage, children, no career	38	26
Career, marriage, no children	4	4
Career, no marriage, no children	2	3
Marriage, no career, no children	1	1
Don't know	3	2

Source: The Roper Organization for Virginia Slims, as cited in Shirley Wilkins and Thomas A.W. Miller, "Working Women: How It's Working Out," Public Opinion, October/November 1985, p. 45.

still more likely to be willing to relocate than men. Fifty percent of the working women as compared to 42 percent of the men said they would be willing to relocate if their spouse was offered a better position.

Indeed, when asked about the desirability of improving the status of women, there has been a considerable shift on the part of male and female respondents (see Table 18.16). For the most part, men's and women's responses were closely aligned. It was not until 1985 that slightly more women than men favored efforts to strengthen women's status.

Given these responses, it is not surprising that between 1974 and 1980 the percentage of men favoring passage of the ERA exceeded that of women. It was not until 1981 that support for the ERA among women equalled the support expressed by men (see Table 18.17).

We could find only one national poll on which men and women were asked to make a judgment about the women's movement and its impact, if any, on family life. When asked in 1977 whether the women's movement has been a major cause of family breakdown ("Has it created a better family structure, or has it not made any difference?"), 43 percent of the men, as opposed to 33 percent of the women, believed that the women's movement has had no major impact on family life (CBS News). Forty-seven percent of the women, as opposed to 41 percent of the men, thought it had been a major cause of family breakdowns;

Table 18.11

In today's society there are different lifestyles and some that are acceptable today that weren't in the past. Regardless of what you have done or plan to do with your life, and thinking just of what would give you *personally* the most satisfying and interesting life, which one of these different ways of life do you think would be the best as a way of life?

	1974		1977*		1985	
	Women	Men	Women	Men	Women	Men
			(in percent)			
1. Marriage where husband and wife share responsibilities. Both work and share housekeeping and childcare responsibilities.	46	44	50	46	57	50
2. Traditional marriage; husband assumes responsibility for providing for family and wife runs house and takes care of children.	50	48	41	47	37	43
3. Living with someone of opposite sex, but not married.	3	3			2	3
4. Remain single and living alone.	1	1			2	1
5. Remain single and live with others of same sex.	--	--			--	--
6. Live in large family of people with similar interests and in which some are married and some are not.	--	4			--	--
7. No opinion/ DK	--	4			1	0

*1977: Only the first two answer categories were included.

Sources: 1977, CBS News/New York Times, October 23-36, as cited in Public Opinion, January/February 1979, p. 37; 1974 and 1985, The Roper Organization for Virginia Slims, as cited in Public Opinion, October/November 1985, p. 47, and Shirley Wilkins and Thomas A. W. Miller, "Working Women: How It's Working Out," Public Opinion, October/November 1985, p. 47.

20 percent of the women, as opposed to 15 percent of the men, perceived the movement as contributing to a better family structure.

Over the past twenty years, abortion has surpassed the ERA as the top priority issue of the women's movement, and has been one of the most publicly debated issues as well. At least as early as 1966, Gallup queried the American public

Table 18.12
Compared to ten years ago, do you think the institution of marriage is stronger, weaker, or about the same as it was then?

Year	Women			Men		
	Stronger	Weaker	Same	Stronger	Weaker	Same
	(in percent)					
1970	5	75	20	5	72	22
1985	15	61	23	16	60	24

Source: Roper Organization for Virginia Slims, latest March 1985, as cited in Public Opinion, December/January 1986, p. 25.

about abortion rights. Public opinion on abortion has changed little over the years. But, unlike attitudes toward the ERA, differences between men and women have consistently been negligible, albeit varying somewhat according to the degree of abortion rights in question.

Prior to the 1973 Supreme Court decision in *Roe v. Wade*, which upheld the right of a woman to obtain an abortion in the first trimester of pregnancy, support for this right had grown among both men and women, but slightly more among men than women (see Table 18.18).

Early on, men and women were in agreement about the desirability of legal abortion in cases that threatened the life of the mother and those in which there was a probability of deformity (see Tables 18.19 and 18.20).

Women were less likely than men to support abortion for economic reasons (see Tables 18.21 and 18.22). After *Roe*, men were slightly more likely than women to support the Court's decision on abortion, although by the mid-1980s there were no differences by gender (see Table 18.23).

In 1988 the public was asked for its views concerning the circumstances under which abortions should be legal. Seventy-five percent did not believe that a family's economic circumstances were legitimate grounds for abortion. Again, more women expressed disapproval than men. The circumstances for which abortion received the strongest support from both women and men were endangerment to the woman's life, whether she was a victim of rape or incest, and severe physical health damage in the absence of abortion. Among the 60 percent who favored abortion if there was a chance that the baby would be born deformed, men were more likely to indicate their approval than women.

In July 1989 the Supreme Court ruled in *Webster v. Reproductive Health Services* that states may pass laws restricting abortions. The public expressed disagreement with that ruling when polled days after it was announced (see Table 18.24). When the public was asked in July 1989 and again in October 1989 for

Table 18.13
Ideal Number of Children

Year	Women (18-39 years)			Men (18-39 years)		
	Two	Three	Four or more	Two	Three	Four or more
	(in percent)					
1941	18	20	52	35	30	26
1945	16	23	55	26	35	37
1953	24	26	48	34	32	33
1957	18	36	48	23	44	25
1959	13	21	51	21	33	35
1966*	13	26	41	23	28	29
1973	53	22	17	57	21	11
1974	45	22	20	48	22	17
1978	60	24	11	51	18	16
1980	54	20	15	51	22	16
1983	61	19	11	55	21	13
1985	63	18	10	53	25	11
1986**	67	14	12	61	20	10

* Includes all ages.
** Includes all ages, and figures cited for 2 children include 1 as well. The category is worded "1 or 2."

Sources: The Gallup Organization, 1941-1959; 1973 and 1978-1985 as cited in Public Opinion, December/January 1986, p. 28.

its views on *Roe v. Wade*, almost twice as many respondents—men slightly more than women—favored retaining the *Roe* decision (see Table 18.25).

CONCLUDING REMARKS

The theme running throughout all of the polls is the growing convergence and shared perspectives of men and women. On none of the ''women's'' issues were there major differences in the opinions and preferences of women and men.

In particular, responses to items about women in the work force belie the image of women perceiving themselves as victims of discrimination and arbitrary treatment. Except for their chances of becoming an executive, the majority of

Table 18.14
Recently, there has been a lot of talk about women's rights. Some people feel that women should have an equal role with men in running business, industry, and government. Others feel that women's place is in the home. Where would you place yourself on the scale, or haven't you thought much about this? (Egalitarian = 1; Traditional = 7)

		Years						
Categories of Women		1972	1974	1976	1978	1980	1982	1984
Employed:								
1	Egalitarian	38	40	37	49	40	47	43
2								
		16	19	26	19	29	23	26
3								
4	Neutral	25	21	19	16	16	17	20
5								
		9	12	12	9	9	9	9
6								
7	Traditional	13	8	6	7	5	5	3
Housewives:								
1	Egalitarian	25	21	24	26	27	29	22
2								
		14	19	13	15	27	18	16
3								
4	Neutral	21	23	25	24	17	19	30
5								
		11	17	16	17	18	14	18
6								
7	Traditional	29	20	23	18	12	19	14

Source: University of Michigan election surveys, as cited in Harmon Aiegler and Keith Poole, "Political Woman: Gender Indifference," Public Opinion, August/September, 1985, p. 55.

women (and men agree with them) believe that they have as good a chance as men to increase their salaries, enhance their responsibilities, and gain promotions.

Men and women also see eye-to-eye on the number of children they would like to have, in their support of efforts that have been made to strengthen women's status, and in their approval of the Equal Rights Amendment. The large majority of women and men believe that the wife should quit her job and relocate with her husband if the husband is offered a more attractive position in another city.

Table 18.15
Suppose both a husband and wife work at good and interesting jobs and the husband is offered a very good job in another city. Assuming they have no children, which one of these solutions do you think they should seriously consider?

Options	Women			Men		
	1979	1980	1985	1979	1989	1985
	(in percent)					
Husband should turn down the job and stay where they are so the wife can continue with her job.	11	10	10	20	18	19
Wife should quit her job, relocate with her husband, and try to get another job in the new place.	85	77	72	76	68	62
Husband should take the new job and move there, the wife should keep her job and stay where she is, and they should get together whenever they can on weekends, holidays, and vacations.	4	4	6	4	4	5
No opinion / DK	--	9	12	--	10	14
If the wife is offered a very good job in another city:						
Wife should turn down the job	--	68	55	--	62	58
Husband should quit his job	--	17	20	--	18	22
Wife should take new job and move/husband should keep his job and stay	--	4	8	--	5	6
No opinion / DK	--	11	17	--	15	14

Sources: The Roper Organization for Virginia Slims, 1979, as cited in Public Opinion, August/September, 1981; 1980 and 1985 as cited in Public Opinion, December/January, 1986, p. 26.

There is no quid pro quo on that issue: if it is the wife who is offered the better job, the majority of women (and men) believe she should turn down the offer so that her husband can continue working at his job. And while there have been changes in attitudes since 1953, more men and women would still rather work for a man than for a woman.

The main message from these data is that most men and women in the United States are not involved in a confrontation about women's rights: men are just as supportive as women of the issues for which the women's movement has struggled. But these data also send out the clear message that the women's movement has not radicalized the American woman: she is still prepared to put marriage and children ahead of career and to allow her husband's status to determine the family's position in society.

Table 18.16
Do you favor or oppose most of the efforts to strengthen and change women's status in society today?

Year	Women		Men	
	Favor	Oppose	Favor	Oppose
(in percent)				
1970	40	42	44	39
1972	48	36	49	36
1974	57	25	63	19
1980	64	24	64	23
1985	73	17	69	17

Source: Roper Organization for Virginia Slims, as cited in Public Opinion, October/November, 1985, p. 45, by Shirley Wilkins and Thomas A.W. Miller, "Working Woman: How It's Working Out."

NOTES

1. The Gallup Report, March 1976.
2. *Ms*, April 1988, p. 76.
3. *Public Opinion*, April/May 1984.
4. Harman Aiegler and Keith Poole, "Political Woman: Gender Indifference," *Public Opinion*, Aug./Sept. 1985.

Table 18.17
Have you heard or read about the Equal Rights Amendment to the Constitution which would give women equal rights and equal responsibilities? Do you favor or oppose this amendment?

	National		Women		Men	
Year	Favor	Oppose	Favor	Oppose	Favor	Oppose
			(in percent)			
1974	78	22	73	27	83	17
1975	58	24	54	25	63	22
1976	57	24	55	26	59	23
1978	58	31	55	33	62	29
1980	58	31	54	34	61	28
1981	63	32	63	32	63	32
1982	56	34	57	33	55	36
1984[*]	63	31	62	32	64	31

[*] Question: Would you please tell me whether you generally favor or generally oppose passage of an equal rights amendment to the Constitution?

Source: The Gallup Organization.

Table 18.18
Would you favor or oppose a law which would permit a woman to go to a doctor to end a pregnancy at any time during the first three months?

Year	Group	Favor	Oppose	No Opinion
		(in percent)		
1969:	National	40	50	10
	Men	40	46	14
	Women	40	53	7
1973:	National	46	45	9
	Men	49		
	Women	44		

Source: Gallup Opinion Index.

Table 18.19
Do you think abortion operations should or should not be legal when the health of the mother is in danger?

1966	Should	Should not	Don't Know
	(in percent)		
National	77	16	7
Men	77	15	8
Women	77	16	7

Source: The Gallup Organization.

Table 18.20
Do you think that abortion operations should or should not be legal when the child may be born deformed?

1966	Should	Should not	Don't Know
		(in percent)	
National	54	32	14
Men	56	30	14
Women	53	34	13

Source: The Gallup Organization.

Table 18.21
Opinions on Whether Abortion for Economic Reasons Should Be Legal

1966	Should	Should Not	Don't Know
		(in percent)	
National	18	72	10
Men	20	68	12
Women	17	75	8

Source: The Gallup Organization, Princeton, NJ, 1966.   Men and women also agreed about the appropriateness of the abortion decision being a matter between a woman and her doctor.

Table 18.22
As you may have heard, in the last few years a number of states have liberalized their abortion laws. Do you agree or disagree with the following statement regarding abortion: The decision to have an abortion should be made solely by a woman and her physician.

1972	Agree	Disagree	No Opinion
		(in percent)	
National	64	31	5
Men	63	32	5
Women	64	31	5

Source: The Gallup Organization.

Table 18.23
Opinions on U.S. Supreme Court Ruling Allowing First-Trimester Abortion

Year	National		Women		Men	
	Favor	Oppose	Favor	Oppose	Favor	Oppose
1974	47	44	43	49	51	38
1981	45	46	43	49	49	44
1983	50	43	46	48	56	37
1986	45	45	45	46	45	43
1988	58	37	58	34	57	38
1989	61	33	58	35	63	32

Source: The Gallup Organization, Princeton, NJ, 1974-1989.

Table 18.24
Opinions on Ruling in *Webster v. Reproductive Health Services*

1989	Approve		Disapprove		No Opinion
	Strongly	Not Strongly	Strongly	Not Strongly	
National	28	9	44	11	8
Women	28	6	47	11	8
Men	29	12	40	11	8

Source: The Gallup Organization, Princeton, NJ, July 1989.

Table 18.25
Opinions on Whether U.S. Supreme Court Should Overturn *Roe v. Wade*

Year		Should	Should Not	No Opinion
July 1989:	National	34	58	8
	Women	34	58	8
	Men	35	57	8
Oct. 1989:	National	33	61	6
	Women	35	58	7
	Men	32	63	5

Source: The Gallup Report, Princeton, NJ, Report 289, October 1989, p. 17; Report 286, July 1989, p. 9.

Selected Bibliography

Archer, Dane, and Rosemary Gartner. *Violence and Crime in Cross-National Perspective*. New Haven, CT: Yale University Press, 1984.

Babchuk, N. "Primary Friends and Kin: A Study of the Associations of Middle Class Couples." *Social Forces* 43 (May 1965): 483–493.

Babchuk, N., and A. P. Bates. "The Primary Relations of Middle-Class Couples: A Study of Male Dominance." *American Sociological Review* 28 (June 1963): 377–384.

Baxter, Sandra, and Marjorie Lansing. *Women and Politics: The Visible Majority*. Ann Arbor: University of Michigan Press, 1983.

Beattie, J. M. "The Criminality of Women in Eighteenth Century England." *Journal of Social History* 8 (1975): 80–116.

Brownlee, W. Elliot, and Mary M. Brownlee. *Women in the American Economy: A Documentary History, 1675 to 1929*. New Haven, CT: Yale University Press, 1976.

Carroll, Jackson W., Barbara Hargrove, and Adair T. Lummis. *Women of the Cloth: A New Opportunity for the Churches*. San Francisco: Harper and Row, 1983.

Chafe, W. *The American Woman: Her Changing Social, Economic and Political Roles, 1920–1970*. New York: Oxford University Press, 1972.

———. *Women and Equality: Changing Patterns in American Culture*. New York: Oxford University Press, 1977.

Cole, J. R., and H. Zuckerman. "Marriage, Motherhood and Research Performance in Science." *Scientific American* 256, 2 (1987): 119–125.

Degler, C. *At Odds: Women and the Family in America from the Revolution to the Present*. New York: Oxford University Press, 1980.

Dexter, Elizabeth Anthony. *Career Women of America, 1776–1840*. Boston: Houghton Mifflin, 1950.

Feinman, Clarice. *Women in the Criminal Justice System*. New York: Praeger, 1986.

Ferree, Myra M., and Beth B. Hess. *Controversy and Coalition: The New Feminist Movement*. Boston: Twayne, 1985.

Flexner, E. *Century of Struggle: The Women's Rights Movement in the United States.* Cambridge, MA: Harvard University Press, 1959.

Freeman, Jo. *The Politics of Women's Liberation.* New York: David McKay, 1975.

Friedan, B. *The Feminine Mystique.* New York: Dell, 1963.

Gilligan, Carol. *In a Different Voice.* Cambridge, MA: Harvard University Press, 1982.

Glancy, Dorothy. "Women in Law." *Harvard Law School Bulletin* 21, 5 (1970): 22–23.

Glazer, Penina Megdal, and Miriam Slater. *Unequal Colleagues: The Entrance of Women into the Professions, 1890–1940.* New Brunswick, NJ: Rutgers University Press, 1987.

Harris, Barbara J. *Beyond Her Sphere: Women and the Professions in American History.* Westport, CT: Greenwood Press, 1978.

Kanowitz, Leo. *Woman and the Law: The Unfinished Revolution.* Albuquerque: University of New Mexico Press, 1975.

Kanter, R. M. *Men and Women of the Corporation.* New York: Basic Books, 1977.

Kirkpatrick, Jeane J. *Political Woman.* New York: Basic Books, 1974.

Kirp, D., M. Yudof, and M. Franks. *Gender Justice.* Chicago: University of Chicago Press, 1986.

Klein, Ethel. *Gender Politics.* Cambridge, MA: Harvard University Press, 1984.

Lapidus, Gail W. *Women in Soviet Society.* Berkeley: University of California Press, 1978.

Lehman, Edward C., Jr. *Women Clergy: Breaking Through Gender Barriers.* New Brunswick, NJ: Transaction, 1985.

Long, J. S. "The Origins of Sex Differences in Science." *Social Forces* 68, 4 (1990): 1297–1315.

Lundberg, F., and M. F. Farnham. *Modern Woman: The Lost Sex.* New York: Universal Library, 1947.

Martin, S. E. *Breaking and Entering: Policewomen on Patrol.* Berkeley: University of California Press, 1980.

Millett, K. *Sexual Politics.* Garden City, NY: Doubleday, 1970.

Montero, D. *Vietnamese Americans: Patterns of Resettlement and Socioeconomic Adaptations in the United States.* Boulder, CO: Westview, 1979.

Proctor, Priscilla, and William Proctor. *Women in the Pulpit: Is God an Equal Opportunity Employer?* New York: Doubleday, 1976.

Reskin, B. F. "Scientific Productivity, Sex, and Location in the Institution of Science." *American Journal of Sociology* 83 (1978): 1235–1243.

Rossi, A., ed. *The Feminist Papers: From Adams to De Beauvoir.* New York: Columbia University Press, 1973.

Rothman, Sheila M. *Woman's Proper Place: A History of Changing Ideals and Practices, 1870 to the Present.* New York: Basic Books, 1978.

Scharf, Lois. *To Work and to Wed: Female Employment, Feminism, and the Great Depression.* Westport, CT: Greenwood Press, 1980.

Schwartz, Felice N. "Management Women and the New Facts of Life." *Harvard Business Review* 89 (January-February 1989): 65–76.

Simon, R. J., and C. Brettell, eds. *International Migration.* Totowa, NJ: Rowman and Allanheld, 1986.

Simon, Rita J., Shirley M. Clark, and Kathleen Galway. "The Woman Ph.D.: A Recent Profile." *Social Problems* 15, 2 (1967): 221–236.

Simon, Rita J., and Gloria Danziger. *Women's Movements in America: Their Successes, Disappointments, and Aspirations*. Westport, CT: Praeger, 1991.

Simon, Rita J., and Jean Landis. *The Crimes Women Commit, the Punishments They Receive*. Lexington, MA: Lexington Books, 1991.

Sokoloff, N. *Between Money and Love: The Dialectics of Women's Home and Market Work*. New York: Praeger, 1981.

Weisberg, D. Kelly, ed. *Women and the Law: A Social Historical Perspective*. Cambridge, MA: Schenkman, 1982.

Weitzman, Lenore J. *The Divorce Revolution: The Unexpected Social and Economic Consequences for Women and Children in America*. New York: Free Press, 1985.

White, James J. "Women in the Law." *Michigan Law Review* 65 (1967): 1051–1122.

Zimmer, Lynn E. *Women Guarding Men*. Chicago: University of Chicago Press, 1986.

Index

About the Author

RITA J. SIMON is Professor of Justice, Law and Society at The American University. She is the author or editor of more than twenty books, including Praeger's *Transracial Adoptees and Their Families*, *Intercountry Adoption*, and *Adoption, Race and Identity* (with Howard Altstein, in 1987, 1990, and 1992), *The Insanity Defense* (with David Aaronson, 1988), *Women's Movements in America* (with Gloria Danziger, 1991), and *The Ambivalent Welcome* (1993).

WITHDRAWN